Accounting for Business Management

Accounting for Business Management

A. I. M. FLEMING
S. McKINSTRY

ROUTLEDGE

First published 1991 by HarperCollins Publishers

Reprinted 1992 and 1995
by Routledge
11 New Fetter Lane, London EC4P 4EE

© 1991 Iain Fleming and Sam McKinstry

Typeset in 10 on 11 point Times by
Computape (Pickering) Ltd, North Yorkshire
Printed and bound in Great Britain by
The University Press, Cambridge

British Library Cataloguing in Publication Data
A catalogue record for this book is available from the British Library

ISBN 0-415-09106-3

Contents

Preface

Accounting textbooks fall into fairly clear categories. There are those aimed at students of accountancy, of necessity narrow in compass and very detailed in treatment. At the other end of the spectrum are the 'appreciation' texts, designed for those who require the flavour of the subject, the 'why' without worrying too much about the 'how', a legitimate enough approach for those for whom that is sufficient. This textbook is intended to fall between these poles. Increasingly, students of engineering, management, computing, business studies and a whole host of other subjects are having to undertake concise but fairly detailed courses in accounting and finance (terms which are seen as interchangeable) in order to qualify for their professional membership, national diploma, certificate or degree. Typically, courses such as these are of about one year's duration. Added to this, the recent push given to small business education has produced a hunger for deeper accountancy knowledge in many of our entrepreneurs. In our experience, there are very few textbooks containing, in a single volume, the right width of coverage at the depth which these students require. This book is our attempt to fill the gap.

The approach we have adopted is a practical one. Accounting theory is explained in plain language, not out of any attempt to be patronizing, but because we firmly believe that it should be, resting as it does on a foundation of sound sense and simple logic. Throughout, we have tried to communicate in a 'user-friendly' way, reducing jargon to a level consistent with the needs of our readers. This means that precise terminology remains, but there is no more of it than we feel there needs to be.

Our aim has been, in one volume, to present a detailed overview of accounting, explained for the benefit of readers whose main perspective will be a managerial one. For this reason we begin with *financial accounting*, proceeding logically and traditionally to *management accounting* and *costing*. Naturally there were choices to be made. In the costing area, for example, we felt that it would not be wise to embark on *process costing* as a distinct study, basing our chapter on the engineering model since it encompasses all the basic principles, which can easily be applied in other situations. On the other hand, we felt it necessary to include a brief chapter on *contract accounts*, an area of accounting study of interest to students of construction and civil engineering. Naturally, we expect teachers and students to omit those subjects outside their respective syllabuses. This is easily done, we feel, since the chapters and many of their subsections are self-contained. While computers and their use in accounting are an area of limited interest to users of accounts, we feel that they cannot be ignored, and have therefore woven references to applications and software into the text and have additionally given two computerized examples in an appendix. The applications involved, *cash flow forecasting* and *budgeting*, should, we feel, be of general interest.

Each chapter has been concluded with a selection of questions of varying types for use in classwork or for student self-testing. Numerical solutions have been provided in an appendix.

Acknowledgements

The authors wish to thank Computer Associates International for their permission to include SuperCalc commands in Appendix III. Thanks are also due to Peter Burns, Aileen Falconer, Linda Hunter, Jeanette Johnstone and Ella Kinninmonth for their help with the wordprocessing of the text.

Finally, our thanks are due to our wives and families who saw a great deal less of us while we worked on this book.

The accounting environment

Introduction

This book is about accounting. Although accounting is the work of accountants, an ever increasing number and range of non-accountants need to understand what accountants actually do and, more importantly, the contribution their work makes to business success.

The purpose of this chapter is to look at the nature of accounting and to examine some of the uses of accounting information. We will also outline some of the main users of this information and why such users may require data which can only be provided by accountants.

All business organizations have, ultimately, one thing in common and that is that they must survive. To survive, they must make money (they have to do many other things besides, but if they do not make money then they can do nothing else – for they are then out of business) and to make money, decisions have to be made. Decisions could be made in a vacuum, based on no information, but if that was the case then there would be no way of ensuring that the decision was the best that could have been made. Information is needed in businesses to help in the decision-making process.

The role of accountants

Accountants provide information – that is why they are paid so much! Not only do they provide information on which decisions can be based but they also provide information on the financial consequences of the possible outcomes if there is a choice of decisions which could be made. Finally, accountants provide information on the financial consequences of the decisions which were actually made.

Accounting can be seen as an information system in its own right. Financial information flows through business organizations and is amassed by those organizations. The role of accounting is to collate that information, organize it in some meaningful way, and then distribute it to those who will make use of it in the decision-making process. This is shown in Figure 1.1.

Thus, the accountant will provide financial information on which decisions can be based. Those decisions will result in actions which will produce results, and those results are then collected and analysed by accountants. The results of that analysis are then passed on to the decision makers so that they can make more decisions, and so on. It is a continuous cycle.

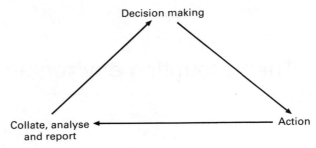

Figure 1.1

Historical development

Accountants, in the sense of being providers of information, are not a modern phenomenon but can be traced back to ancient Egypt and hieroglyphics showing details of past transactions. Roman accounts also exist which show details, maintained by servants, of money collected, spent and due to their masters.

Accounting developed as commercialization developed, so that by the late fifteenth century an Italian mathematician, Luca Pacioli, had described the essential elements of financial recording which are still used today. What Pacioli described was sufficient for the information needs of an essentially non-industrial society. The advent of the 'Industrial Age' saw an increased use of financial information by different groups of people (considered in the next section) which resulted in accounting progressing from the recording and distributing of basic data to business owners to the position it finds itself in today.

Modern accountants are now required to provide a wide variety of financial data to many groups of users with different needs. Accounting started off as the recording of past information but is now much more concerned with the provision of information for future decision making.

The decision makers

The decision makers referred to above need not just be the management of a company but will include everyone who has an interest in how well a company is doing. Different people will be interested in different aspects of a company's performance and will have different decisions to make about the company. Ideally, accountants would be able to supply the appropriate information for all decision makers.

Owners and investors

The owners of businesses invest their money (capital) and expect, in so doing, to make more money. Apart from the smallest firms, investors do not actively manage the business and, consequently, are not in a position to ensure that their money is being put to the best possible use.

Owners, therefore, normally have two distinct information requirements; they need to know:

(a)   What profits are they earning?
(b)   Is their money being efficiently used and properly managed?

Based on the answers to these questions, the owners can then make informed decisions about whether or not the level of profit is satisfactory to them, if their managers are acting properly and, if not, what they should perhaps do about the situation.

Potential investors

Such people are in a similar position as existing investors in that they will also want information about a firm's ability to earn profits for them and to make good use of their money. They will want such information so that they can make the best choice of investment – they can compare different firms and select, for them, the best.

There is a difference between the information needs of potential and existing investors, but the type of information is similar. The difference concerns the time covered by that information. Existing investors are concerned about how much profit has been, and is being, earned, whereas potential investors will want to know how much will be earned.

Note, however, that existing investors will also want to know about the future (is it worthwhile keeping their money in the firm?), and potential investors will also want to know about past results (if only to use as an indicator for the future). It is a question of emphasis.

Management

If a firm's managers are to manage the business effectively they must have the necessary information on which to base their decisions. If they are employed by the owners, they will have to have information if they are to account for their actions to the owners. They will also have to have information if they are to measure their performance and to control the firm.

Managers, therefore, will need a wide variety of financial information simply because their needs are so diverse. In summary their information needs are those which will answer the following questions:

(a)   How well have they performed in the past?
(b)   What is their current level of performance?
(c)   What are their future plans?
(d)   Are they properly controlling the business?

In addition, they will need information to help them make business decisions. Since there could be an almost endless list of possible management decisions that could arise, the following must be seen as only a very restricted list of questions which would require answers from a firm's management:

(a)   Should the firm increase its prices? If so, what will be the effect on profits, particularly since some customers may be lost?
(b)   Should the firm replace an old machine, or keep on repairing the old one?
(c)   Should the firm give credit to its customers? If so, how much and for how long?
(d)   Should the firm expand? If so, how, where, at what cost, and with what results?

To make sensible decisions about these and all the other management problems, the managers need information, and it is the accountant who is expected to supply that information.

Lenders

People who lend money are not particularly interested in how much profits a firm earns, or can earn, since they will not be sharing in those profits. Nor are they necessarily concerned about whether or not the firm is making the most efficient use possible of its financial resources.

Lenders will only lend money after carefully considering the following questions:

(a)   Will their loan be repaid on the due date?
(b)   Will they receive their interest when it is due?

The information needs of lenders are, therefore, concerned with the security that the firm can offer and with the firm's ability to pay a particular cost – their interest.

Creditors

Creditors are people who are owed money by a firm and are due that money in the relatively near future. They normally consist mostly of other firms which have supplied goods on credit and are willing to wait a month or so before being paid.

Their information needs are similar to those of lenders in that they will want to know if the firm will survive in the near future and pay them the money that is owed. They will not be concerned with the firm's profits or long-term viability, only whether or not the firm will have sufficient cash to pay its bills over the next few months.

Employees

Employees have an obvious interest in a firm's financial health, perhaps, as some people have argued, an even greater interest than the investors. Investors invest their money, but employees invest their livelihoods in a business.

If the firm goes bankrupt, investors lose their money but employees lose their jobs and their wages.

Employees should, therefore, require to know about the long-term financial viability of their company as a means of assessing their own personal futures. The employees of some firms may also need information about the profitability of their firm if their wages are profit-linked or if they want to claim higher wages on the basis of increased profitability (it is debatable that they would want to claim lower wages on the basis of decreased profitability, however).

Government

The government requires information about the performance of businesses in two ways.

(a) It needs to know how firms are doing in total so that it can assess the performance of the total economy and, if necessary, plan its economic policy. Such information, of course, will not be about individual firms but will be about firms in aggregate.

(b) More specifically, the government also requires information about the profitability and level of sales of individual firms in the recent past. This information is required by the Inland Revenue and Customs and Excise so that the correct levels of tax and VAT can be collected.

Types of accounting

In thinking about the various kinds of information which different decision makers require, it becomes obvious that the accountant is asked to present different types of accounting data. For example, the Inland Revenue wants to know how much was earned last year; potential investors want to know how much will be earned in coming years; managers want information which will help them choose the correct option; and so on. This leads to the possible conclusion that there is no such thing as 'accounting', and , indeed, that is the case. The word 'accounting' is a generic term which describes different tasks which, although they may have money as their central theme, are substantially different. There are, in fact, different types of 'accountant' just as there are different types of 'engineer'.

The accounting profession has become very specialized, but there are three main streams:

- Financial accounting
- Management accounting
- Financial management.

Financial accounting

Financial accounting is concerned with the supply of financial information about the past. Financial accountants collect information about costs and income as they occur and then collate those data and present them to show what has happened in the past (usually over the past year) and what the current position is.

Financial accountants produce the well-known *profit and loss accounts* and *balance sheets*. They are also concerned with anything to do with such data. Thus, auditors are also financial accountants since their task is to verify the presented information.

Management accounting

Financial accountants normally present information to the firm's owners and outside third parties. Management accountants, however, are concerned with the effective internal management of the business.

It is the management accountant in business who provides management with information on which to base managerial decisions. He assists in planning the future of the company, in determining costs, and in the internal analysis of performance.

Financial management

Financial management is concerned with ensuring that the firm is maximizing the use of the money available to the business. It is this aspect of accounting which tries to make sure that the firm is being as efficient and effective as possible with the funds entrusted by the investors.

The accountancy profession

In the UK, anybody can call himself, or herself, an accountant since there is no legal restriction on the use of that word. Indeed, there are many very able people working in business as accountants who have never sat, far less passed, an accounting exam. However, most accountants are qualified.

As was shown above, the work of the accountant is very varied and this is reflected in the organization of the qualified accountancy profession. There are six accountancy bodies each producing highly qualified accountants with differing specialisms:

(a)   Institute of Chartered Accountants of Scotland.
(b)   Institute of Chartered Accountants in Ireland.
(c)   Institute of Chartered Accountants in England and Wales.
(d)   Chartered Association of Certified Accountants.
(e)   Chartered Institute of Management Accountants.
(f)   Chartered Institute of Public Finance and Accountancy.

Members of the first three bodies (the *chartered accountants*) are essentially financial accountants, as are members of the fourth body, although the certified accountants are more firmly based in industry than chartered accountants. Members of the fifth body specialize in management accounting whereas members of the last body specialize in the financial affairs of the government, local authorities, health boards and suchlike.

There is a suspicion that some accounting qualifications are 'better' than others. This is rather unfair and untrue. Members of the different bodies are highly trained in their own specialisms and comparisons are hard to make and justify.

Business organizations: the legal framework

Accountants provide information to, and about, businesses. However, there are different formats of businesses in the UK, each with its own peculiarities, and the accountant is expected to be aware of the differences and special needs of each type.

The three most common types of business format are:

(a)   Sole traderships.
(b)   Partnerships.
(c)   Limited liability companies.

There are other formats, such as cooperatives, banks and investment trusts, but they are either very specialized with their own accounting methods or relatively rare. This book will concentrate only on the three common formats.

Sole traders

As the name suggests, such businesses are 'one-person shows'. They are owned exclusively by one person who is responsible for all policy decisions such as what the business will do and how it will work. The name does not mean that the business has only one person in it – there could be many employees. It simply means that there is only one owner.

There are really no formalities involved in starting as a sole trader, it is just a question of finding a niche in the market and getting going.

Being a sole trader means that the owner has total control over the management of the business, shares its profits with nobody and need tell nobody about its success or otherwise (except for the Inland Revenue). There are disadvantages, however, notably that the burden of responsibility cannot be shared, and the owner's liability is unlimited.

Legally, there is no distinction between the sole trader's business and the sole trader as a person. Unlimited liability is just an extension of that idea, so if the business goes bankrupt then the business owner is personally liable for all of the debts of the business.

Partnerships

This form of business is created when two or more people agree to form and run a business jointly. With few exceptions, there cannot be more than twenty partners in a partnership (although, as with the sole trader, there can be any number of employees).

The partners can agree among themselves the basis of the partnership, but, if they do not, the Partnership Act of 1890 will dictate for them what the duties and rights of each partner are. Starting formalities may be negligible although it is advisable that prospective partners consult a solicitor first unless they want to abide by the contents of the 1890 Partnership Act.

The benefits of a partnership include the fact that responsibility can now be shared while retaining managerial control among very few individuals. Unlimited liability still remains a problem, meaning that the partners are personally liable for the debts of the partnership. Added to that is the fact that the partners are said to be jointly liable for the business debts (and severally in Scotland). This means that if one partner cannot pay his/her share of the business debts then the remaining partners, in addition to paying their share, must also pay the share of the partner who cannot.

Limited liability companies

The limited liability company is created by the law and, in the eyes of the law, has a corporate personality; that is, as far as the law is concerned, the limited company is a 'person' in its own right and exists independently from its owners. In fact, the owners of this form of business do not own it in the same way as the owners of sole traders and partnerships own these businesses. Rather, individuals own shares in the company and it is only the ownership of shares which confers (somewhat restricted) rights.

The starting formalities can be quite onerous and complex. Since the law creates the limited company, it is not too surprising that the law also states a wide range of formalities which must be gone through before the company may start trading. Essentially, the new company must prepare a *memorandum of association* and the *articles of association* which, together, form the rules and constitution of the company. These documents state how a company will be run and what it will do and if the company tries to do anything outside these rules, it is breaking the law.

The principal advantage of this format of business is that the owners, the shareholders, have limited liability. Thus, if the business goes bankrupt, the owners do not have to make good the debts of the company. Also, because the law recognizes the company's independent existence, the death of the shareholders does not mean the death of the business (obviously the death of a sole trader will have a rather profound effect on the existence of his/her business!). Similarly, if a shareholder is personally bankrupt that does not affect the company.

The price to be paid for these advantages may be considered by some to be considerable. All limited companies must abide by the content of the Companies Acts which, among other things, require companies to prepare annual accounts in a strict format. The affairs of limited companies are not secret, since anybody can see copies of these annual accounts.

One final disadvantage is that the owners do not control their firm directly. They have to elect a *board of directors* who have the responsibility of managing the company. Indeed, individual shareholders do not have the right of access to any of the books of account of their company. This may seem a rather stringent limitation on the rights of the owners, but there is a good reason for it. If shareholders did have the right of access to the internal management of their company, a rival firm could buy one share and then take advantage of its ownership of the one share and demand access to the firm's secrets – undoubtedly to the disadvantage of the company.

Questions

1.1   Outline the role of the accountant in business.
1.2   Who are the main users of accounting information? What information do they require and why?
1.3   Explain the distinction between financial and management accounting.
1.4   What type of accountant would be most suitable for the following tasks:

   (a)   Establishing the cost of producing a product.
   (b)   Calculating a firm's tax liability.
   (c)   Auditing a firm's annual accounts.
   (d)   Preparing a firm's budget for the coming year.
   (e)   Producing a firm's annual accounts.
   (f)   Measuring managerial performance.

1.5   Outline the principal features of:

   (a)   Sole traders.
   (b)   Partnerships.
   (c)   Limited liability companies.

1.6   What are the main advantages and drawbacks inherent in each of the three most common business formats in the UK?
1.7   What does 'unlimited liability' mean and what are the possible consequences for the owners of firms which are said to be unlimited?

2 The basics of financial accounting

Introduction

Most non-accountants have heard of the *profit and loss account* and of the *balance sheet*. Although these terms have become part of everyday language and refer to the two most important financial statements in use in business, they are still widely misunderstood.

The next three chapters will examine these two financial statements in detail, showing how they are constructed and the rules and assumptions which underpin them, and start to dispel the myth that they are exact statements of fact.

The principal financial statements

The profit and loss account and the balance sheet are normally produced annually by all profit-orientated organizations, for tax purposes if for no other, but can be produced more regularly. In fact, most larger firms produce these statements monthly for management purposes.

Each statement provides the reader with a different view of the financial health of an enterprise, thus

- The *balance sheet* shows the financial status of a firm at a precise moment in time by stating everything that a firm owns (its assets) and how much, and to whom, the firm owes money (its liabilities).
- The *profit and loss account* shows how successfully a firm has traded over a given time period and how it has moved from the situation shown in one balance sheet to that shown in the next one. Put simply, it shows how much has been earned and what costs have been incurred in an accounting period.

A moment's thought will show why there are two financial statements – the balance sheet shows the current situation, and the profit and loss account shows a summarized picture of what has happened over time.

The need for accounting rules

The contents of the balance sheet and the profit and loss account may appear straightforward, but the process of their creation can be complex. As a simple analogy, the game of football is basically very simple – score more goals than the other team. However, the game of football must be circumscribed by rules if it is not to degenerate into total anarchy. There must be rules regulating, for example, the number of players in each team, the number of goalkeepers allowed, the definition of fair tackling, and so on.

Without rules, the construction of financial statements would be similarly anarchic. Consider the following questions:

THE BALANCE SHEET

(a) Should assets be shown at cost or market value?
(b) Should it show a value for all assets owned by a firm, no matter how insignificant they may be?
(c) Should it show the value of having a good relationship with customers?
(d) Should it show the value of money owed to the firm even if the person owing the money is unlikely to repay the debt?

THE PROFIT AND LOSS ACCOUNT

(a) Should income be defined in terms of cash received or value earned?
(b) Similarly, should costs only be included if the cash has actually been paid?
(c) Should all income be included, including loans received?
(d) Should all costs be included? If a firm buys a factory, should the cost be included in that month's profit and loss account?

It should begin to be clear that, without rules covering the construction of financial statements, any that are drawn up would be quite meaningless. They would only have meaning to the accountant who prepared them, as only he/she would know the bases which had been used in their compilation.

Unfortunately, there are many accounting rules (hundreds of them). Some of the more important and fundamental ones are discussed below.

Boundary rules

Boundary rules are those rules which define the parameters of accounting.

Accounting periods

For a person there is only one real time period – the time between that person's birth and death. Breaking time down into years, days , hours, and so on, is quite artificial. We only do so because we find it useful, but there is no real reason why a year should be 365 days or that one hour should be 60 minutes.

Similarly, the only natural choice of a time period for a firm would be one which covered the whole life of that firm. In such a period, the accountant would be able to say clearly how well the firm had performed, but it would be a very long time period to wait for such information. Owners, and other interested parties, need to know about a firm's performance regularly; indeed it is highly unlikely that the Inland Revenue would be willing to wait until the demise of a firm before it could assess it for tax.

The Companies Acts and tax law require limited liability companies to prepare accounts every year, but there is no logical reason why this time period should not be two years or 196 days, or anything else for other users.

Whatever time period is chosen, it will always be the result of arbitrary choice and so must always be shown on the face of the accounts. Readers will then know exactly what length of time is being evaluated.

Going concern

The normal assumption is that a firm will not fail but will carry on doing business indefinitely and that the annual accounts display only a slice of an ongoing activity – rather like a clip from a film. All acounting rules are based on this assumption and, as such, it is important to ensure that the firm is, in fact, a going concern.

If the firm is not a going concern then the underlying assumptions in many accounting rules will be invalid and revised rules will have to be applied.

Money measurement

Financial statements only measure transactions which involve money. It is a mistaken idea that such statements measure the company; they only measure, and can only measure, the financial status of the firm and the financial results of decisions made within it.

Companies, being essentially human organizations, have attributes which cannot be quantified in monetary terms, for example, all firms have work-forces, and some have highly skilled workforces. Financial statements will only show the financial consequences of the workforce (how much it has been paid) for that is the only quantifiable and objective statement that can be made. There are no objective measures of skill, and even if there were, it would still remain difficult to quantify that skill and compare it with, for example, the cost of a new machine.

Relevance (or materiality)

The financial records of large firms can contain a whole plethora of financial information, most of which will involve relatively small sums. The relevance rule means that time, and money, should only be expended on those items which are sufficiently large as to make the cost of extracting or analysing those figures worthwhile.

Determining which figures are relevant and which are not will require a degree of subjectivity by the accountant, but it will appear reasonable if extremes are considered. For example, in valuing the stock of a pub, the value ascribed to the stock of beer is obviously relevant whereas the value of the publican's stock of paperclips is not.

Consistency

There are few, if any, accounting rules which must be adhered to by all firms for all time. Each rule does allow for discretion; for example, a firm may have selected an accounting period which runs from 1 April to 31 March, but the firm need not always have such an accounting period. If it wished, it could easily change to 1 January to 31 December.

The consistency rule, however, requires firms to adopt specific interpretations of the basic rules and apply them consistently, year after year, unless there are good reasons why a revised interpretation should be followed.

The reason for this rule is simply that if a firm's financial performance is to be comparable year on year, then the underlying bases of each year's accounts must be similar. If they are not, then no legitimate comparison can be made between years, as such a comparison would not be on a 'like with like' basis.

Measurement rules

Measurement rules are those which define the level of income or expenditure.

Cost basis

Given that transactions have to be objectively measured in monetary terms, it follows that the measurement must be in terms of historic cost. Any other basis, such as value, would involve subjectivity – the only true objective measure is historic cost.

Attempts have been made in the past to produce accounts which use a basis other than cost, usually in an attempt to remove the distorting effects of inflation. However, there has never been a genuine consensus on what the revised basis should be and such innovations have largely fallen by the wayside.

Matching

As a direct result of the accounting period rule, it follows that all income and expenditure must be allocated to identifiable time periods. Thus income is defined as income earned in a period, and expenditure is defined as costs incurred and/or relevant to a specific time period.

This can cause problems. For example, some costs may be incurred in one time period but are relevant to another such as the prepayment of insurance premiums or the purchase of long-term equipment. In such cases, the costs would have to be allocated to the 'correct' accounting period. Thus, if the insurance premium for year 2 was paid in December of year 1, then it would be treated as a cost for year 2 and not as a cost of year 1.

Simply because cash was spent in one time period does not necessarily mean that it refers to that time period and should be accounted for in it, nor does the non-payment of a cost necessarily mean that such a cost was not incurred.

Capital and revenue

Costs which are incurred in one time period and will have a lasting benefit in further time periods have to be distinguished from those costs which have only a one-off immediate benefit. Consider a firm which has projected profits over the next four years as follows:

	Years				
	1	2	3	4	Total
Profits	£10,000	10,000	10,000	10,000	£40,000

The firm could buy a machine in year 1 for £16,000 and in so doing would increase all profits by 50%. If the full cost of the machine was charged against that year's profit level, the result would be:

	Years				
	1	2	3	4	Total
New profit	£15,000	15,000	15,000	15,000	
less Cost of machine	16,000	—	—	—	
Net profit	£(1,000)	15,000	15,000	15,000	£44,000

It is manifestly unfair that year 1 should suffer a loss and subsequent years show increased profits. What should happen is that the cost of the machine, although incurred in year 1, should be matched to the income that it will earn in the subsequent years.

To overcome this problem, expenditure is classified as either *revenue expenditure* or *capital expenditure*. Revenue expenditure is defined as those costs which can be attributed to only a single accounting period, such as the cost of wages, rent and power. Capital expenditure is costs whose benefits will be seen in a number of accounting periods, such as the purchase of premises or machinery.

The distinction between capital and revenue expenditure is important, since profit is defined as the difference between *revenue income* (normal business earnings) and *revenue expenditure*. Thus capital expenditure is excluded from the definition of profit.

Prudence

Accountants are frequently seen as tight-fisted, conservative individuals who always see the negative side of life. This may be the result of applying the prudence rule so often. This rule basically urges accountants to be cautious when preparing financial statements and, if faced with a choice, to choose the option which minimizes profit. It is seen to be better to be slightly pessimistic than to be disappointingly optimistic.

The application of this rule is seen in many accounting axioms such as:

- 'recognize losses when they become apparent but profits only when they are realized' – that is, prepare for the worst and do not count your chickens until they are hatched;
- 'lower of cost and net realizable value' – that is, if a firm has stock which cost £1,000 but whose resale value is £800, abandon the cost basis rule and choose the lower value; if, however, the resale value is £1,200, stay with cost basis rule.

Dual Aspect

This rule does no more than state the obvious fact that every transaction made by a firm affects that firm in two ways. Thus if a firm pays out money, it must also have received something in return; or if it receives money, it must also have either sold something or have borrowed the money.

The importance of this rule lies in the fact that it forms the basis of the financial recording systems of every large firm irrespective of whether the system is the old manual method or computerized. A complete understanding of accounting and the mechanics of financial account preparation would not be possible without an understanding of the underlying basis of how the raw data are both recorded and stored. Consequently, some time will now be devoted to this aspect of accounting.

You are recommended to study this section thoroughly before moving on to further chapters.

Double entry book-keeping

The fundamentals of double entry book-keeping lie in three suppositions:

(a)   that every transaction can be described;
(b)   that similar transactions may be aggregated;
(c)   that every transaction made by a firm will affect that firm in two ways.

The *account* is the basic storage unit of all financial information; thus there will be an account for every transaction made by a firm. Firms are likely to make a number of transactions of a similar type, such as sales, and it would not make much sense to have a separate account for every single sales transaction – if that was the case, just imagine the number of accounts for sales that would be necessary in a firm like ICI Plc. Rather, similar transactions are recorded and stored in the one account, in this case the *sales account*. Thus not only do all accounts record and store financial information, but the total figure in each account will be a summary of all transactions of that type made by the firm.

Accounts can increase as well as decrease. Remaining with the example of the sales account, all sales made by the firm would increase this account, but if a customer returned faulty goods and was reimbursed then the total value of sales shown in this account would decrease by the value of the reimbursement.

As mentioned earlier, every transaction has a dual aspect; it affects the firm in two ways; thus every time one account is adjusted, another must also be adjusted. If the sales account is increased because of a sale, then the *cash account* must also be increased to account for the money received from the sale. It could become quite tedious if accountants were continually to refer to 'increasing' or 'decreasing' an account; it could also become rather confusing. To overcome this, accountants refer to *debit* and *credit* when describing the effect of a transaction on an account.

The terms 'debit' and 'credit' can be confusing, probably because they have been adopted into everyday language and are then used in ways which are inconsistent with their use in accounting. The first thing to realize is that they are just words. Just as the words 'increase' and 'decrease' cause no confusion, neither should 'debit' and 'credit'.

The sales account could be shown pictorially thus:

One side would record all increases and the other would record all decreases. The difference between the two sides, the balance, would then be the net value of sales made by the firm.

If, for no other reason than that it seemed a good idea at the time, the left-hand side is called the *debit*, then the right side is the *credit*. Within an account, debit and credit are synonymous with increase and decrease, or plus and minus – they simply refer to opposites. Again in the sales account, to increase it would be to *credit* that account, and to decrease that account would be to *debit* it.

There is another accounting maxim which says that 'every debit has a credit'. (This is a maxim you would do well to remember.) All that it means is that every transaction has a dual aspect, that no account may be adjusted on its own, and that every time an account is, say, credited, then another account (or accounts) must be debited with a similar sum. This will ensure that the dual aspect rule is maintained and forms the basis of double entry book-keeping.

Suppose in our example the firm had made a sale for cash amounting to £1,000, then the sales account would be credited with £1,000 thus:

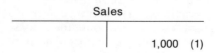

There would have to be a debit to another account, the cash account, thus:

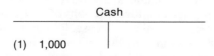

The debit to the cash account could therefore be said to be increasing that account.

Sales are *income* and cash is an *asset*, so what could now be said is:

- *Debit* increases an asset account; and
- *Credit* increases an income account.

Also, since within accounts debit and credit are simply opposites:

- *Credit* decreases an asset account; and
- *Debit* decreases an income account.

If the firm then spent £200 on buying raw materials, then the cash account would decrease (be credited) and the *materials account* would also be affected – since *cash* was credited, *materials* would have to be debited. Thus:

- *Debit* increases an expense account; and conversely
- *Credit* decreases an expense account

That is:

	Cash				Materials	
(1) 1,000		200 (2)		(2) 200		

Again, if the firm then borrowed £500 the effect would be to increase the cash account (that is, it would be debited) and the dual aspect would be to *credit* the *loan account*, thus:

	Cash				Loan	
(1) 1,000		200 (2)				500 (3)
(3) 500						

- *Credit* increases a liability; and
- *Debit* decreases a liability.

Every transaction made by a firm can be classified as:

(a)   income;
(b)   expense;
(c)   asset;
(d)   liability;

and summarising the above:

- *Debit* –   increases an asset;
          increases an expense;
          reduces a liability;
          reduces income.
- *Credit* – increases a liability;

increases income;
reduces an asset;
reduces an expense.

Choice of accounts

Large firms can have hundreds, if not thousands, of accounts, and in recording a particular transaction it is not an uncommon problem as to which accounts should be adjusted. Often the solution is straightforward and obvious – if the firm made a sale for cash then the obvious accounts will be the *cash account* and the *sales account*. If there is any uncertainty, the easiest solution is to open another account. If a firm has hundreds of accounts, one more will make little difference. Besides, the annual financial statements, which are based on the individual accounts, require many accounts to be amalgamated and one more account again will make little difference in that amalgamation process.

Double entry example

Sarah Scott started her business on 1/1/19xx. She invested £1,000 of her own money and borrowed £750. Her initial transactions were as follows:

2/1/19xx – bought equipment for £350 and raw materials for £400.
3/1/19xx – made sales to the value of £275.
4/1/19xx – paid £100 for rent, £50 for raw materials and made sales of £600.
5/1/19xx – repaid £75 of the loan.
6/1/19xx – refunded £20 to a dissatisfied customer.

Required: show these transactions in Sarah's books of account.

	Bank				Capital				Loan	
(1)	1,000	350	(3)					(8) 75		750 (2)
(2)	750	400	(4)			1,000	(1)			675
(5)	275	50	(6)							
(7)	600	75	(8)							
		20	(9)							
	2,625	995								
	1,630									

	Equipment			Materials			Sales	
(3) 350			(4) 400			(9) 20	275 (5)
			(6) 50				600 (7)
			450			20	875
							855

	Rent	
(6) 100		

The first thing that Sarah did was to introduce £1,000 of her own money into the business. The dual effect of that was:

(a)   Assets (the bank) increased, therefore debit that account.
(b)   Her business now owed her money, that is, liabilities were increased, therefore some account had to be credited. The account in question has to be the Capital Introduced account (or Capital).

The next thing was she borrowed money, and the dual effect here is:

(a)   Bank (an asset) increased; therefore debit the Bank account.
(b)   Loans (a liability) increased, therefore credit Loans.

You are now recommended to follow Sarah's remaining transactions into their respective accounts.

If it is difficult to remember which accounts should be debited and which should be credited, it may help to consider the problem in terms of cash, as all financial transactions will, ultimately, involve either cash coming into the business or cash going out of it. Also remember that cash is an asset; and to increase an asset, that account is debited and to reduce it, the account is credited.

For any transaction, ask the question, 'Will this involve cash coming in or cash going out?' Whatever the answer, you will have the debit (or credit), and the other account will have to be credited (or debited). Sometimes it will not be obvious. For example, Sarah may sell goods worth £150 on credit to ABC Ltd. Asking the question 'Does this involve cash coming in?' provides no immediate answer as there is no cash involved in a credit sale. But it will, when ABC Ltd pay their debt. The answer is to debit the account that will, ultimately, result in cash coming in, the Debtors account, and so credit the other account, Sales.

Trial balances

The *trial balance* is not part of the double entry process but is a useful means of summarizing the balances on all of a firm's accounts and of ensuring that the double entry process has properly worked. It does so by simply listing all debit and credit balances in all accounts and summing each list. Since 'for every debit there must be a credit', it follows that the sum of all debit balances must equal the sum of all credit balances. If the two totals do not agree, an error must have been made somewhere. The trial balance is also a useful starting point in preparing a firm's financial statements as it has summarized all accounts and transactions made by a firm in an accounting period.

In the case of Sarah Scott, her trial balance would be:

Sarah Scott

Trial balance

	Debit	Credit
Bank	£1,630	
Capital		1,000
Loan		675

Equipment	350	
Materials	450	
Sales		855
Rent	100	
	£2,530	2,530

Simply because the trial balance balances, it should not be taken as proof that it is 'correct'. Certainly, if it does not balance, that can be taken as proof that an error has been made, but even in a balanced trial balance errors can be made which will not affect the balancing. The more common errors include:

(a) Debiting (or crediting) the wrong account. For example, a sale for £274 cash would result in

> Debit Cash 274
> Credit Sales 274

If, instead, the following entry had been made

> Debit Debtors 274
> Credit Sales 274

then the trial balance would still balance (since every debit has a credit) but it would still be wrong by understating cash and overstating debtors.

(b) The complete omission of a transaction will not affect the balancing of the trial balance, but it will make the summary wrong.

(c) Reversing the entry will also make the summary wrong but will not affect its balancing. In the above example, if it had been entered as

> Debit Sales 274
> Credit Cash 274

such an entry would be wrong but it would not affect the balance.

(d) Transposing numbers can also affect the summary. For example, if instead of £274, £247 had been entered thus

> Debit Cash 247
> Credit Sales 247

it is obviously wrong, but it will still balance.

The transposition of numbers is a common error, easily made, particularly when a large volume of numbers are being manipulated. It is usually common that the transposition is made only once such as debiting cash with £247 but sales being properly credited with £274. Such an error will produce an unbalanced trial balance. If it is suspected that an unbalanced trial balance arises from the transposition of one number, this can be checked quite easily. If the difference between the two totals is exactly divisible by 9 then the chances are that the reason is transposition (this is not proof positive, it merely indicates a high probability). In the case of £274 and £247, the difference is £27 and this is exactly divisible by 9 to £3.

A FULLER EXAMPLE

Steven Scott, Sarah's brother, also started business on 1/1/19xx. He started by injecting £3,000 capital, by borrowing £2,000, and by introducing his car which had a value of £1,800.

His first transactions were as follows:

2/1/19xx – bought equipment costing £2,200 and materials for £1,200.
3/1/19xx – paid rent of £150, insurance of £360, and stationery for £70. He also made sales of £176 on credit.
4/1/19xx – Sales were £724 for cash. He bought more materials for £220 and paid £16 delivery charges.
5/1/19xx – Sales were £561 for cash. He paid £100 interest   on the loan and purchased a telephone for £66 and other office equipment for £350.
6/1/19xx – He paid himself £100 and his employees £240. Sales were £1,392 on credit. He returned faulty materials to his supplier and was refunded £56. Petrol cost him £25.

Required: show Steven's accounts, journal entries, and trial balance up to 6/1/19xx.

Note that journal entries are simply written statements which explain the recording of financial information and any adjustments that may be necessary from time to time.

Journal entries

(1)	Debit Bank	£5,000	
	Credit Capital		3,000
	Loan		2,000

This introduces his own money as Capital and also the loan raised.

(2)	Debit Vehicles	1,800	
	Credit Capital		1,800

The vehicle is just another asset (like cash, only in a different form) which Steven introduced. The Capital account shows the value of all assets introduced into the business by Steven.

(3)	Debit Equipment	2,200	
	Materials	1,200	
	Credit Bank		3,400

Cash paid for equipment and materials.

(4)	Debit Rent	150	
	Insurance	360	
	Stationery	70	
	Credit bank		580

Cash paid for those expenses.

(5)	Debit Debtors	176	
	Credit Sales		176

Sales made on credit. The debit must be to the Debtors account indicating an increase in assets.

| (6) | Debit Bank | 724 | |
| | Credit sales | | 724 |

Sales made for cash.

(7)	Debit Materials	220	
	Delivery	16	
	Credit Bank		236

Cash paid for listed expenses.

| (8) | Debit Bank | 561 | |
| | Credit Sales | | 561 |

Cash received from sales.

(9)	Debit Interest	100	
	Office equipment	416	
	Credit Bank		516

Payment of listed costs. Note that the cost of the telephone and of other office equipment have been amalgamated into the one account – Office Equipment. Two separate accounts could have been opened, but as the telephone is office equipment it makes more sense to have just the one account.

(10)	Debit Drawings	100	
	Wages	240	
	Credit Bank		340

Expenses paid. Note that in sole trading firms, money drawn out of the firm by the owner is not described as *wages* but as *drawings*, or *personal drawings*. The reason is that the owner puts money into the business and any money that he/she takes out is just the firm repaying him/her his/her own money. As an analogy, it is like an individual putting money into the bank and then withdrawing some of it. In so doing, the individual is not paying him/herself a wage.

| (11) | Debit Debtors | 1,392 | |
| | Credit Sales | | 1,392 |

More sales made on credit and treated in the same way as journal entry number (5).

| (12) | Debit Bank | 56 | |
| | Credit Materials | | 56 |

Reimbursement for faulty goods. Note that the Materials account is being reduced by the credit entry.

| (13) | Debit Travel costs | 25 | |
| | Credit Bank | | 25 |

Costs incurred.

Accounts

Bank			
(1) 5,000	3,400	(3)	
(6) 724	580	(4)	
(8) 561	236	(7)	
(12) 56	516	(9)	
	340	(10)	
	25	(12)	
6,341	5,097		
1,244			

Capital	
	3,000 (1)
	1,800 (2)
	4,800

Equipment	
(3) 2,200	

Loans	
	2,000 (1)

Materials	
(3) 1,200	56 (12)
(7) 220	
1,420	56
1,364	

Vehicles	
(2) 1,800	

Rent	
(4) 150	

Insurance	
(4) 360	

Sales	
	176 (5)
	724 (6)
	561 (8)
	1,392 (11)
	2,853

Stationery	
(4) 70	

Interest	
(9) 100	

Delivery	
(7) 16	

Office equipment	
(9) 416	

Drawings	
(10) 100	

Wages	
(10) 240	

Travel costs	
(13) 25	

Debtors	
(5) 176	
(11) 1,392	
1,568	

After the balance on each account has been determined by finding the difference between the sum of all debits and credits within each account, a *trial balance* can be drawn up. Bear in mind that the trial balance will not prove that the entries to each account are correct. If it balances, the trial balance will only say that the double entry process has probably been carried out properly.

Trial balance
as at 6/1/19xx

	Debit	Credit
Bank	£1,244	
Capital		4,800
Loans		2,000
Vehicles	1,800	
Equipment	2,200	
Materials	1,364	
Rent	150	
Insurance	360	
Stationery	70	

Sales		2,853
Delivery charges	16	
Interest	100	
Office equipment	416	
Drawings	100	
Wages	240	
Travel costs	25	
Debtors	1,568	
	£9,653	9,653

The use of computers

Microcomputers have had a substantial impact on accounting perhaps more so than in any other aspect of management. This is probably because accounting is, basically, little more than the manipulation of numbers (in the form of financial data), and computers perform this task of 'number crunching' extraordinarily well. Many programs have been developed which perform the basic task of recording financial transactions. Some are relatively cheap (costing about £150), others are more expensive (well over £1,000); but they all work on basically the same principle of double entry and ledger accounts.

All programs require the user to create the necessary ledger accounts – such as for sales, purchases, debtors, creditors, bank and all the usual expenditure accounts – giving each account a unique code number. Once created, the user then feeds in the transactions and the accounts are automatically updated. For example, assume a firm sells a product on credit to ABC Ltd for £100. The user will have to define a code for Sales and another one for the debtor ABC Ltd. Once done, the £100 will have to be entered as a debit to the debtor account and a credit to the sales account except that the user will not have to use the terms' 'debit' and 'credit'. By using the account codes, the computer will perform the appropriate posting. Adjusting journal entries can also be input into the system.

The benefits are obvious. Little, or no, knowledge of book-keeping is required to maintain 'perfect' books, as the machine does that automatically. So long as the proper codes are used, the records will always be accurate, and, probably the most useful benefit, all this can be performed at speed.

Imagine a small firm with a manual book-keeping system. It has 4 sales accounts (because it has 4 different types of product to sell), 35 expenditure accounts, 150 individual debtor accounts and 35 individual creditor accounts, together with the usual capital accounts, bank, cash and VAT accounts. All in, this small firm could have over 220 accounts.

A simple transaction of Debit Telephone : Credit Bank will take some time since the book-keeper will have to search the 220 accounts to find the Telephone account, post the debit, search again for the Bank account and then post the credit. Using a computer, the program will do all this at the speed of electricity!

The drawbacks are, perhaps, equally obvious. Errors can still be made and such errors will also be made at the speed of electricity. You will remember that a balanced trial balance does not prove that the individual accounts are correct – only that the double entry process has been performed correctly. In the above example, suppose that the Telephone account had a code number 3129 and that the Personal Drawings code was 3192. If the user types in code 3192 instead of 3129 (an easy error to make) the trial balance will still balance but will be wrong. It will also be very difficult to spot.

Another problem area is disk security. Computer disks are very sensitive, and, if they become corrupted, all the data on them can be lost. If that happens, many hours of work will be lost, and the data will have to be reconstructed from the primary documents (invoices, receipts, and so on). This book was written using a microcomputer. The disk which held Chapter 6 did become totally corrupted, and from bitter personal experience we can confirm the heartache of losing data and having to reconstruct them.

To prevent this happening, users of computers should always make back-up copies, on separate disks, of all work done.

Chapter summary

This chapter was mainly concerned with the basic accounting rules. As a reminder, these rules were:

Boundary rules

- *Accounting periods*: financial statements should always identify the discrete time period to which they refer.
- *Going concern*: unless stated otherwise, accounts are prepared on the assumption that the firm has an infinite life.
- *Money measurement*: accounting is only concerned with transactions which involve the movement of money.
- *Relevance*: accounting is only concerned with identifying significant values.
- *Consistency*: firms may not reinterpret their accounting rules each year without very good reasons.

Measurement rules

- *Cost basis*: firms must account for transactions in terms of cost and not value.
- *Matching*: transactions should be accounted for in the time period for which they are relevant and not necessarily when they are incurred.
- *Capital and revenue*: only revenue income and expenditure are considered in defining profit.
- *Prudence*: when a choice of options is available, that which minimizes profit should be chosen.
- *Dual aspect*: the basic book-keeping rule which requires every debit to have an equal and corresponding credit.

Questions

2.1   Why does financial accounting need rules?

2.2   To what extent does the *cost basis* rule produce financial statements which fail to disclose a firm's true worth?

2.3   Distinguish capital expenditure from revenue expenditure.

2.4   Explain the following accounting concepts:
   (a) Matching
   (b) Going concern
   (c) Accruals
   (d) Prudence
   (e) Money measurement.

2.5   Double-entry book-keeping is based on the *dual aspect* rule. Explain this rule.

2.6   Explain which accounting rule would be applied in the following circumstances:
   (a) The purchase of premises for £75,000 in 1974 and which has a resale value of £450,000 in 1990.
   (b) A customer, who is facing bankruptcy, owing £5,150.
   (c) A phone bill incurred in the current year ended 31/12/19x8 but which will not be paid until 16/1/19x9.
   (d) Small levels of stock of stationery valued at £75. Ordinary stock has a value of £76,500.
   (e) The value of having a good sales manager. If he/she left, the firm's annual level of sales would fall by £300,000.
   (f) The demand by shareholders to be told exactly how much was spent on every identifiable cost in the past year.
   (g) Management's wish to change the basis of calculating depreciation.

2.7   Adam Brown started his own business on 1/1/19x9. The following is a list of his transactions in January of 19x9.
   (a) Introduced his own cash of £7,000 and paid it all into a business bank account.
   (b) Paid £3,600 by cheque for the purchase of machinery.
   (c) Bought raw materials for £1,200, paying by cheque.
   (d) Made sales of £600. He banked £250 and kept £350 in cash.
   (e) Paid January's rent of £250 by cash.
   (f) Paid wages of £190 by cheque.
   (g) Bought a second hand typewriter for £60 cash.

   Required: Prepare *journal entries* for these transactions.

2.8   At the start of Arthur Brown's business, he paid £1,000 of his own money into a business bank account. He also raised a bank loan of £750 which was also paid into the bank. The following transactions then took place:
   (a) Made sales, for cash, of £700.
   (b) Bought raw materials, by cheque, for £235.
   (c) Made more sales of £525, again for cash.
   (d) Deposited £1,100 into the bank. (This money came from sales made above.)
   (e) Bought raw materials for £315 on credit.
   (f) Paid casual wages of £60 by cash.
   (g) Made a sale for £100, on credit.

   Required: prepare *journal entries* for the above transactions. From the journal entries, prepare appropriate *ledger accounts* and then produce a *trial balance*.

2.9   After posting all transactions, Robin Jones closed off her ledger accounts and listed the balances as follows:

Cash	£ 500
Raw materials bought	12,000
Owner's capital	6,000
Loans	2,500
Rent paid	2,500
Debtors	2,000
Sales	22,500
Machinery	3,000
Personal drawings	3,000
Interest received	500
Wages paid	4,000
Interest paid	200
Car	5,800

Required: prepare a *trial balance* for Ms Jones.

2.10   Which of the following errors would cause unequal totals in a trial balance? Which accounts would be wrong?

(a) A £200 cash payment for a typewriter recorded as a £20 debit to Office Equipment and a £20 credit to Cash.
(b) A payment of £1,200 to a creditor was recorded as a £1,200 debit to Creditors and a £2,100 credit to the Bank.
(c) The collection of £750 from a debtor was recorded as a £750 debit to Debtors and a £750 debit to Owner's Capital.
(d) A payment, by cheque, of £172 to a creditor was recorded as a debit of £172 to Creditors and a debit of £172 to Cash.

2.11   Joe Sow is a trader in leather goods who sells his products at an indoor market. He trades on both cash and credit terms. At the start of a week he had stock which had a resale value of £2,500 but which had cost him £1,100, £500 in his bank account, and debtors of £1,250. He had no other assets except for his stall which had cost him £1,000, and had no liabilities.

During the week he sold goods for £3,000 and received cash, and made credit sales of £1,250. Some old debtors settled their accounts and Joe received £350. His purchases of stock amounted to £2,150 for which he had paid cash.

At the end of the week, he still had his stall, stock which had cost him £1,150, his debtors, £1,000 in the bank, and some cash.

Required: Write *journal entries* to account for this information, prepare his *ledger accounts* and then extract a *trial balance*.

2.12   On 1/1/19xx Ms Julie Granger opened up a small shop. She withdrew £6,000 from her bank account and opened a business account with that money. She borrowed a further £14,000 and promptly spent it on buying her shop. It cost £2,500 to buy a till, counter, shelves and a window display, but she has only paid £2,000 so far. She bought £2,700 worth of stock, obtaining credit for £1,900 of it. Ms Grainger recently bought a car for herself for £2,000 but finds that she now uses it exclusively for her business. She bought a microwave cooker for £300 for her personal use, using the business's chequebook, and also lent £300 to a friend using the same account.

Required: prepare Ms Granger's *ledger accounts* from the above information.

2.13   On 31/12/19x8 M. Jarvis's ledger contained the following list of balances;

Owner's capital	£9,600
Equipment	6,500
Vehicles	2,700
Loans	3,000
Stock	2,900
Overdraft	1,500
debtors	2,000

Jarvis only maintains a cash book and a summary of that cash book showed the following totals for the year to 31/12/19x9:

Income	
Sales	£39,584
Capital introduced	5,000

Expenditure	
Raw materials	£10,950
Wages	4,700
Heat and light	1,900
Rent and rates	3,500
Equipment	6,300
Administration	400
Miscellaneous	4,450

His bank account showed that he had paid £44,584 into the account during the year and had written cheques totalling £32,200.

On speaking to Jarvis, you find that he writes up his cash book only when he pays money into the bank or when he writes a cheque. Accordingly, the following information is unrecorded:

(a) his closing debtors of £1,600;
(b) his closing creditors for:

raw materials £1,500
heat and light   370
accounting fee   425;

(c) closing stock which cost £3,600.

In addition, you discover that included in Raw Materials in the cash book is £570 spent on wages, and that he took £85 per week out of weekly takings for personal use and recorded only the balance as sales.

Required: Prepare *ledger accounts* to account for the above information and then produce a *trial balance*.

3 The financial statements

Introduction

Having prepared the trial balance, it is now possible to start to prepare the financial statements: the *profit and loss account* and the *balance sheet*.

To recap, the profit and loss account is the statement which measures a firm's activities over a period of time, profit being defined as the excess of *revenue income* over *revenue costs*. The balance sheet, however, is a 'moment-in-time' document which summarizes a firm's financial standing at a particular date. It will show all that a firm owns (its assets) and the sources of funding for those assets (its liabilities).

The profit and loss account

The objective of the profit and loss account is to determine the level of profit, or loss, which has been earned by a firm over an accounting period. It does this by listing all revenue income and then deducting all revenue costs, which have been matched to the accounting period being considered.

The first task, then, is to examine the trial balance and identify all revenue items. To facilitate matters at this stage, the following definitions may help:

- *Revenue income* would include all income that a firm would normally expect to earn in an accounting period. For the majority of firms, this would normally be restricted to *sales*, *fees* earned and *interest* received. It would not include sources of cash such as capital introduced, loans raised, grants received or income from the sale of assets. Such sources are not 'normal' or renewable.
- *Revenue costs* would include all costs which a firm would normally expect to incur every year. They are recurrent costs and the firm receives nothing permanent in return. Examples of such costs would be *wages*, *raw materials*, *power*, *interest paid* and *rent*.

   Costs which provide a firm with something permanent, such as a new vehicle, would be excluded since that would be *capital expenditure* (or the provision of an asset). The repayment of loans would also be excluded (although money is spent on repaying a loan, there is no real cost incurred in returning to somebody that person's own money).

The format of the profit and loss account is normally divided into two parts. First, there is the *trading account* (or *manufacturing account* if the firm is in manufacturing), which identifies the profit made in simply buying in units and then selling them. The manufacturing account identifies the profit made in making something and then selling it. This difference, in either the trading profit or the manufacturing profit, is referred to as the firm's *gross profit*.

The profit and loss account starts with the gross profit and deducts from that all the remaining revenue costs incurred. Although there is a distinction made between the trading account and the profit and loss account, this distinction is normally only seen in the accounts of large organizations. The accounts of smaller firms normally do not distinguish between the two accounts except by highlighting the gross profit.

Using as an example the trial balance of Steven Scott, his profit and loss account can now be drawn up as follows:

Steven Scott
Trading and profit and loss account
for the period 1/1/19xx to 6/1/19xx

Sales			£2,853
less Cost of sales			
	Purchase of raw materials		1,364
	Gross profit		£1,489
less Expenses			
	Rent	£150	
	Insurance	360	
	Stationery	70	
	Delivery	16	
	Interest	100	
	Wages	240	
	Travel costs	25	
			961
	Net profit		£ 528

Points to note:

(1)   The title of the account always states the name of the firm and that it is a profit and loss account. The phrase, 'for the period . . .', is included to show the time period being covered by the account.

(2)   As the amount of sales (£2,853) indicates, the profit and loss account shows the value of sales earned in a period, not just the cash received. The £2,853 is made up of sales which produced cash in the period (£1,285) and sales on credit (£1,568).

(3)   All expenses are *revenue* costs. None have resulted in the firm acquiring something permanent (assets), nor do any of the costs relate to the repayment of loans.

(4)   The section down to gross profit is, in fact, the trading account, the remainder being the profit and loss account proper. No formal distinction is made simply because the size of the business does not warrant such a detailed division.

The balance sheet

The balance sheet shows the financial status of a firm at any given moment in time. It shows the items which are owned by the firm, its assets, and sets this off against a list of claims on these assets by those who provided funds with which to buy those assets, its liabilities. The balance sheet, therefore, can be likened to a photograph of the financial state of the business showing, on the one hand, what the firm has and, on the other, where the money came from to acquire those assets.

The balance sheet will always balance. This is because of the dual aspect rule and the fact that every debit has a credit. If a balance sheet does not balance, then an error has been made in recording the fundamental dual effect of transactions made by the business.

Assets

Assets are those things of value aquired by a firm at some cost to the business. The balance sheet does not simply list those assets but displays them in a logical order by subtotalling *fixed assets* (or long-term assets) and *current assets* (or short-term assets). Conventionally, the distinction between fixed and current assets has been one year. Thus, if the asset is expected to remain in the firm in an unaltered form for more than one year, it is classed as a fixed asset; if not, it is classed as a current asset.

FIXED ASSETS
The permanent assets which a firm could have are fairly common to almost all firms and would normally be classified as follows:

- Land and buildings.
- Plant, machinery and equipment.
- Fixtures and fittings.
- Motor vehicles.
- Investments.

Expenditure on such assets does not appear in the profit and loss account; it appears in the balance sheet alone.

CURRENT ASSETS
Again, the classification of current assets is common to most businesses and would appear as follows:

- Stock.
- Work in progress.

- Finished goods.
- Debtors (people who owe the firm money).
- Bank.
- Cash.

The order in which current assets appear in the balance sheet (as well as fixed assets) is said to be in the reverse order of liquidity; that is, the most permanent comes first, and that asset which is closest to being turned into cash comes last.

The above distinction between fixed and current assets need not always hold true. For example, lorries would normally be considered to be fixed assets except in a firm whose business is to sell lorries. In such a case, any lorries it has would be more properly classed as its *stock*, that is, as a current asset.

A more useful distinction, therefore, may be that fixed assets are those assets which are acquired to enable the firm to function on a long-term basis, whereas current assets allow the firm to function on a day-to-day basis or are the result of everyday transactions.

Liabilities

Liabilities should not be regarded as debts (although they frequently are) but as sources of finance – where the money came from to buy the firm's assets. As for assets, liabilities do not appear as a simple list in the balance sheet but are distinguished between *long-term* and *short-term* liabilities (short-term liabilities being called *current liabilities*). The general one year rule applies to separate them.

CURRENT LIABILITIES

Current liabilities are generally debts which a firm is legally bound to repay within one year. The normal current liabilities to be expected in a balance sheet are:

- Trade creditors.
- Taxation.
- Value added tax.
- Short-term loans.
- Dividends payable (for limited companies only).
- Bank overdrafts.

Included in trade creditors are all suppliers of goods and services who are awaiting payment at the date of the balance sheet and could include any cost which a firm is likely to incur.

LONG-TERM LIABILITIES

These are the sources of finance which have been supplied on a long-term basis and are not due for repayment in less than one year. It is normal to see such liabilities categorized into those supplied by the owners of the firm (*owners' capital*) and those supplied by other third parties such as banks.

The *owners' capital* is normally shown thus:

> Capital introduced (or Opening balance)
> *plus* Current year's profit
> *less* Personal drawings

Note that it is normal, except in the case of limited companies, to show the personal drawings, or personal wages, of the owners as a deduction from capital, since, theoretically, all money in a firm belongs to them and they can, if they wish, take everything out, not just what they have decided to take.

Using as an example the trial balance of Steven Scott (Chapter 2), his balance sheet can be drawn up:

Steven Scott
Balance sheet
as at 6/1/19xx

Fixed assets			
Equipment			£2,200
Office equipment			416
Vehicle			1,800
			£4,416
Current assets			
debtors		£1,568	
bank		1,244	
		£2,812	
less Current liabilities			
Creditors		—	
			2,812
Net assets			£7,228

as financed by:

Opening capital	£4,800
add Profit	528
	£5,328
less Personal drawings	100
	£5,228
Long-term loans	2,000
	£7,228

Points to note:

(1) The phrase in the title 'as at 6/1/19xx' indicates that the balance sheet applies only to that moment in time. The balance sheet of 7/1/19xx could be different. If, for example, Steven withdrew another £20 on 7/1/19xx then the Bank figure would differ as would the personal drawings figure.

(2) The figures are at cost price. The market value of assets could be, and probably is, quite different.

(3)   Note the format of the balance sheet. There are a number of formats which could be used in presenting a firm's assets and liabilities but this particular method is most common nowadays for firms which are not limited companies.

This particular format balances net assets with long-term sources of finance (the opening capital, retained profits and long-term loans). Current assets are netted off against current liabilities, as it is more sensible to display similar items together. In this case, current assets and current liabilities are the result of the normal operations of a firm and, as such, are linked to each other. The difference between current assets and current liabilities is called the *working capital*. This represents the cost of current assets which have not been acquired on credit but have been financed by the firm itself.

Adjustments to the trial balance

The example of Steven Scott above is a rather simplified introduction to the construction of financial statements. There are a number of complications which can, and do, arise in practice. Some of these complications will now be considered.

The trial balance of a firm is incomplete in that it does not always show all transactions up to a given date. It will not show the value of stock on hand at the balance sheet date, nor will it show debts which the firm will have incurred but for which the firm has yet to receive a bill. For example, presumably Steven Scott has a telephone which he has used. Obviously, in using the telephone, he is incurring costs, but these will not be shown in the trial balance if British Telecom has still to invoice him.

The trial balance has to be adjusted and the principal adjustments which will now be considered are for:

- Stock.
- Depreciation.
- Accrued charges.
- Prepayments.

Stock adjustments

Firms which are in either retailing or manufacturing will buy in large quantities of stock during a year either for resale or for use in the manufacturing process. At the end of each year, such firms will undoubtedly have unsold or unused stock on hand.

The matching principle requires that only the cost of purchasing stock, sufficient to account for the volume of sales made in an accounting period, should be used in determining profit. This means that excess stock purchased during the year must be discounted when determining the value of the cost of goods actually sold.

Theoretically, this is a relatively simple process; for example, if a firm has 100 units of stock at the start of a year, buys in 1,200 units during the year and has 150 units on hand at the end, then the volume used, or sold, would be:

Opening stock	100
add Bought in	1,200
Total available for use	1,300
less Closing stock	150
Total used	1,150

By applying unit costs to the volumes of stock, quantities would become values, and the *total used* figure would become the *cost of sales* value for inclusion in the profit and loss account.

The value for cost of sales is, therefore:

```
    OS (opening stock)
 +     P (purchases made in year)
 −     CS (closing stock)
```

Stock Valuation

In practice, valuing stock and hence cost of sales is not quite so simple. Two main problems present themslves:

(a) Large quantities of various items of stock may exist, thus making it difficult to ascertain the true volumes on hand.

(b) It is often difficult to determine the actual cost of closing stock. As a simple illustration, imagine a firm which has to buy in only nails, all of which are one inch long. During the past year the cost of nails increased (by six increments) from £1.00 per kilo to £2.50 per kilo. At the end of the year the firm has 100 kilos of nails in stock. What is the cost of those nails? Some will have been bought at £1.00 per kilo, some at £2.50 and others at the various prices in between. Unfortunately, one nail looks exactly like any other nail and has no way of identifying its purchase price. The cost of those 100 kilos could be £100, or £250, or anything in between.

To overcome these problems, techniques have had to be developed which will estimate the cost of closing stock and, hence, cost of sales. It should be noted that there is no way of accurately valuing stock. All methods must result in an approximation only. Since the value of closing stock affects the value of cost of sales in the profit and loss account, and since closing stock is subject to some subjectivity, the level of profit disclosed must also be the subject of some subjectivity.

Assume that a firm has just reached its year end and that its stock records show:

	Stock in			Stock out
Date	Volume	Unit cost	Value	Volume
1/2/19x9	100	£1	£100	
1/4/19x9	150	2	300	
1/6/19x9				125
1/8/19x9	200	3	600	
1/9/19x9				225
	450		£1,000	350

Thus, during the year, 450 units were bought at a cost of £1,000. During the year 350 units were used, thus leaving 100 units in stock at the year end. What value should be given to those 100 units? Three methods of valuation are shown below.

FIRST-IN-FIRST-OUT (FIFO)

This method assumes that the stock which was purchased first will be the first to be used. Therefore any remaining stock would be valued at the latest unit costs, that is:

Date	In		Out	Balance		
1/2/19x9	100 @ £1			100 @ £1		£100
1/4/19x9	150 @ £2			100 @ £1		£100
150 @ £2	300	£400				
1/6/19x9			100 @ £1	125 @ £2		£250
			25 @ £2			
1/8/19x9	200 @ £3			125 @ £2	£250	
				200 @ £3	600	£850
1/9/19x9			125 @ £2	100 @ £3		£300
			100 @ £3			

Using FIFO, the end stock would be valued at £300, and the cost of sales would be (assuming no opening stock):

Purchases	£1,000	
less Closing stock	300	
	£ 700	

LAST-IN-FIRST-OUT (LIFO)

This method assumes that stock is used from the most recent intake of stock. Thus:

Date	In	Out	Balance		
1/2/19x9	100 @ £1		100 @ £1		£100
1/4/19x9	150 @ £2		100 @ £1	£100	£400
			150 @ £2	£300	

1/6/19x9		125 @ £2	100 @ £1	£100	£150
			25 @ £2	£ 50	
1/8/19x9	200 @ £3		100 @ £1	£100	£750
			25 @ £2	50	
			200 @ £3	600	
1/9/19x9		200 @ £3	100 @ £1		£100
		25 @ £2			

Using LIFO, the end stock is valued at £100 and the cost of sales would be:

Purchases	£1,000
less Closing stock	100
	£ 900

AVERAGE COST (AVCO)

As the name suggests, this method requires that, on receipt of new stock, the value of all stock is taken as the average value of all stock received so far after deducting stock used. Stock used is deemed to have been used at the prevailing average cost at the time of usage.

Date	In	Out	Average cost of stock held	Number of units held	Value
1/1/	100 @ £1		£1	100	£100
1/4/	150 @ £2		£100 + (150 × £2)		
			100 + 150		
			= £1.60	250	£400
1/6/		125 @ £1.6	£1.60	125	£200
1/8/	200 @ £3		£200 + (200 × £3)		
			125 + 200		
			= £2.46	325	£799
1/9/		225 @ £2.46	2.46	100	£246

Using AVCO gives a closing stock valuation of £246, and a cost of sales of:

Purchases	£1,000
less Closing stock	246
	£ 756

It is clear that each method gives a different closing stock value, a different cost of sales value, and, hence, a different ultimate profit value. None are wrong.

The method of stock valuation which should be adopted will often be determined by a firm's pattern of stock usage. For example:

- FIFO may be appropriate in firms which have good stock procedures, where new intakes of stock are stored behind existing stock.
- LIFO may be appropriate in firms which have stock in loose bulk such as stocks of coal. New intakes will be dumped on top of existing stock and, obviously, will be used first.
- AVCO may be appropriate in firms where new stock must become mixed with existing stock such as in garages. New stocks of petrol will mix with existing levels and it would be impossible to identify which drop of petrol was new stock and which was old.

Depreciation adjustment

As mentioned earlier, the purchase of assets does not appear in the profit and loss account. One of the reasons that this is so is that an asset is going to endure over more than one time period and affect more than one time period's profits. It was previously explained that it would be 'unfair' if the cost of an asset were to be charged against one year's profits when subsequent years would also benefit.

Depreciation is simply a means of allocating the original cost of an asset over the years in which it will be used. In accounting, depreciation is not an attempt to measure the decline in value of an asset; it is just a means of equitably spreading the cost over an asset's useful life.

All assets (except, usually, land) have a finite life, although the length of that life may be determined by various factors such as:

(a)   normal wear and tear;
(b)   obsolescence;
(c)   passage of time;
(d)   technological advance.

No matter the reasons which cause assets to have finite lives, given that they do then all assets ought to be depreciated over their expected periods of economic usefulness.

As with the valuation of stock, there are a number of ways that the annual depreciation can be calculated. Three methods in particular, however, predominate in business – the *straight line method*, the *reducing balance method* and the *sum of years digits method*.

Straight line method

In this method the net cost of an asset is depreciated evenly throughout the expected life of an asset. Thus, each year will bear an equal proportion of the cost.

As an example, assume a firm has bought a machine for £10,000. It is expected to have a useful life of five years after which it will be valueless. (Note: the value to be depreciated is the net cost of the machine to the business. In this case the net cost is £10,000. If, after five years the machine could be sold for scrap for £1,000, then the cost to be depreciated would be

£9,000, since that would be the net cost of the machine to the firm.) The annual depreciation charge is:

$$\frac{\text{(net cost) £10,000}}{\text{(useful life) 5 years}} = \text{£2,000}$$

Depreciation is not just a cost to the profit and loss account but its effect is also seen in the balance sheet. It may help to look at fixed assets in the balance sheet as a 'holding bay', where the cost of the asset is held until it can be transferred to the profit and loss account, thus:

	1	2	3	4	Years 5
Opening balance	10,000	8,000	6,000	4,000	2,000
less Depreciation (shown in P&L account)	2,000	2,000	2,000	2,000	2,000
Balance (value in each year's balance sheet)	8,000	6,000	4,000	2,000	—

Reducing balance method

In this method, rather than each year having an arithmetically equal share of the cost, each year bears an equal percentage of the asset's value. In the above example, this could be 40%. The percentage is applied not to the original cost but to the reduced balance after deducting previous years' depreciation (hence this method's name). Thus:

	1	2	Years 3	4	5
Opening balance	10,000	6,000	3,600	2,160	1,296
less Depreciation (shown in P&L account)	4,000	2,400	1,440	864	518
Balance (shown in balance sheet)	6,000	3,600	2,160	1,296	778

Sum of years digits method

This method is somewhat similar to the reducing balance method in that future years will bear a progressively smaller depreciation charge. The annual charge is a reducing fraction applied to the original net cost of an asset, the fraction being found by:

(a) the numerator is the year number, counting backwards
(b) the denominator is the sum of the years of the expected life of the asset.

In the above example, the fraction for year 1 would be 5/15 (5 since that is the last year and 15 since that is the sum of the years 1–5). Year 2's fraction would be 4/15 and so on down to year 5 where the fraction would be 1/15, thus:

	Years				
	1	2	3	4	5
(Applicable fraction)	5/15	4/15	3/15	2/15	1/15
Open balance	10,000	6,667	4,000	2,000	667
less Depreciation charge	3,333	2,667	2,000	1,333	667
Balance	6,667	4,000	2,000	667	—

As can be seen, different methods of depreciation produce different annual depreciation charges. The result must, therefore, be that different profit levels are possible. Assume that the above firm which purchased the machine had earned £15,000 profits before depreciation. The difference in net profit under the three methods in year 1 would be:

	Straight line	Reducing balance	Sum years digits
Profit	£15,000	£15,000	£15,000
less Depreciation	2,000	4,000	3,333
Net profit	£13,000	£11,000	£11,667

As with the different methods of stock valuation, all profit levels are correct for year 1. It all depends on which depreciation method is chosen.

The appropriate journal entry to account for depreciation would be:

Debit Depreciation (P&L account)
Credit Fixed assets (balance sheet)

Choosing the appropriate depreciation method

Which method ought to be adopted will depend on the expected wear pattern of an asset over its useful life. The three methods described above have different annual depreciation charges: the straight line method has an even charge over the asset's life; the reducing balance method has high charges in the earlier years and low charges in the later years (the charge becoming exponentially smaller); and the sum of years digits method basic-ally echoes the reducing balance method except that the annual charge becomes arithmetically smaller. This can be shown graphically, as in Figure 3.1.

If the expected wear of an asset were plotted over time on a graph and its curve were similar to any of the above curves, then that would be the method to choose.

As an example, a car wears out very quickly in its early years, but the wearing out becomes less and less severe as the years pass. In fact, it is

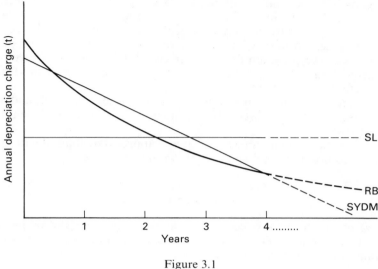

Figure 3.1

doubtful if the car would ever be valueless. That being the case, the reducing balance method would seem to be the most appropriate.

Accruals adjustment

An *accrual* is an estimate of a bill which the firm knows is due at the year-end but for which it has yet to be invoiced. The usual accruals would consist of the telephone account and the heat and light account, although other accounts may also have to be accrued.

The effect of an accrual will be to increase the expense in the profit and loss account and increase the sums due (creditors) in the balance sheet. It is not uncommon to see in the balance sheet, under current liabilities, a separate account headed 'Accruals'.

Example: a firm last paid its telephone bill on 31/1/19x9. Its year end is 31/3/19x9 and at that date it estimated that the cost of the phone from 1/2/19x9 to 31/3/19x9 was £275. This £275 would have to be accrued in the firm's annual accounts. It could not appear in the trial balance if only because the invoice has yet to be received.

In the workings to produce the accounts the following journal entry would be required:

```
Debit Telephone           275
   Credit Accruals (or creditors)       275
```

Prepayments adjustment

The accruals adjustment is required for expenses which, although incurred, have not yet been invoiced. The opposite can also happen; that is, a firm could incur expenditure in one year which is relevant to the subsequent year. As an example, a firm may have a year-end 31/12/19x9. If this firm paid its annual insurance premium for the year ended 31/12/19x0 in December of the current year, the expenditure would have been incurred in 19x9 but would refer to the year 19x0.

The prepayments adjustment is used to apply the matching rule and, in the above case, remove the cost of the premium from 19x9 and include it in the costs of 19x0.

If the insurance premium were £350, the appropriate journal entry in the workings to produce the final accounts would be:

Debit Prepayments	350
Credit Insurance	350

The effect on the final accounts would be to increase the prepayments account (a current asset, similar to debtors) and decrease the expense of insurance in the profit and loss account.

A comprehensive example

The following is an example which draws on all the points previously discussed. You are advised to follow through the example and then try it yourself without referring to the answer. If you have any problems, re-read the appropriate section of this chapter which covers your area of difficulty and try again. Do not proceed unless you are happy with the basics of financial accounting.

EXAMPLE

Mary Matthews has owned her newsagent's shop for some years. Her trial balance for the year ended 31/3/19x9 was:

	Debit	Credit
Sales		£67,400
Purchases	£49,750	
Rent and rates	3,000	
Shop fittings	5,500	
Office equipment	1,700	
Van	3,000	
Debtors as at 31/3/19x9	250	
Creditors as at 31/3/19x9		760
Stock as at 1/4/19x8	950	
Wages	4,200	
Personal drawings	5,000	
Bank loan as at 31/3/19x9		3,500

Bank account	360	
Repairs	200	
Heat and light	950	
Motoring costs	1,200	
Capital account		4,850
Loan interest	450	
	76,510	76,510

You are given the following additional information:

(1) Stock was valued at £1,070 on 31/3/19x9.
(2) Depreciation is charged at 25% on the van and at 10% on all other assets.
(3) One of Mary's debtors has moved away and she does not know where to. This debtor owes her £75.
(4) The last electricity bill was for the quarter to 31/1/19x9. Mary estimates that she has used £200 of power since then.
(5) A bill from her garage, dated 30/3/19x9, for £150 has not been entered in her books.

Required: prepare Mary's financial accounts for the year ended 31/3/19x9.
The following procedure should be used in such questions:

STEP ONE
Identify all the accounts which have to be adjusted. These will always be shown in the additional notes. Working notes should then be prepared to account for the adjustments.

(1) *Stock and cost of sales*

Opening stock	£ 950	(from TB)
add Purchases	49,750	(from TB)
	£50,700	
less Closing stock	1,070	(from note 1)
	£49,630	

(2) *Depreciation*

	Fittings	Equipment	Van	Total
Depreciation rate	(10%)	(10%)	(25%)	
per trial balance	£5,500	1,700	3,000	
Depreciation	550	170	750	£1,470
Book value at 31/3/x9	£4,950	1,530	2,250	

(3) *Bad debts*

Debtors at 31/3/19x9	£250	(from TB)
less Bad debts	75	(from note 3)
	£175	

(Note: a bad debts cost of £75 will also appear in the profit and loss account.)

(4) *Electricity*

Heat and light	£ 950	(from TB)
add Accrued charge	200	(from note 4)
	£1,150	

(5) *Garage bill*

Motoring costs	£1,200	(from TB)
add Outstanding bill	150	(from note 5)
	£1,350	

(6) Creditors

per Trial balance	£ 760
add Electricity accrual	200
add Garage bill outstanding	150
	£1,110

STEP TWO

Prepare the trading and profit and loss account for the accounting period. Most figures will come straight from the trial balance. However, do not forget that some revenue costs have been adjusted. In those cases, the figure which will appear in the profit and loss account will be the adjusted figure, not the 'raw' figure in the trial balance.

The figures in brackets refer to the working notes which show their calculations.

Mary Matthews, Newsagents
Trading and profit and loss account
for the year ended 31/3/19x9

Sales		£67,400
less Cost of sales (1)		49,630
Gross profit		£17,770
less Expenses		
Rent and rates	£3,000	
Wages	4,200	
Repairs	200	
Heat and light (4)	1,150	
Motoring costs (5)	1,350	
Bad debts (3)	75	
Depreciation (2)	1,470	
Interest paid	450	
		11,895
Net profit		£ 5,875

STEP THREE

Prepare the balance sheet.

Mary Matthews, Newsagents
Balance sheet
as at 31/3/19x9

Fixed assets		
Shop fittings (2)		£4,950
Office equipment (2)		1,530
Vehicle (2)		2,250
		£8,730
Current assets		
Stock	£1,070	
Debtors (3)	175	
Bank	360	
	£1,605	
less Current liabilities		
Creditors (6)	1,110	
		495
		£9,225

as financed by:

Owner's capital	
Opening balance	£4,850
add Profit (from P&L account)	5,875
	£10,725
less Personal drawings	5,000
	£5,725
Long-term loans	
	3,500
	£9,225

Questions

3.1 Outline the content and function of both the profit and loss account and balance sheet.

3.2 Why does the balance sheet balance?

3.3 'The balance sheet shows what a company is worth.' Discuss.

3.4 'A persistent myth is that financial statements reflect a high degree of precision, and that the values shown in them are both accurate and correct.' Discuss.

3.5 Explain the following terms:

(a) Net current assets.
(b) Gross profit.
(c) Accrued charges.
(d) Revenue expenditure.

(e) Loan capital.
(f) Owners' capital.

3.6   What is the difference between fixed assets and current assets? Why is this difference important in the preparation of financial accounts?

3.7   What is depreciation? Outline the mechanics of two methods of depreciation with which you are familiar.

3.8   Discuss the assertion that depreciation and stock valuation are both highly judgemental yet of crucial importance in reporting a firm's financial position.

3.9   Outline the mechanics of three methods of stock valuation with which you are familiar.

3.10 An extract of the balance sheet of Acecars as at 31/12/19x8 shows:

Fixed assets

	Premises	Equipment	Vehicles
Cost	£75,000	£120,000	£80,000
less Depreciation to date	—	43,200	32,000
Value as at 31/12/19x8	£75,000	£ 76,800	£48,000

The firm has adopted the following depreciation policies:

(a) Premises – no depreciation charged.
(b) Equipment – at 20% reducing balance.
(c) Vehicles – evenly over 5 years.

Required: calculate the depreciation charge for 19x9 and show the figures for fixed assets as they would appear in the balance sheet as at 31/12/19x9.

3.11 The Home Bright Company has the following depreciation policies:

(a) Charge a full year's depreciation in the year of a purchase.
(b) Charge no depreciation in the year of a disposal.
(c) Depreciate vehicles evenly over 4 years.
(d) Depreciate machinery at 25% reducing balance.

The firm's balance sheet at 31/12/19x8 showed

Fixed assets

	Machinery	Vehicles
Cost	£200,000	£120,000
less Accumulated depreciation	87,500	60,000
	£112,500	£ 60,000

In the year ended 19x9, the following assets were disposed of:

Asset	Year of Acquisition	Cost
Machinery	19x8	£20,000
Machinery	19x7	40,000
Vehicles	19x7	28,000

In addition, the firm bought new machinery costing £60,000 in 19x9.

Required: calculate the depreciation charge for 19x9 and show the fixed assets as they would appear in the balance sheet as at 31/12/19x9.

3.12   On 1/1/19x9 Blue Brothers Company had 1,200 units of stock on hand which had cost £2,400. During that year, the following stock movements took place:

| | *In* | | *Out* |
	Quantity	Value	Quantity
1/2/19x9	16,400	£41,000	
1/4/19x9			14,000
1/5/19x9			400
1/6/19x9	11,000	£33,000	
1/7/19x9	4,000	£14,000	
1/9/19x9			3,000
1/10/19x9			4,000
1/11/19x9			3,000

Required: prepare a schedule which will show the value of stock on hand at the end of each month when there was movement in stock. (The firm adopts the FIFO method of stock valuation.)

3.13   The Hawk Company uses material X in manufacture. The following information refers to receipts and issues of that material in the first quarter of 19x9.

Jan.	1	opening balance	100 units @ £2.00 each
	10	received	300 units @ £2.00 each
	15	issued	90 units
	31	issued	150 units
Feb.	10	received	240 units @ £2.50
	15	issued	200 units
	28	issued	170 units
Mar.	10	received	270 units @ £3.00
	11	issued	50 units
	15	issued	110 units
	31	issued	50 units

Required: prepare a table which will show *receipts*, *issues* and *balances* (in terms of quantity and cost/value) according to the date of occurrence assuming that the firm uses AVCO and hence the end stock valuation. What would the end stock valuation have been if FIFO had been used?

3.14   Jane Smith owns a small manufacturing firm, and at the end of her financial year, 31/3/19x9, her accounting records contained the following information:

	Debit £	Credit £
Sales		164,000
Opening capital		73,500
Premises	96,000	
Machinery	55,000	
Debtors	24,000	
Opening stock	10,000	
Manufacturing costs	24,000	
Creditors		25,000
Long-term loans		62,000
Personal drawings	10,000	
Overdraft		· 2,000

Overheads	31,000	
Raw materials	76,500	
	326,500	326,500

In addition, you are informed that Ms Smith had £14,000 worth of stock on hand at the year end and that her machinery is to be depreciated at 20%.

Required: prepare the profit and loss account and balance sheet for Ms Smith as at 31/3/19x9.

3.15   The following figures were taken from the books of account of the Eagle Company on 31/7/19x9:

	Debit £	Credit £
Owner's capital		160,000
Plant and machinery	90,000	
Premises	160,000	
Vehicles	25,000	
Sales		400,000
Purchase of raw materials	150,000	
Sales returned	10,000	
Stock at1/8/19x8	20,000	
Heat and light	2,000	
Insurances	1,000	
Creditors		15,000
Other expenses	36,000	
Bank	5,000	
Debtors	12,000	
Wages	75,000	
Long-term loan		10,000
Loan interest	1,000	
Purchases returned		5,000
Telephone	3,000	
	590,000	590,000

The following information is also available:

(a) Stock at 31/7/19x9 was valued at £25,000.
(b) Plant and machinery are to be depreciated at 10%.
(c) Vehicles are to be depreciated at 25%. There is to be no depreciation on premises.
(d) There are accrued charges of £2,000 for raw materials to be accounted for.

Required: prepare the profit and loss account and balance sheet for the Eagle Company as at 31/7/19x9.

3.16   Vanilla cone runs a successful fleet of motorized grocery shops and the following information was taken from her records for the year ended 31/12/19x9:

Opening capital account	£ 30,000
Sales	176,600
Vans at cost	25,000

Opening stock	14,300
Bank	18,400
Purchases	128,300
Wages	14,000
Debtors	16,500
Creditors	18,200
General costs	4,100
Motor costs	6,300
Insurance	1,000
Bad debts	200
Depreciation to 31/12/19x8	10,000
Personal drawings	8,500
Discounts received	1,800

Before the annual accounts can be prepared, the following additional information must be considered:

(a) Doubtful debts amount to £900 and must be provided for.
(b) Unsold stock at the year end cost £18,000 but had a resale value of £30,000.
(c) Employer's National Insurance contributions for December have not yet been paid or recorded. These amount to £100.
(d) Included in Insurance is a payment of £200 which refers to next year's insurance premium.
(e) The vans are to be depreciated at 20% straight line.
(f) Included in Motor Costs is a payment for road taxing Ms Cone's private motor car. This amounted to £55.

Required: prepare the financial accounts for Ms Cone as at 31/2/19x9.

4 Manufacturing accounts and partnerships

Introduction

The previous chapter discussed the general principles in preparing a firm's financial statements. The firms involved were relatively simple in that they were sole traders and trading organizations only. This chapter will examine some complications which can arise when a firm is neither a sole trader nor a simple trader. However, it should be borne in mind that all possible complications are only variations on the general theme of Chapter 3.

More specifically, this chapter will consider:

- Manufacturing accounts.
- Partnership agreements.
- Partnership accounts.

Manufacturing accounts

In trading firms which do little more than buy in goods and then resell them, *gross profit* is defined as *sales* less *cost of sales*. Cost of sales is found by:

Opening stock
+ purchases
− closing stock

Despite the problems involved in valuing stock, this calculation of cost of sales is a relatively easy process simply because the firm has nothing to do with the purchases, except sell them, after they have been bought.

The problem facing a manufacturer is that, after buying in raw materials, the firm must use that stock and convert it into something else before sales can be made. At the year-end, a manufacturer will have a variety of stock, made up of:

- Raw material – unused purchases.
- Work in progress – part-completed items.
- Finished goods – completed items waiting to be sold.

In addition, the gross profit of a manufacturer is defined as the difference between sales and the costs incurred in the manufacturing process. It is not

just the difference between sales and purchases. The cost of sales calculation, therefore, must take into account not just the adjusted purchases figure
but also all additional manufacturing costs.

The most obvious additional manufacturing cost is the cost of manufacturing labour such as the shop-floor workers' wages. Another manufacturing cost would be cost of heat and light to the factory or the cost of the shop-
floor foreman's wages.

So far four manufacturing costs have been identified:

- Raw materials.
- Employees' wages.
- Factory heat and light.
- Foreman's wage.

In considering the cost of production, there are two types of cost:

- *direct costs*; and
- *indirect costs*.

Direct costs are those costs such as the cost of raw material and employees' wages which are easily identifiable with the end product. Indirect costs
are those costs which are inescapable in production but which are not
readily identifiable in the finished product. For example, consider this book
and the costs involved in its production. It is easy to imagine the cost of the
paper (the raw material) and the wages of the printer – these would be the
direct costs. But the book had to be printed in a factory which used power,
and the printers had to have a foreman. It is much more difficult to 'see'
these costs in the finished article, yet they had to be paid – these are the indirect costs.

The *manufacturing account* has to account for all direct and indirect costs
of production, normally in three sub-categories of *materials, labour* and
overheads ('overheads' being the term used to describe all other costs except
materials and labour). Thus, in a manufacturing account, you would normally expect to find:

Direct	Materials
	Labour
	Overheads
Indirect	Materials
	Labour
	Overheads

Construction of the manufacturing account

It is normal to see direct costs and indirect costs distinguished in the manufacturing account. The adjustments for the difference between opening and
closing work in progress and finished goods are also separately disclosed.

That apart, the construction is very similar to the calculation of cost of sales for a trading firm.

EXAMPLE

Lucien Fino's firm manufactures specialized chemicals. The following information has been extracted from his records as at 31/3/19x9:

Stock at 1/4/19x8	
Raw materials	£ 5,000
Work in progress	2,000
Finished goods	1,000
Factory wages	20,000
Purchases	40,000
Foreman's salary	9,000
Factory power	3,000
Lubricating oil	500
Sales	100,000

On 31/3/19x9 he had stocks of raw materials, work in progress and finished goods valued at:

Raw materials	£6,500
Work in progress	1,500
Finished goods	3,000

Required: show Lucien's manufacturing account.

Lucien Fino
Manufacturing account
for the year ended 31/3/19x9

Direct costs (Note 1)			
Opening stock of raw materials	£ 5,000		
add Purchases in year	40,000		
	£45,000		
less Closing stock	6,500		
		£38,500	
Direct labour		20,000	
Prime cost (note 2)			£58,500
Indirect costs (note 3)			
Indirect material (oil)		£ 500	
Indirect labour			
(foreman's salary)		9,000	
Indirect overhead (power)		3,000	
			12,500
Work in progress adjustment (note 4)			
Opening value	£2,000		
less Closing value	1,500		
		£ 500	

Finished goods adjustment (note 5)

Opening value	£1,000		
less Closing value	3,000		
		(2,000)	
			(1,500)

Total manufacturing costs	£69,500

Points to note:

(1) Opening and closing stocks of raw material are adjusted in the section dealing with direct costs. This is exactly the same as the adjustment for the trading firm as, in so doing, the resulting figure (£38,500) represents the cost of raw materials used in earning sales of £100,000.

(2) *Prime cost* is the term used to describe the total expenditure on direct costs. In this case, direct costs were for raw materials and factory wages.

(3) The indirect costs are all those costs (as identified in the account) which, although essential to the manufacturing process, cannot be readily identified in the overall cost of an individual product. For example, what share of the cost of lubricating oil can be identified to a single unit of production? An impossible question to answer, so the total cost is shown as an indirect cost.

(4) The *work in progress adjustment* is really little more than an extension of the cost of sales calculation. In this case, Lucien had opening WIP of £2,000 but closing WIP of only £1,500. This must mean that he has 'used up' £500 of WIP during the year.

(5) Similarly, to some extent, the *finished goods adjustment* is also an extension of the basic cost of sales calculation. In this case, Lucien has more finished goods at the end of the year than he had at the start. This must mean that the excess is the result of manufacturing for stock rather than for sales and so should be ignored in calculating the cost of goods which were actually sold.

The above example shows the layout of a typical manufacturing account. The only additional complications which can arise are the introduction of more indirect manufacturing costs and the presentation of the data in an apparently complex way.

A fuller example will be given at the end of the next section and will be incorporated into a partnership accounts problem. Before moving on, you are recommended to study the format and construction of the manufacturing account until you are certain that you understand it.

Partnership accounts

Partnerships consist of two or more individuals who come together with the intention of running a business. They are fundamentally no different from the sole tradership since, like the sole trader, partnerships have unlimited liability; that is, the individual partners could be held personally liable for the firm's debts if the firm was not able to honour them. With very few exceptions, partnerships may not have more than twenty partners, although, of course, they can have as many employees as they wish. The main exceptions to this 'maximum of twenty' rule are firms of lawyers and accountants.

A partnership can come into being by the simple decision of the partners; indeed, a partnership can legally exist by the actions of the partners or be implied simply by what they say. Normally it is advisable that a parnership be properly constituted at the start by means of a legal contract stating the rights and duties of the individual partners. Without such a contract, severe problems can arise in the future as to what is expected of each partner and what each partner is entitled to from the firm.

Partnership agreements

Partners do not have to contribute exactly the same amount of capital to the firm. Some partnerships, in fact, have partners who have contributed nothing to the firm's capital but still share in its profits. Normally, however, such partners will be contributing something else other than money – their skills, for instance. Similarly, all partners do not necessarily share profits equally among themselves – the normal practice, however, being to share profits in the same ratio as the amount of capital initially introduced by each partner.

The partnership agreement will regulate the rights and responsibilities of the partners among themselves and with third parties. From the account-ant's point of view, the main clauses should cover at least:

(a)   the amount of capital to be introduced by each partner;
(b)   the salary, interest and drawings due to each partner;
(c)   the profit and loss sharing ratio;
(d)   voting rights;
(e)   duration of the partnership, if it has to have a finite life;
(f)   arrangements for the dissolution of the partnership; and
(g)   arbitration procedures in case of disagreements.

Unless otherwise stated in a formal partnership agreement, the law in the form of the 1890 Partnership Act will be deemed to apply. Among its main provisions are the assumptions that:

(a)   all partners have equal rights and duties;
(b)   all partners have equal powers;
(c)   all partners will receive an equal share of profits and bear an equal share of any losses;
(d)   no partner is entitled to a salary or interest.

It makes sense, therefore, that if partners do not want the provisions of the 1890 Act to apply, then they should draw up a partnership agreement. The reason is that the partnership can have its own provisions so long as they are contained in a formal partnership agreement. If they are not, then the 1890 Act is deemed to apply.

Partnership accounts

The main differences between the financial accounts of a sole trader and a partnership are:

(a) In the profit and loss account of a partnership there is normally an *appropriation account*. This account is used to share out the firm's profits among the partners. There is no need for such an account for a sole trader, since all profits belong to him/her, but a partnership has to share them out among two or more people in the agreed profit-sharing ratio.

(b) The capital account of the sole trader in his balance sheet is a simple matter of

opening balance
\+ profits for year
− personal drawings

In a partnership there must be a difference, since there is more than one person contributing capital, owning the profits and withdrawing money. The capital accounts of the partnership show the same detail as that of the sole trader except that there will be separate accounts for each partner. The capital accounts show the value of each partner's share in the partnership.

These two basic differences will now be examined in more detail.

Appropriation accounts

This account is shown after net profit has been calculated and is normally seen as an appendix to the firm's profit and loss account.

Profit is calculated in the normal way as explained in Chapter 3 except that no deduction is made, in determining profit, for partners' wages nor for interest due to the partners on the capital they introduce into the firm (even if the partners have agreed that interest should be paid on their capital account balances).

The appropriation account starts with the *net profit*. From this is deducted the partners' wages and any interest due to them. The resulting balance is then shared out among the partners in their profit-sharing ratio.

EXAMPLE

Smith, Wares, and Cooper are in partnership sharing profits 3:2:1 respectively. They have agreed that interest and salaries should be paid each year as follows:

	Smith	Wares	Cooper
Salaries	£3,000	£2,500	£2,000
Interest	150	200	250

In the year just ended, net profits of £18,300 have been earned before any drawings by the partners.

Required: Show the firm's appropriation account.

Smith, Wares and Cooper
Appropriation account

Net profit brought down			£18,300
less Salaries			
Smith	£3,000		
Wares	2,500		
Cooper	2,000		
	⎯⎯	£7,500	
Interest			
Smith	£ 150		
Wares	200		
Cooper	250		
	⎯⎯	600	
		⎯⎯	8,100
			⎯⎯⎯
Distributable profit			£10,200
			⎯⎯⎯
distributed thus:			
Smith			£ 5,100
Wares			3,400
Cooper			1,700
			⎯⎯⎯
			£10,200
			⎯⎯⎯

Points to note:

(1)   In this case, salaries and interest are deducted before arriving at the profit which can be shared among the three partners. As details such as this are covered in the partnership agreement, it is quite possible to vary this order, that is, to share out net profits first and then deduct each partner's salary and interest, although that would be unusual.

(2)   The phrase 'distributable profit' refers to the profit level which must be allocated to the partners.

(3)   The distributable profit in this case has been shared out in the profit-sharing ratio – 3:2:1. Thus Smith receives $\frac{1}{2}$, Wares receives $\frac{1}{3}$, and Cooper receives $\frac{1}{6}$ of distributable profits of £10,200.

Capital accounts

The capital accounts in the balance sheet of a partnership are used to record the money introduced into the business by the partners, their share of profits and personal drawings made by them. There are two ways that partnerships can account for the capital of partners:

(a)   by having only capital accounts for each partner – in this way, all personal transactions are made through the one capital account; and

(b)   by having separate accounts, one for everyday transactions and one for a permanent investment in the firm, for each partner – in this case, the permanent investment account is normally referred to as the *fixed*, or *capital*, *account*, and the account which is used for normal transactions (such as drawings and adding shares of profit) is the *current account*.

Which of the two methods will be adopted by a particular firm ought to be determined in the firm's partnership agreement.

EXAMPLE

Morrison and Wilson are in partnership sharing profits 2:1. On 1/1/19x9 their capital accounts were as follows:

	Morrison	Wilson
Fixed capital account	£10,000	£ 5,000
Current account	4,500	5,500
	£14,500	£10,500

In the year just ended, the firm made £18,000 distributable profits. Morrison withdrew £7,000 and Wilson withdrew £4,500 for personal use. The two partners have agreed that their investment in the fixed accounts may not be adjusted.

Required: show the partners' capital accounts as at 31/12/19x9.

	Morrison	Wilson	Total
Fixed accounts	£10,000	£5,000	£15,000
Current accounts			
Opening balance	£ 4,500	£ 5,500	
Add Profit share	12,000	6,000	
	£16,500	£11,500	
less Personal drawings	7,000	4,500	
Closing balance	£ 9,500	£ 7,000	16,500
			£31,500

Points to note:

(1)   The investments of both partners in the firm are clearly distinguished. Each partner's accounts show how much money has been contributed to the firm's financing by each partner.

(2)   The fact that the fixed and current accounts are kept separate arises only because the partners have agreed that this should be so. If there had been no such agreement, then all money would have appeared in the one account for each partner headed 'Capital account'.

(3)   Personal drawings are just that, drawings made by each partner. If they

had been described as 'wages', or 'salaries', they would have been deducted from net profits in the appropriation account.

A FULLER EXAMPLE

(Note that this example also requires the construction of a manufacturing account.)

Some time ago, Scott and Fino (from Chapters 2 and 3) decided to combine their talents and form a partnership manufacturing wool dyes, sharing profits 3:2 respectively. For the year just ended, 31/12/19x9, the following information has been extracted from the books of the firm:

	Debit £	Credit £
Sales		250,000
Purchase of raw materials	120,000	
Factory wages	30,000	
Administration salaries	15,000	
Foremen's salaries	16,000	
Carriage inwards	1,000	
Stocks at 1/1/19x9		
Raw materials	27,000	
Work in progress	9,500	
Finished goods	8,000	
Rent and rates	10,000	
Selling costs	22,256	
Debtors	32,000	
Creditors		26,200
Machinery	38,000	
Vehicles	18,000	
Bank balance		11,800
Capital accounts		
Fixed – Scott		30,000
Fino		23,000
Current – Scott		4,000
Fino		5,000
Salaries – Scott	8,000	
Fino	7,500	
Other personal drawings		
– Scott	2,100	
Fino	324	
Accumulated depreciation		
Machinery		13,680
Vehicles		6,000
Heat and light costs	5,000	
	369,680	369,680

Additional notes:

(1)   Closing stocks were:

Raw materials	£30,000
Work in progress	8,000
Finished goods	11,000

(2)   Assets are to be depreciated thus:

Machinery – 20% reducing balance
Vehicles – Straight line over 6 years

(3)   The factory occupies 75% of the firm's premises and uses 80% of its power requirements.

Required: prepare the *manufacturing*, *trading*, and *profit and loss* accounts and *balance sheet* as at 31/12/19x9.

('Carriage inwards' is the term used to describe the costs paid by the firm for the delivery of raw materials to the factory.

The 'Accumulated depreciation' values in the trial balance show the amount of depreciation charged so far. The figures for the assets themselves must, therefore, be their original cost. Their net book values on 1/1/19x9 are the asset costs less accumulated depreciation.)

Working notes

Depreciation

	Machinery	Total depreciation
Original cost	£38,000	
less Accumulated depreciation	13,680	
Opening book value	£24,320	
Depreciation charge (20%)	4,864	£4,864
Closing book value	£19,456	

	Vehicles	
Original cost	£18,000	
less Annual charge (1/6)	3,000	3,000
	£15,000	£7,864
less Accumulated depreciation	6,000	
Closing book value	£ 9,000	

Scott and Fino
Manufacturing account
for the year ended 31/12/19x9

Direct costs

Opening stock of raw materials		£ 27,000
+ Purchases		120,000
		£147,000
− Closing stock of raw materials		30,000
		£117,000
Direct labour	30,000	
Direct overheads (carriage inwards)	1,000	
		31,000
Prime cost		£148,000
Indirect costs		
Indirect labour		16,000
Indirect overheads (share of R&R, H&L)		11,500
Work in progress adjustment		
Opening value	£ 9,500	
− Closing value	8,000	
		1,500
Finished goods adjustment		
Opening value	£ 8,000	
− Closing value	11,000	
		(3,000)
Total cost of manufacture		£174,000

Scott and Fino
Trading, and profit and loss account
for the year ended 31/12/19x9

Sales		£250,000
less Cost of sales		174,000
Gross profit		£ 76,000
less Expenses		
Administration salaries	£15,000	
Rent and rates	2,500	
Heat and light	1,000	
Selling costs	22,256	
Depreciation	7,864	
		48,620
Net profit		£ 27,380

Appropriation account

Net profit brought down		£ 27,380
less Salaries:		
Scott	£8,000	
Fino	7,500	
		15,500
Distributable profit		£ 11,880

distributed thus:

Scott (3/5)	£ 7,128
Fino (2/5)	4,752
	£ 11,880

Scott and Fino
Balance sheet
as at 31/12/19x9

Fixed assets

Machinery (1)			£19,456
Vehicles (1)			9,000
			£28,456

Current assets

Stocks – Raw materials		£30,000	
Work in progress		8,000	
Finished goods		11,000	
		£49,000	
Debtors		32,000	
		£81,000	

less Current liabilities

Creditors	£26,200		
Overdraft	11,800		
		38,000	
			43,000
			£71,456

as financed by:

Partners' capital accounts

	Scott	Fino	Total
Fixed accounts	£30,000	23,000	£53,000
Current accounts			
Opening balance	£ 4,000	5,000	
+ Profit share	7,128	4,752	
	£11,128	9,752	
− Personal drawings	2,100	324	
	£ 9,028	9,428	18,456
			£71,456

Points to note:

(1)   In this example, the manufacturing account has been kept separate

from the main financial statements. The figure in the trading, and profit and loss account for cost of sales is the total cost of manufacture calculated in the manufacturing account.

(2) The appropriation account only shows how profit has been distributed. This excludes personal drawings as this need not refer to a withdrawal of profits. If they wanted, the partners could take out much more than their profit share, in which case the firm would be repaying capital introduced. Payments for personal drawings, as opposed to salaries, wages and interest, are therefore more properly dealt with in the capital accounts in the balance sheet.

(3) The factory cost element of rent and rates, and heat and light, has been charged to the manufacturing account as indirect overheads (75% of rent and rates, and 80% of heat and light, that is, £7,500 for rent and rates, £4,000 for heat and light). Only the difference is shown in the profit and loss account.

Questions

4.1 What clauses would you expect to see in a formal partnership agreement? What are the potential consequences for any partnership which does not have such a formal agreement?

4.2 The accounts of a partnership show both *fixed* and *current* capital accounts. Distinguish between the the two types of account. Why should a partnership have two types of capital account?

4.3 In partnership accounting, what is an *appropriation account*? What should it contain?

4.4 To what extent are partners' salaries a business expense as opposed to being personal drawings?

4.5 The following data have been extracted from the records of Arran Products, a firm which manufactures wooden toys, at the end of a year's trading on 31/3/19x9:

Opening stock	
– Raw materials	£ 20,000
– Work in progress	15,000
– Finished goods	50,000
Closing stock	
– Raw materials	35,000
– Work in progress	10,000
– Finished goods	55,000
Raw materials bought	100,000
Direct labour	80,000
Sales salaries	5,000
Administration costs	3,000
Sales	275,000
Insurance	
– Factory	9,000
– Administration	2,000
Glue and nails	2,300
Paint	4,500
Rent (factory)	1,500

Required: prepare a manufacturing account and draft profit and loss account for Arran Products.

4.6 The following trial balance has been extracted from the books of Wares, Fino and Morrison on 31/12/19x9:

	Debit £	Credit £
Fixed capital		
– Wares		10,000
– Fino		8,000
– Morrison		6,000
Current accounts		
– Wares		4,000
– Fino	500	
– Morrison		2,000
Long-term loans		5,000
Plant and equipment	15,000	
Vehicles	8,000	
Debtors	29,000	
Creditors		12,000
Stock at 1/1/19x9	15,500	
Bank	3,000	
Sales		250,000
Wages	50,000	
Purchases	125,000	
Rent and rates	5,000	
Other costs	35,000	
Salaries		
– Wares	6,000	
– Fino	3,000	
– Morrison	2,000	
	297,000	297,000

The following information is also available:
(a) The profit sharing ratio is 3:2:1 for Wares, Fino and Morrison respectively.
(b) All assets are to be depreciated by 20%.
(c) Closing stock has a value of £18,000.
(d) All capital transactions are to be conducted through the partners' current accounts.
(e) At the year end, the partners agreed to increase each fixed capital account by 10% by transferring funds from their current accounts.

Required: prepare the financial accounts of this partnership for the year to 31/12/19x9.

4.7 On 1/1/19x9 Andrew, Pat and Frances form a partnership agreeing to make the following total capital contributions:

Andrew	£30,000
Pat	20,000
Frances	10,000

The agreement specifies that fixed capital accounts are to be maintained holding £5,000 from each partner. Further, each partner should receive 10% interest per annum on the balance of all his/her accounts at the start of the year, that Frances should receive a salary of £4,000 per annum, and thereafter that profits should be shared 4:3:3 amongst Andrew, Pat and Frances respectively.

In the year ended 31/12/19x9, the firm made profits, before any appropriation, of £40,000.

Required: Prepare the firm's appropriation account and the capital accounts of each partner at the year end.

5 The accounts of limited companies

Introduction

The potential for failure exists in all business ventures and none can be seen as being totally risk free. In the case of sole traders and partnerships, should the firm become bankrupt, then the owners can become personally bankrupt also; their liability for the debts of the firm is unlimited.

In limited companies the owners' – the shareholders' – liability is limited only to the extent of their shareholding. Thus, if the firm cannot pay its debts, the owners cannot be held responsible for them. This obviously means that everyone dealing with a limited company is taking on an additional risk. To warn prospective third parties of this additional risk, all limited liability companies have to identify themselves as such.

Limited companies

There are two types of limited liability company.

- A public limited company must have a minimum authorized share capital of £50,000, and its shares must be freely available to the general public. Such companies are normally distinguished by the letters 'Plc' after the name of the firm.
- A limited company is, normally, relatively small and private. Very often the entire issued share capital is owned by members of a family or a handful of individuals, this form of company often being seen as an alternative to forming a partnership. This need not always be the case, however. The principal feature which distinguishes a limited company from a Plc is that its shares are not freely available to the general public. Limited companies are denoted by the letters 'Ltd' after the company name.

Operations and management

The management of either type of limited company is vested in the firm's *board of directors*. Shareholders, although the ultimate owners of the company, have no right to manage the firm on a day-to-day basis. Rather, they must elect annually directors to manage the firm on their behalf.

Directors are normally elected for three or five years (although the tenure of their office could be at the company's discretion) and must be re-elected at the end of that period. It is the directors who are responsible for what the company does and how the firm does it. The directors are required to report back to the shareholders at the end of each business year (the stewardship function from Chapter 2).

The shareholders (the owners) have very few rights – for example, they have no right of access to the firm's books of account – and, if they want changes to be made, they must either convince the directors to implement the changes or appoint new directors.

Regulation of companies

All limited companies (both Plc and Ltd) are under a legal obligation to publish financial accounts annually. Such accounts, and other information, must be sent to the Registrar of Companies and, for a small fee, are available for inspection by the general public. This can be contrasted with the accounts of the sole trader and partnership which are totally private to the owners.

The format of a company's accounts and the level of disclosure of information are prescribed by the law and by the accountancy profession, the main regulatory functions being contained in:

(a)   Statements of Standard Accounting Practice, and
(b)   the Companies Acts.

Statements of standard accounting practice (SSAPs)

SSAPs describe methods of accounting practice which have been deemed, by the professional accounting bodies, to be appropriate in the construction and disclosure of the accounts of businesses. They attempt to show 'best practice' and also ensure that all accounts are prepared on a broadly similar basis so as to allow legitimate comparisons to be made both between companies and from one year to the next.

Such statements are not legally enforceable, but do have the backing of the professional bodies whose members are expected to comply with them at all times. If a departure from an SSAP is thought desirable, then firms should give the reason for the departure together with the financial effects caused by that departure.

The Companies Acts

One of the drawbacks of limited companies is that the law, which created the company, also dictates what information must be disclosed by the company and the format that information must be given in. There have been numerous Companies Acts, but the principal Act which governs the operation and disclosure requirements of limited companies is the 1989 Companies Act.

Annual reports

All limited companies publish annual accounts which normally form part of the firm's *annual report*. This report is made available to every shareholder and is meant to show what has happened to their investment over the past year. These reports generally have a standard format, many parts of which are requirements, taking the following form (shown here together with the appropriate requiring 'body'):

(a)   Chairman's report (by custom – not a requirement).
(b)   Profit and loss account (Companies Act).
(c)   Earning per share statement (SSAP).
(d)   Balance sheet (Companies Act).
(e)   Notes to accounts (Companies Act and SSAP).
(f)   Sources and uses of funds statement (SSAP).
(g)   Directors' report (Companies Act).
(h)   Auditor's report (Companies Act, but form defined by the accounting bodies).
(i)   Group accounts (Companies Act).

It should be noted that, although most firms' annual reports will contain the above points, they need not be shown in the order described.

The remainder of this chapter will be devoted to a closer examination of the content of the annual report.

The chairman's report

This is not a legal requirement but is normally part of the annual report. It summarizes the results of the company in a non-technical manner, high-lighting profitability and dividend proposals. A summary of the results of operating divisions may also be given, together with prospects for the future. Again, this would be in non-technical terms aimed, primarily, at share-holders who do not have a firm grasp of accounting.

The profit and loss account

The Companies Act 1981 introduced four formats of profit and loss account, and all limited companies must adopt one particular format and retain it. (Two formats are in vertical form, the other two being a reiteration of the vertical forms expressed horizontally, with income being shown on the left-hand side and expenditure on the right.) Format 1 is the format adopted by most UK companies and classifies costs by operational function, for example, Cost of Sales would include manufacturing wages. Format 2 classifies costs by type, thus all wages, including manufacturing wages, would be shown under the heading of Staff Costs.

Format 1 requires the profit and loss account to be shown thus (note that Format 2 is described in Appendix I):

Alba Plc
Profit and loss account
for the year ended 31/12/19x9

Turnover	(2)		£10,000,000
Cost of sales			6,000,000
Gross profit			£4,000,000
Distribution costs	(3)	£1,000,000	
Administration costs	(3)	750,000	
Other operating income	(4)	(50,000)	
			1,700,000
Operating profit	(5)		£2,300,000
Income from shares in participating companies	(6)	£50,000	
Income from other fixed asset investments	(7)	25,000	
Other income receivable	(8)	10,000	
Interest payable	(9)	(40,000)	
			45,000
Profit on ordinary activities before taxation	(10)		£2,345,000
Tax on profits on ordinary activites			925,000
Profit on ordinary activities after taxation			£1,420,000
Minorities interests	(11)		370,000
Profit attributable to members before extraordinary items	(12)		£1,050,000
Extraordinary items	(13)		250,000
Profit for year	(14)		£800,000
Dividends paid and proposed	(15)		200,000
Retained profits for year			£600,000
Earnings per share			Xp

The numbers in brackets refer to the explanatory notes below:

(1)   In addition to the current year's figures, comparable figures must also be given for the previous year.

(2)   *Turnover* is usually defined as the net sales made by the company. A geographic and functional analysis of turnover must also be given if the company trades overseas or if it has two or more types of product.

(3)   The Companies Act does not define what should be described as *distribution or administration costs*. It only requires a company to make that distinction.

(4)   *Other operating income* would include other revenue earned by the company apart from normal sales and interest, for example rents received.

(5)   Additional information about certain costs must be given by way of a note to the accounts at this stage. The main costs to be disclosed are:

(a) Costs of the hire of plant and machinery.

(b) Remuneration of the firm's auditors.

(6) A 'participating company' is a firm where a large number of its shares are owned by another firm, but not so many that the other firm can control its activities. In such cases, the owning firm must show its share of the profits/losses of the participating firm and not just the dividends received.

(7) *Fixed asset investments* do not refer to the fixed assets in the balance sheet such as plant and machinery. This item refers to long-term investments in other firms, and so it refers to income from such investments.

(8) *Other income receivable* would normally be interest from loans made by the company.

(9) *Interest payable* may be shown in total in the profit and loss account, but a separate note must also disclose that interest split between loans repayable:

(a) in less than five years;

(b) in more than five years.

(10) More detailed information must be given about certain other costs, notably:

(a) Directors' remuneration, including the remuneration of chairman and the highest-paid director.

(b) Total wages paid, total social security costs, total pension costs and the average number of employees over the year.

(c) Total depreciation charged for the year.

(Such additional information is usually given in the same note referred to in point 5 above).

(11) If the reporting company has subsidiaries but does not own all of the shares in those subsidiaries (that is, only owns a majority voting rights of more than 50%), then the minority shareholders are entitled to their share of profits. This section requires parent companies to disclose the amount of profits due to the minority shareholders.

(12) This is the net profit earned on the ordinary activities of the company after tax, which, theoretically at least, belongs to the shareholders and could be paid to them by way of dividends.

(13) *Extraordinary items* are those items of income and expenditure which result from events outside the normal activities of the company, which are unlikely to recur, and are of a material size. SSAP No. 6 identifies a number of such events including:

(a) The costs incurred in closing down part of the business.

(b) The sale of fixed assets.

(c) The write-off of intangible assets due to unusual developments.

(14) This is the total net profits which could be paid out to the shareholders.

(15) *Dividends paid and proposed* state how much of total net profits are, in fact, being paid to the shareholders.

(16) *Earnings per share* are discussed in the next section.

Earnings per share

SSAP No. 3 requires that the *earnings per share* (EPS) be shown on the face of the profit and loss account. It is normally shown in pence and discloses the share of total earnings which is attributable to each ordinary share in the company. This can be of importance to potential and existing shareholders as it shows how much each share is earning and, hence, could be used to calculate the return that is being made on the investment. For example, if a firm has shares which have a market value of £2.50 each and has an EPS of 30p then the rate of return that investment is earning is:

$$\frac{0.30}{2.50} \times 100\% = 12\%$$

This can then be compared with other possible investments.

Earnings per share is calculated thus:

$$\frac{\text{profits after tax but before extraordinary items}}{\text{number of ordinary shares}}$$

If a firm also has preference shares, then the figure in the numerator is after any preference share dividends.

The balance sheet

The 1989 Companies Act also prescribes the layout and content of published balance sheets. A choice is offered between a horizontal presentation (where all assets are shown on the left-hand side and liabilities are shown on the right) and a vertical presentation similar to that used in Chapter 3. Although the same information must be given in each format, the main difference between the two is that in the horizontal format current liabilities are kept apart from current assets. In the vertical presentation current liabilities are deducted from current assets to disclose 'net current assets'.

The Act lays down very strict guidelines on what must be disclosed and how that information must be presented. It also introduces new terminology in some cases. Also to be shown are comparative figures for the previous year.

The vast majority of firms in the UK have adopted the vertical form of presentation and, as such, only that format will be discussed in the following example:

Alba Plc
Balance sheet
as at 31/12/19x9

Called-up shares not paid	(1)	£10,000
Fixed assets		
Intangible assets	(2)	50,000
Tangible assets	(2)	2,500,000
Investments	(3)	500,000
		£3,060,000

Current assets		
Stock	(4)	£200,000
Debtors	(5)	650,000
Investments	(3)	100,000
Cash and bank		30,000
		£980,000
Prepayments	(6)	20,000
		£1,000,000
less Creditors: amounts falling due		
within one year	(7)	
		700,000
Net current assets	(8)	
		300,000
Total assets less Current liabilities		£3,360,000
less Creditors: amounts falling due		
after more than one year	(9)	
		360,000
		£3,000,000
Provisions for liabilities	(10)	
		£100,000
		£2,900,000
Capital and reserves	(11)	
Called-up share capital	(12)	£1,750,000
Share premium account	(13)	150,000
Revaluation reserve	(14)	100,000
Other reserves		50,000
Profit and loss account	(15)	850,000
		£2,900,000

EXPLANATION OF TERMS

(1) *Called-up capital.* Shares in a company can be sold requiring the buyers to pay the full cost either immediately or by 'calls', that is, to pay only proportions of the cost as and when the firm asks them to pay. The total amount actually paid at the balance sheet date is the *called-up share capital.* Some shareholders may not pay their 'call', the sum of which is the *called-up shares not paid.*

(2) *Intangible* and *tangible assets.* When a company spends money, it would normally expect to acquire something 'real' such as a new piece of machinery or equipment. Such assets are tangible assets in that they physically exist, and can be seen and identified. In respect of each major class of tangible fixed asset, the following additional information must be given:

(a) Cost or value at the start of the year.
(b) Revaluations and acquisitions during the year.
(c) Disposals during the year.

(d) Cumulative depreciation at the start of the year.
(e) Depreciation charged during the year.
(f) Cumulative depreciation at the end of the year.
(g) Net book value at the end of the year.

Other types of expenditure may give a company a lasting benefit but will not provide it with something 'real'. An example of such expenditure would be the purchase of a patent right. Owning a patent right would allow the firm to make money either by using that right or by leasing the right to use the patent to other firms. Such expenditure will be correctly identified as capital expenditure but there is a difference between the purchase of a machine and that of a patent right. The latter would be defined as an intangible asset. The 1985 Companies Act requires that intangible assets be further categorized into:

(a) Development costs.
(b) Patents, trade marks, etc, and so on.
(c) Purchased goodwill.

(3) *Investments* made by a company can be either *long-term* or *short-term*. The Act requires that this distinction be made clear in the balance sheet by separately disclosing each either as a fixed asset or as a current asset. The difference between long- and short-term investments is whether or not the company intends to keep them for more or less than one year.

(4) The *stock* figure in the balance sheet must be further classified into:

(a) Raw materials.
(b) Consumables.
(c) Work in progress.
(d) Finished goods.

(5) Similarly, *debtors* have to be further categorized into:

(a) Trade debtors.
(b) Other debtors.

(6) *Prepayments* are simply sums of money paid by a firm in advance of receipt of the goods or services to which they relate. At a firm's discretion, prepayments may be included in the general debtors figure. If so, they must be separately identified.

(7) *Creditors: amounts falling due within one year.* This is a new title for what used to be called (and still is in the accounts of unincorporated firms) *current liabilities.* Such creditors have to be categorized into:

(a) Trade creditors.
(b) Bank overdraft/short-term loan.
(c) Other creditors, including tax.
(d) Accrued charges.

(8)   *Net current assets* are the difference between current assets and creditors: amounts falling due in less than one year. This is commonly referred to as the firm's *working capital* except in the annual accounts!

(9)   *Creditors: amounts falling due in more than one year.* Such liabilities are long-term, that is, they do not have have to be paid in the coming year, and are due to third parties. They have to be categorized into:

   (a)   Bank loans.
   (b)   Trade creditors.
   (c)   Tax.
   (d)   Debentures.
   (e)   Other creditors.

   Debentures are formal, long-term loans made to a company. The company creates a legal deed and issues certificates as evidence of the debt. The legal deed will specify the rate of interest to be paid and when the debenture will be repaid (normally the redemption date is very wide, for example '1994–9'. This means that the debenture will be repaid at some time between these years at the company's discretion.
   In terms of security offered, debentures are fixed, floating, or unsecured. *Fixed* debentures have specific assets as collateral (usually the firm's premises). *Floating* debentures have no specific assets as collateral, but the firm's general assets have been offered as security. *Unsecured* debentures have no assets as security.

(10)   *Provisions for liabilities.* Occasionally there may be circumstances when a firm thinks that it might have liabilities in the future in excess of those which it is certain that it does have – for example, if a firm is being sued and, at the balance sheet date, the case has still to go to court. The firm may lose, have large legal costs to pay and perhaps be required to pay substantial damages. In such a case, the firm may think it wise to provide for such possible liabilities by way of this provision.

(11)   *Capital and reserves.* This section displays the financing of the firm from shareholders' funds and how that financing is made up.

(12)   *Called-up share capital.* The figure in the balance sheet is only the summary of all issued share capital. Further details must be given covering:

   (a)   The nominal values of each class of share.
   (b)   The authorized and issued capital for all classes of share.

   The market value of shares is, of course, the price at which such shares can be bought and sold on the open market. The *nominal value*, however, is no more than the face value printed on the share certificate and has little significance other than as a means of identifying the share. It would be nothing more than coincidence if the market value and nominal values were the same. The nominal value is often referred to as the *par* value.
   The *authorized capital* of a company is the maximum number, and

value, of shares which a company may legally issue to shareholders. The *issued capital* is simply the number of shares that the firm has decided to issue and which have been bought. Naturally, the issued capital may equal the authorized capital but can never exceed it.

A share represents a proportion of a company. However, many companies do not just have 'shares' but may have a number of different types, or classes, of share capital – the two most common classes being *preference shares* and *ordinary shares*.

Preference shares have a stated, fixed rate of dividend payable each year but only if a dividend is declared. If no dividend is declared then no preference share receives a dividend. In the winding-up of a company, preference shareholders receive their money back after all creditors have been paid and before ordinary shareholders receive anything. The word 'preference' refers to such shareholders being preferred in receiving a dividend and their money back before ordinary shareholders.

Ordinary shares entitle the owners to a dividend of varying rates if one is declared and, in theory, the residue of all profits earned by a company after all due payments have been made including preference share dividends. They also share all the proceeds on the winding-up of the company, again after everyone else has been repaid.

Ordinary shareholders are the ultimate risk-takers in a company. For their investment, they receive no security or guarantee and are last in line to receive anything. But, if the company is successful, they share in that success.

(13)   When a company sells its shares, of any class, it may do so at a price higher than those shares' nominal value. The difference between the actual price and the nominal value is the share premium, and all such premiums must be shown separately in the balance sheet. This money cannot be repaid to the shareholders except in very unusual circumstances.

(14)   When a firm's assets increase in value both substantially and irreversibly, some firms decide to show such assets at their increased values rather than at cost. The difference between the cost price and the revaluation must be credited to the *revaluation reserve account* in the balance sheet and may not be distributed to the shareholders. Normally it is only a firm's land and buildings which are revalued.

(15)   *Retained profits* from each year are to be accumulated in this *reserve account*.

Note: all the additional information described above does not have to be shown in the balance sheet itself. Normally it is disclosed by way of notes to the accounts which can often run to many pages in length.

Statement of sources and uses of funds

Looking at the profit and loss account and balance sheet of a company alone does not give a full picture of the finances of a firm. The balance sheet shows the end of year position, and the profit and loss account shows profits earned during the year. However, since the profit and loss account concerns itself with revenue items only, any changes of a capital nature during a year will not be easily seen. For example, a firm may raise new loans or spend substantial sums on acquiring new assets, but such income and expenditure will not be immediately obvious.

Another problem with the annual accounts is that they do not concern themselves with liquidity. That is, they do not consider the flow of cash, or funds, within the year.

To help in overcoming these deficiencies, the accounting profession requires that all companies with a turnover of more than £25,000 a year produce a further statement showing changes in liquidity and how a firm acquired, and used, all funds raised in the year – the *statement of sources and uses of funds*.

By comparing the balance sheets from two time periods, all differences in capital income and expenditure can be noted, since the balance sheet shows, at any moment in time, a firm's assets and indebtedness. The profit and loss account shows revenue profits. By considering the capital differences and revenue earned a statement can be drawn up combining the two, and it is just that which the statement of sources and uses of funds does.

From the profit and loss account come increases in funds from profits, and from the balance sheet come funds raised from other sources. The balance sheet will also disclose non-revenue uses of these funds (revenue expenses will have been accounted for already in determining profits).

Although there is no formal layout for funds statements, most of those which are produced contain three sections:

(a) a section showing the sources of funds;
(b) a section showing the main uses of funds;
(c) a section showing the changes in working capital.

EXAMPLE

Iona Ltd has just produced its balance sheet for the year to 31/3/19x9 (together with the previous year's comparative figures), and condensed profit and loss account:

Profit and loss account

Net profit before depreciation	£27,500
less Depreciation	11,000
Net profit before tax	£16,500
less tax	2,000
	£14,500
less Proposed dividend	1,000
Retained profit	£13,500

Balance sheet

	19x8		19x9
Fixed assets (net of depreciation)	£95,000		£100,000
Current assets			
Stock	£15,000	£20,000	
Debtors	3,000	10,000	
Bank	2,000	5,000	
	£20,000	£35,000	
less Current liabilities			
Trade creditors	£10,000	£12,000	
Tax	1,000	2,000	
Proposed dividends	500	1,000	
	£11,500	£15,000	
Net current assets	8,500		£20,000
Total net assets	£103,500		£120,000
Ordinary shares	£70,000		£70,000
Retained profits	18,500		32,000
	£88,500		£102,000
Long-term loans	15,000		18,000
	£103,500		£120,000

Note:
During the year, assets costing £16,000 were acquired. Also during the year extra funds were raised from two sources:

(a)   Profits of £27,500. Profits must be before depreciation, since that is not a cash cost. It is just a book adjustment. The tax figure is just an estimate and, again, it involved no cash flowing out of the business. The same point applies to proposed dividends.
(b)   New loans of £3,000. That is the difference between the long-term loans in two balance sheets.

Money was also spent on the following:

(a)   Acquiring new assets of £16,000. We are told this.
(b)   Increasing stocks by £5,000 (the difference between the two balance sheets).
(c)   Increasing debtors by £7,000 (again, the difference).
(d)   Increasing the bank balances by £3,000.

However, current liabilities have also increased by £3,500. This means that not all of the additional expenditure was paid for; some of it was financed by increased indebtedness.

The statement of sources and uses of funds rearranges this information into some meaningful form. Since there are no imposed formats, companies will present their funds statement in different ways. A common format would be as follows:

Iona Ltd
Statement of sources and uses of funds
for the year to 31/3/19x9

Sources of funds			
Profits before tax	(1)		£16,500
add back Adjustments for non-cash movements	(2)		
Depreciation			11,000
Total generated from operations	(3)		£27,500
Funds from other sources:	(4)		
New loans raised			3,000
			£30,500
Uses of funds			
Acquisition of fixed assets	(5)	£16,000	
Dividends paid	(6)	500	
Tax paid	(7)	1,000	
			17,500
			£13,000
Changes in working capital	(8)		
Increase in stock		£5,000	
Increase in debtors		7,000	
Increase in creditors		(2,000)	
			10,000
	(9)		£3,000
Movement in liquid assets			
Increase in bank balance	(10)		£3,000

Points to note:

(1)   As mentioned earlier, the tax in a profit and loss account is only an estimate of the tax liability on those profits. The tax has still to be paid. In considering the funds generated from profits, the figure must be, therefore, profits before tax, since the tax has not yet involved any money going out of the business.

(2)   Similarly, depreciation does not actually involve any cash payments, and so any figure for depreciation used in defining profits must be added back to arrive at the funds which were generated.

(3)   This subtotal is used to distinguish funds generated from the normal work of the business, making profits, and from other 'abnormal' sources.

(4)   This will normally arise from either the issue of more shares or the raising of more long-term loans. It will be found by comparing the respective values in two balance sheets.

(5)   Although the figure is given, it could have been calculated:

Book value at the end of the year (after depreciation)	£100,000
add back depreciation deducted	11,000
Theoretical opening book value	£111,000

However, the real opening book value was only £95,000. The difference, £16,000, could only arise if there had been a net acquisition of assets at that cost.

(6)   The *use of funds* in respect of dividends is the cash which was actually spent, not the proposal in the profit and loss account – that has still to be spent. Assume that the creditor in the 19x8 balance sheet for dividends had never been paid; what would the liability have been at the end of 19x90? The answer must be:

Opening creditor	£500
add Current year's proposal	1,000
Amount owed at the end of 19x9	£1,500

But the balance sheet for 19x9 shows that only £1,000 is owing. That must mean that £500 has been paid in the year.

(7)   Calculating the tax which was actually paid in the year uses the same method used to find the dividends which were paid in point 6 above; that is:

Opening creditor	£1,000
add Current year's estimate	2,000
	£3,000
less Closing creditor	2,000
Cash paid in year	£1,000

(8)   Increases in current assets are seen as uses of funds; for example, if stock levels have increased from £15,000 to £20,000 then funds must have been used to acquire that additional stock.

Increases in current liabilities are seen as a source of funds. In this example, trade creditors have increased by £2,000, probably because the firm increased its stock levels. Stock levels increased by £5,000, but the firm did not have to pay cash for all of that increase; it bought £2,000 of it on credit. The firm had to finance only £3,000 of the increase by itself – the remainder is being financed by the trade creditors.

(9)   This figure accounts for all funds coming in and going out and shows that £3,000 more funds came in than went out.

(10)   The account is balanced off to the increase over the two years' bank balances. Since £3,000 more funds came in than went out, it would be expected that the bank balance would have increased by a similar amount. That is so!

Although statements of sources and uses of funds attempt to assist non-accountants in understanding financial statements, it is doubtful if they succeed. To fully understand these statements requires an understanding of the construction rules and content of balance sheets and profit and loss accounts, since it is from these financial statements that the statement of sources and uses of funds is directly produced. It has been argued that if a reader understands the balance sheet and the profit and loss account then he/she has no need for the funds statement; but if he/she does not understand the basic financial statements then he/she cannot fully understand and appreciate the significance of funds statements.

The directors' report

The 1985 Companies Act requires the directors of a company to produce an annual report to the shareholders of the company, and attach it to the firm's annual accounts.

The contents of the *directors' report* are supposed to give the readers more information about the firm than is disclosed in the annual accounts and would include, at least, the following:

(a) A statement on the principal activities of the firm.
(b) A fair review of the year just past and an indication of future developments.
(c) A statement identifying any significant changes in the firm's fixed assets.
(d) An indication of any material difference between the market value and book value of the firm's land and buildings.
(e) A statement on the proposed final dividend, together with a note of profits which are being transferred to reserves.
(f) The names of all directors who held office during the year, together with details of each director's shareholding in the firm and of any interest a director may have had in contracts entered into by the company.
(g) A statement showing details of any of its own shares which have been purchased by the company.
(h) The total amounts of donations made by the company to political organizations and charities.
(i) If the company has more than 250 employees, a note explaining the firm's employment policies.

The auditor's report

All limited companies must hire a qualified accountant to audit their annual accounts and to prepare a report giving his/her opinion on them to the shareholders of the company. The auditor must be totally impartial and unconnected with the company save in his/her capacity as auditor.

The audit report is only a statement of whether or not the annual accounts show a true and fair view of the financial status of the company at the year end and of the profits disclosed in the profit and loss account for the year. The report does not state categorically that the accounts are correct or that there was no fraud in the company (as we have seen, there is no such thing as a 'correct' set of accounts – there could be several).

If the auditor is satisfied that the accounts do show a true and fair view of the company's finances, then he/she produces an unqualified audit report – a rather bland statement, normally just stating that the accounts do give a true and fair view. If his/her opinion of the accounts is that some aspects do not give a true and fair view, then he/she produces a qualified report drawing the attention of the shareholders to the aspect he/she has doubts about.

Qualified audit reports used to be a fairly serious matter but they are becoming more and more common nowadays and their impact may well be diminishing.

Auditors have to ensure that the accounts abide by the Companies Acts and SSAPs. Any deviation may result in a qualified opinion, even if the deviation is minor. For example, SSAP No. 12 requires that all assets be depreciated. Some firms do not depreciate their buildings since they see such assets increasing in value and argue that to show them decreasing in the balance sheet because of depreciation is patent nonsense and, indeed, may be misleading. Such an omission could result in a qualified audit report, but it is hardly in the same league as deliberate misrepresentation which would also attract a qualified opinion.

Group accounts

Many companies own shares in other companies and, if they own more than 50% of another firm's voting rights, can control the affairs of that other company.

For example, if Company A owns 75% of the shares in Company B, then, because of its majority voting rights, A can dictate to B what B must do. If B pays dividends, then A will receive its share; but, more importantly, A can dictate what B must pay. Therefore, not only does A control the affairs of B but it can also control B's profits. In presenting its accounts to its share-holders, A would be wrong if it ignored its majority shareholding in B and so ignored the assets and profits of B which it controls. *Group accounts* are the means by which A has to account for its effective ownership of B.

The 1989 Companies Act requires companies which are 'parent under-takings' to produce group accounts and also introduced two important definitions:

- A *parent undertaking* is a firm which can exercise control over a *subsidiary undertaking*.
- A *subsidiary undertaking* is a firm over which control may be exercised by another firm (the *parent*) whether because of the ownership of a majority of voting rights or some other reason.

The 1989 Companies Act requires every parent company to publish, in addition to its own accounts:

(a)   A *group* (or *consolidated*) *balance sheet* which would include all the net assets of subsidiaries which are attributable to the holding company.
(b)   A *group* (or *consolidated*) *profit and loss account* which would include all the earnings attributable to the holding company.

In addition, a *consolidated statement of sources and uses of funds* is required by the accountancy profession.

In producing this information, the shareholders of the parent company are given the opportunity to examine the total earnings and net assets attributable to the firm in which they have an interest.

The accounts of limited liability companies – an example

Keith Ltd is a toy manufacturer, and the following information has been extracted from its books of account for the year ended 31/12/19x1:

	£
Sales	10,000,000
Purchases	8,500,000
Plant and machinery	1,500,000
Vehicles	200,000
Wages (manufacturing)	200,000
Wages (administration)	75,000
Distribution costs	250,000
Rent and rates	180,000
Stock at 1/1/19x1	950,000
Cash	10,000
Bank loan (repayable 19x2)	200,000
Loan interest	20,000
Debenture interest	75,000
Ordinary shares of £1	500,000
Profit and loss account reserves	160,000
Debtors	150,000
Accumulated depreciation at 1/1/19x1	
Plant and machinery	200,000
Vehicles	100,000
Dividends paid	50,000
12.5% debentures (19x6–x9)	500,000
Trade creditors	400,000
Tax (due 19x2)	150,000
Goodwill	50,000

The following additional information is available:

(a)   The authorised share capital is 750,000 ordinary shares of £1.
(b)   Plant and machinery are depreciated at 20% and vehicles at 25% using the reducing balance method.
(c)   Tax for the current year is estimated at £75,000. This will not be paid until 19x3 and, as yet, has not been entered in the firm's books.
(d)   Closing stock comprises:

Raw materials	£800,000
Work in progress	250,000
	£1,050,000

Required: prepare, in good form, the financial accounts of Keith Ltd for the year ended 31/12/19x1. (Note: 'good form' simply means that the accounts must comply with the disclosure requirements of the 1989 Companies Act.)

At first glance (and also perhaps at second glance), this may seem a daunting question. However, there is nothing new in the construction of the accounts – you have met all possible difficulties in Chapter 3, and overcome them. The only new aspect is that the accounts must be in the required format, but that is just a question of knowing the format.

WORKINGS

(1) *Cost of sales*

Opening stock at 31/12/19x0	£950,000
add Purchases	8,500,000
Manufacturing wages	200,000
Depreciation (see note 2 below)	285,000
	£9,935,000
less Closing stock at 31/12/19x1	1,050,000
Cost of sales	£8,885,000

The Companies Act does not state what should go into the calculation of cost of sales or administration costs. In this case, since plant causes the most depreciation, it would seem more logical to describe it as a cost of sales than as anything else.

(2) *Depreciation*

	Plant (20%)	Vehicles (25%)
Cost	£1,500,000	£200,000
less Depreciation to 31/12/x0	200,000	100,000
Book value at 1/1/19x1	£1,300,000	£100,000
Depreciation charge for year	260,000	25,000
Book value at 31/12/19x1	£1,040,000	£75,000

(3) *Administration costs*

Wages (administrative)	£75,000
Rent and rates	180,000
	£255,000

Keith Ltd
Profit and loss account
for the year ended 31/12/19x1
notes

Turnover			£10,000,000
Cost of sales (workings 1)			8,885,000
Gross profit			£1,115,000
Distribution costs		£250,000	
Administration costs (workings 3)		255,000	
			505,000
Operating profit			£610,000
Interest payable	(1)		95,000
Profit on ordinary activities before taxation			£515,000
Taxation			75,000
Profit after tax attributable to members			£440,000
Dividends paid			50,000
Retained profits for year			£390,000
Earnings per share	(2)		£1.03

Keith Ltd
Balance sheet
as at 31/12/19x1

Fixed assets			
Intangible assets	(3)		£50,000
Tangible assets	(4)		1,115,000
			£1,165,000
Current assets			
Stock	(5)	£1,050,000	
Debtors		150,000	
Cash		10,000	
		£1,210,000	
Creditors: amounts falling due within one year	(6)	750,000	
Net current assets			460,000
Total assets less current liabilities			£1,625,000
Creditors: amounts falling due in more than one year	(7)		575,000
			£1,050,000
Capital and reserves			
Called-up share capital	(8)		£500,000
Profit and loss account	(9)		550,000
			£1,050,000

Notes to the accounts:

(1) *Interest payable*
On loans due in less than five years
   (the bank loan)   £20,000
On loans due in more than five years
   (on the debentures)   £75,000

(2) *Earnings per share:*

$$\frac{\text{Profit before tax}}{\text{Number of shares}} = \frac{£515,000}{500,000} = £1.03$$

(3) *Intangible assets*

Goodwill   £50,0000

(4) *Tangible assets*

	Plant	Vehicles
Cost	£1,500,000	£200,000
Depreciation at 1/1/19x1	£200,000	£100,000
Depreciation for year	260,000	25,000
Depreciation at 31/12/19x1	£460,000	£125,000
Book value at 31/12/19x1	£1,040,000	£75,000

(5) *Stock*

Raw materials	£800,000
Work in progress	250,000
	£1,050,000

(6) *Creditors: amounts due within one year*

Trade creditors	£400,000
Taxation	150,000
Bank loan	200,000
	£750,000

(7) *Creditors: amounts falling due in more than one year*

Taxation	£75,000
12.5% debentures (19x6–9)	500,000
	£575,000

(8) *Called-up share capital*

	Authorized	Issued
Ordinary shares of £1	£750,000	£500,000

(9) *Profit and loss account*

Balance at 1/1/19x1	£160,000
Retained profits for year	390,000
Balance at 31/12/19x1	£550,000

Computers and financial accounts

As was explained in Chapter 2, packages can be bought which will maintain a firm's financial records. Such packages will perform the routine book-keeping work very quickly and efficiently, and will also produce balanced trial balances.

The cheaper packages will normally also produce pre-defined profit and loss accounts and balance sheets. Such pre-defined accounts will only be suitable for management purposes since their format will not be very 'presentable'. The main advantage is that firms are able to get up-to-date profit and loss accounts as and when required, literally at the press of a button.

The more expensive packages allow the user to define the format of the final accounts which the computer will produce. This will be of use for partnerships which have many partners, for those with complicated capital accounts and also for limited companies which can define the format in such a way as to comply with the Companies Acts.

Limited company accounts will still have to be audited, however, and if such firms are going to use computers for keeping their records and accounts production then the packages used will also have to be able to produce an audit trail; that is, the package will have to show how each account was constructed.

Questions

5.1 What are Statements of Standard Accounting Practice? What purpose do they serve?

5.2 What are the principal constituent parts of a firm's *annual report*? Which parts identified by you are legally required?

5.3 Distinguish between the following:

    (a)   *Authorized* and *issued* share capital.
    (b)   *Tangible* and *intangible* assets.
    (c)   *Preference* and *ordinary* shares.

5.4 What should be contained in the *directors' report*?

5.5 When should a firm publish *group accounts*? (Explain any terms you use.)

5.6 Do *statements of sources and uses of funds* provide the reader of accounts with any new or useful information? Why?

5.7 The Nairn Company Ltd has produced the following draft profit and loss account for the year to 31/3/19x9:

Opening stock	£375,000	Sales	£3,475,000
Purchase of raw material	2,260,000	Closing stock	562,000
Factory wages	425,000	Interest	37,500
Administration costs	176,500		
Dividends paid	29,000		
Dividends proposed	34,000		
Taxation	58,000		

Delivery costs	40,000	
Interest paid	28,500	
Profit	648,500	
	£4,074,500	£4,074,500

Required: prepare the profit and loss account in a form suitable for publication and distribution to the company's members.

5.8   The draft balance sheet of S. O. Poor Ltd as at 31/12/xx is shown below:

Fixed assets

	Cost	Depreciation	Net
Plant and equipment	£11,000	£3,000	£8,000
Motor cars	4,000	1,000	3,000
Goodwill	2,500	–	2,500
			£13,500

Current assets

Stock	£4,000	
Debtors	7,000	
	£11,000	

less Current liabilities

Creditors	£8,000		
Overdraft	2,500		
		10,500	
			500
			£14,000

as financed by:	
Ordinary shares of £1	£5,000
Revenue reserves	7,000
	£12,000
Long-term loans	2,000
	£14,000

Required: redraft the balance sheet in a form suitable for publication and distribution to the firm's shareholders.

5.9   The following trial balance has been prepared from the books of account of the Alpha Company Ltd for the year ended 31/12/19x1:

	Debit £	Credit £
Ordinary shares of £1		100,000
6% preference shares of £1		15,000
Sales		550,000
sales returned	10,000	
Retained profits		75,000
10% debentures (19x7)		25,000
Trade creditors		45,000
Trade debtors	65,000	
Purchases	240,000	
Stock at start of year	35,000	

Factory premises	185,000	
Plant and machinery	80,000	
Bank balance	5,000	
Office salaries	72,000	
Other office expenses	100,000	
Advertising and other selling costs	15,500	
Debenture interest	2,500	
	810,000	810,000

Notes:

(a)   Stock at the end of the year had a value of £50,000.
(b)   Depreciation has to be provided at 4% on premises and at 20% on plant and machinery.
(c)   The authorized share capital of the firm is:

Preference shares	£50,000
Ordinary shares	£200,000

(d)   Preference share dividend has to be provided for, as has an ordinary share dividend of 20% of profits attributable to the ordinary shareholders.

Required: prepare, in good form, the financial accounts of the company for the year ended 31/12/19x1.

5.10   The following list of balances was extracted from the books of Iona Plc on 31/12/19x2:

Ordinary shares of £1	£200,000
5% preference shares of £1	70,000
Share premium reserve	90,000
Revenue reserves	50,000
Opening stock	73,000
Sales	1,000,000
Purchases	550,000
Administrative salaries	60,000
Equipment at cost	125,000
Vehicles at cost	100,000
Accumulated depreciation	
– Equipment	60,000
– Vehicles	20,000
Other administration costs	25,000
Distribution costs	90,000
Directors' fees	40,000
Trade debtors	300,000
Trade creditors	55,000
10% debentures (19x9)	20,000
Cash	200,000
Debenture interest	2,000

Notes:

(a)   Stock on hand at 31/12/19x2 was valued at £150,000.
(b)   The current year's depreciation has to be provided as follows:

Plant and machinery – at 20% of cost
Vehicles – at 25% of the written down value

(c)   The following expenses are still outstanding at 31/12/19x2:

Audit fees	£14,000
Rates	£15,000

(d)   The estimated tax liability for 19x2 is £30,000.
(e)   The directors propose paying the preference share dividend and an ordinary share dividend of 10%.
(f)   The firm's authorized capital is:

Ordinary shares	£500,000
Preference shares	£200,000

Required: prepare, in good form, the financial accounts of the firm for the year just ended.

5.11   From the following abridged profit and loss account and balance sheet of IBK Ltd as at 31/3/19x9, you are required to produce the firm's *sources and uses of funds statement.*

IBK Ltd
Profit and loss account
for the year ended 31/3/19x9

Sales		£24,000,000
Cost of sales		13,000,000
Gross profit		£11,000,000
less Expenses		
Miscellaneous	£6,500,000	
Depreciation	1,000,000	
		7,500,000
		£3,500,000
less Taxation		1,200,000
		£2,300,000
less Dividends		700,000
Transfer to reserves		£1,600,000

Balance sheet
as at 31/3/19x9

	19x9	19x8
Fixed assets	£7,500,000	£5,000,000
Current assets		
Stock	£1,500,000	£1,100,000
Debtors	2,350,000	2,000,000
Bank	50,000	10,000
	£3,900,000	£3,110,000
less Current liabilities		
Creditors	£1,150,000	£700,000
Tax	1,500,000	510,000
Dividends	900,000	500,000
	£3,550,000	£1,710,000
Net current assets	£350,000	£1,400,000
Total net assets	£7,850,000	£6,400,000
Ordinary shares	£2,000,000	£1,500,000
Preference shares	500,000	500,000
Share premium account	550,000	–
Revenue reserves	2,800,000	1,200,000
	£5,850,000	£3,200,000
10% debentures	1,500,000	3,000,000
Bank loan	500,000	200,000
	£7,850,000	£6,400,000

6 Deficiencies in historic accounts

Introduction

The previous four chapters have examined the content and construction of the financial accounts of different types of businesses – the sole trader, partnership, manufacturer and limited company. As was explained and shown, different types of businesses require different types of accounts, although none contravened basic accounting principles.

If there is one essential similarity among the various types of account considered so far, it is possibly that they have all been produced under the historic cost accounting rule or convention. All of the accounts considered have been backward looking, trying to show what has happened to the business in the past, and have concerned themselves solely with cost.

This chapter will look at the reasons why this is so, at the main deficiencies which are thrown up because of that and also at recent attempts by accountants to overcome these deficiencies.

Why historic accounts?

This question could have two meanings:

- Why do accounts say only what has happened in the past?
- And why do accounts only report in cost terms?

Why only the past?

Financial accounts need not report only what has happened in the past; they can be prepared to show what is expected to happen in the future.

Reporting what is expected in the future is 'Budgeting', and this will be examined in some detail in Chapters 9 and 10. Final budgets will, indeed, take the form of a profit and loss account and a balance sheet, and these statements will be produced using the same rules and conventions as historic accounts. Their main advantage will be to show the firm's managers where the firm should be going financially. With this information, they can compare actual results to what was expected and, if there are any variations, perhaps try to do something to correct the situation before it gets out of hand.

Financial accounts are not just for the past, then; they can also be used to show what the future ought to be like.

The last three chapters have considered the past, however, for two good reasons:

(a) For stewardship reporting. Financial accounts are primarily prepared for the owners of a business (although there may be other interested readers, as was explained in Chapter 1). The owners of a business put money into that business, and the financial accounts tell them how that money has been used and what return they have earned from their investment. In many firms, particularly limited companies, the owners do not manage the business; managers are appointed to do that. Managers are entrusted with investors' money, and the financial accounts show the owners if their trust has been well founded. Without financial accounts, it would be similar to you lending money to someone you do not know, for an unknown purpose, and then the lender not telling you if you have made any money on the investment.

(b) For tax purposes. Tax is charged on all income, including profits. That being so, accounts have to be prepared so that tax can be charged properly on earned profits, and those accounts must be of the past.

Why at cost?

Perhaps the honest answer is that reporting of cost is the easiest way of reporting and certainly the most objective. However, there are again two main reasons why accounts are reported at cost:

(a) The stewardship function (again). As the stewardship function implies that the managers of a firm are reporting to the owners, it makes sense that they tell the owners what they have done with the owners' money. To do so, it must be at cost. At the most basic, financial accounts are saying, 'You, the owners, gave us, the managers, £X and this is what we spent it on.'

(b) The second reason has previously been considered, and that is, if accounts are not to be at cost, what else is there? The obvious answer may be that accounts should show value, how much assets are worth, and so on. The question which then arises is, 'What is value?' If a firm is to show its accounts at value, should it be at the market value as a whole or as individual parts? The whole may or may not be more valuable than the sum of the individual parts. Either way, the value must be highly judgemental, whereas the cost is always the cost.

Costs could be adjusted for inflation, and, indeed, this has been tried, as will be shown later on in this chapter. But this, too, raises problems. Should costs be adjusted by the general rate of inflation or by the rate applicable to the particular business? What should be done with costs which have different rates of inflation, because in times of inflation not all costs rise at a uniform rate?

The simplest solution is to report only on cost. Doing so has the added advantage of everyone understanding what is meant by 'cost', whereas people may have different perceptions of value and the effects of inflation.

Deficiencies of historic costs

Given that financial accounts are prepared under the historic cost convention, perhaps for very good reasons, it is well worth remembering that such accounts will have inherent deficiencies which could be misleading if the reader was unaware of them.

The four main deficiencies concern:

- Distinguishing between capital and revenue costs.
- Depreciation.
- Stock valuation.
- Accruals estimation.

Capital and revenue costs

Since profits are defined as the difference between revenue income and revenue expenditure, it follows that the distinction between capital and revenue must be exact. If there is any uncertainty, the profit disclosed in accounts which have that uncertainty must, in turn, be questionable.

Certain costs are clearly revenue, for example, the annual rates bill is clearly a revenue cost. Similarly, the cost of a new factory is clearly a capital cost. Some costs are not so easily distinguished.

Consider a firm which in the current year has spent £1,000,000 on developing a new product. If the development is a success then the product may last up to ten years and make the firm profits over that time. If it is not successful then the expenditure would have been all for nought. Should that £1,000,000 be classed as a revenue cost or a capital cost? Should it all be charged to one year's profits or should it be capitalized and depreciated over ten years? The answer, of course, is that it all depends on whether or not the product is going to be successful, and at the year end it is quite possible that no one knows.

There must be some uncertainty no matter how the £1,000,000 is classified which means that there must be some uncertainty about the end profit figure.

Depreciation

Even with expenditure which is clearly capital, there is still the problematic area of depreciation. The objective of depreciation is to write off the cost of a capital asset over that asset's useful life; but, as we have seen, how that is done can result in different annual depreciation charges. A range of possible depreciation charges, all of which are equally valid, will result in a range of equally valid profit figures.

Profits are also susceptible to the estimates of assets' useful lives. The shorter the estimated useful life, the higher the annual depreciation charge and, consequently, the lower the end profit. For example, assume a firm has profits of £10,000 before charging depreciation. It has one asset which cost £20,000 and its useful life is believed to be five years. The firm's net profit is, therefore:

Profit before depreciation	£10,000	
less Depreciation	4,000	(straight line over 5 years)
Net profit	£ 6,000	

If the asset had a useful life of only 4 years, the result would have been:

Profit before depreciation	£10,000	
less Depreciation	5,000	(SL over 4 years)
Net profit	£ 5,000	

This small change has resulted in profits falling by 16%, but who can say with any certainty how long an asset will last? How long will a brand new car last? How confident are you with your answer?

Stock valuation

Again, the problems involved in the valuation of stock have previously been considered. Just as there are different methods of depreciation, each capable of producing different annual depreciation charges, so there are different stock valuation methods each of which will produce different stock values.

The different stock valuation methods arose because of the need to identify the cost of stock at the year end (as opposed to its value) so that historic cost accounts for discrete periods of time may be produced. Unfortunately, perhaps, different stock figures will result in different profit figures because of the calculation of cost of sales (opening stock + purchases in year – closing stock).

Although a particular method of stock valuation may appear appropriate to various companies, the actual selection of a method remains a subjective choice which, ultimately, means that the final accounts must also be the result of subjective assessment.

Accruals

The subjectivity and deficiency inherent in financial accounts which are prepared for artificial periods of time can best be seen when considering accrued charges. Accrued charges are little more than 'best guesses' of costs incurred by a firm within a period of time but for which it has yet to be billed. They are necessary if a firm is to account for all expenditure incurred within a given time period but, by their very nature, they must be seen as highly judgemental and subjective.

Accruals will certainly be based on costs already incurred. For example, a firm's accrual for telephone charges will be based on the telephone bills which have already been paid, but the one thing that can be said about any accrual is that it will not be the same as the actual account when it is received. Anyone who can foretell to the penny how much a telephone bill is going to be has a future somewhere else other than as an employee in a company!

Deficiencies in meeting user needs

Chapter 1 identified the main users of accounting information and outlined the information needs of each. A little thought will show that historic accounts are insufficient to meet all of the various requirements of these different users. For example:

(a)   Investors require information about future financial performance, but historic accounts only show what has happened in the past.
(b)   Management needs to know about past, present and future perform- ance – historic accounts only tell them about past performance.
(c)   Most lenders will be looking for security, probably over a firm's assets. Financial accounts, unfortunately for such lenders, show only a book value for assets which will probably have little resemblance to actual value. Such book values are of little use in assessing the level of security inherent in the underlying asset.
(d)   Employees require to know about the prospects for long-term viability. Financial accounts are for one year only, normally, and on their own cannot be taken as a reliable guide to the future.

Overcoming the deficiencies

Accountants are aware of the imperfections in historic cost accounts and have introduced new ways of presenting accounting information. They would, however, also point out that these innovations have, as an underlying basis, the very statements which caused the initial confusion. Either that, or the innovations have even more levels of subjectivity than the originals!

At the very least, accountants would say that historic cost accounts are the best way of presenting information that has been devised so far. They may give a slightly distorted picture but at least it is better than no picture at all. In addition, so long as you know the rules, allowances can be made and the picture becomes sharper.

The main innovations which have been introduced in an attempt to present a clearer picture include:

(a)   Statements of sources and uses of funds.
(b)   Employee reports.
(c)   Valued added statements.
(d)   Financial summaries.
(e)   Inflation adjusted accounts.

Statements of sources and uses of funds

These statements have already been discussed in Chapter 4. The main point to note is that they are created directly from two historic balance sheets and the intervening profit and loss account. Consequently, statements of sources and uses of funds do not eliminate any of the deficiencies and subjectivity inherent in the 'primary' statements.

Since these statements have been discussed and described in Chapter 4, we will not be re-examining them here.

Employee reports

The 1985 Companies Act requires annual accounts to be prepared for shareholders only. It does not require companies to report to their employees. Nonetheless, many larger companies do prepare reports for their employees.

Most employee reports try to move away from formal financial accounts while still retaining the essential information. Employee reports generally try to give financial data in a non-technical way that is more easily understood by non-accountants. Some firms have adopted new formats for the profit and loss account and balance sheet and renamed them in terms of:

- How we made money (the profit and loss account).
- Where the money went to (the balance sheet).

Most firms make extensive use of graphs and pictures to display such information, such as Figure 6.1. Many employee reports try to avoid formal accounting terminology (although some do not), attempting to make them more 'user friendly' and more easily understood.

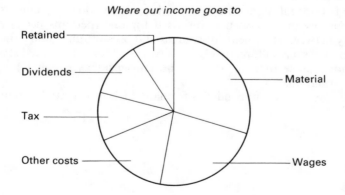

Figure 6.1

Since the majority of individual shareholders are not accountants and do not really understand the full significance of financial accounts, it may be regarded as a pity that such simplified versions are not also supplied to them. However, simplification of the accounts is probably the major drawback in employee reports.

Financial accounts contain a wealth of information, most of which is glossed over or omitted in employee reports. These reports can often be fairly compared to thirty-page comic versions of literature classics – they may contain the essence of the story but there is no detail or explanation (and it is often the detail which is interesting and important). Employee reports are often very condescending in that they treat the employees as being unable to understand full accounts but make no similar assumptions about individual shareholders!

Value added statements

A study in 1975 commissioned by the accountancy profession first recommended the publication of value added statements. Such statements were to show how wealth was created in a firm and how that wealth was then distributed within the company and to those who have an interest in the wealth of the firm.

Value added was defined as the difference between the earnings of a firm and the money which had to be paid by the firm in earning that income (excluding the payment of wages).

The distribution of the wealth was seen as going to four main destinations:

(a)   to pay employees;
(b)   to pay the providers of capital;
(c)   to pay the government;
(d)   to maintain and expand the firm's assets.

The percentage of value added which was absorbed by each category was also to be shown.

There is no legal requirement to produce value added statements, nor is the accounting profession pressing hard for one (perhaps because of the similarity between statements of sources and uses of funds and value added statements). As a result, relatively few firms produce value added statements and, among those that do, there is no consensus as to what form these reports should take.

The 1975 study recommended a format which is, essentially, reproduced below:

Alba Ltd
Value added statement
for the year ended 31/12/x9

Turnover	(1)	£10,000,000	
Other income	(2)	50,000	
		£10,050,000	
less Bought-in materials			
and services	(3)	4,850,000	
Value added	(4)	£ 5,200,000	
			%
Distribution of value added	(5)		
To pay employees	(6)	£ 4,000,000	77
To pay providers of capital	(7)		
Dividends		£400,000	
Interest on loans		150,000	
		550,000	10.5
To pay the government	(8)	250,000	4.8
To maintain and expand	(9)		
Depreciation		£300,000	
Retained profits		100,000	
		400,000	7.7
Value added		£ 5,200,000	100.0

Points to note:

(1) *Turnover* is the total net sales earned by the firm.
(2) *Other income* would consist of all sources of revenue income other than sales.
(3) *Bought-in materials and services* are basically the cost of all materials and services to the business from sources outside the firm. It would exclude all wages since that is not a bought-in cost – employees are part of a firm.
(4) The *value added* is the increased wealth created by the firm. This has been earned by buying in materials, using them, and then selling them at a profit.
(5) This section shows what the firm did with the wealth created at point 4.
(6) Part of the wealth created, normally a large proportion, went to pay the firm's employees.
(7) *Providers of capital* would include shareholders and long-term lenders. The costs would consist, therefore, of dividends and interest.
(8) Included here would be the payment of all taxes.
(9) This would be the charge for depreciation (maintenance of assets) and retained profits (expansion of assets).

The value added statement is little more than a rewrite of the profit and loss account since all the information given in a value added statement comes from the published profit and loss account (and hence all the deficiencies will be transferred also).

If there are any benefits in a value added statement, they would be:

(a)   It shows where a firm's wealth went to in a clear and easily understood way.
(b)   The percentages show how much of the wealth is taken by the three most interested parties in a firm and how much has been retained by the firm.

Financial summaries

Most large companies now include in their annual reports summaries of results covering the previous five to ten years. Such summaries are not intended to eliminate any weaknesses in historic cost accounts – they cannot, since many are simply reiterating such accounts. They do, however, show trends through time; and because the time span is so long, the distorting effects resulting from arbitrary choices of depreciation and stock valuation methods can be reduced.

The information disclosed in financial summaries is left to the discretion of individual companies. This can be, and is, as little or as much as the firm chooses. The following two examples show the range of information disclosed by two leading UK companies.

Company A

Turnover	£x
Trading profit	£x
Profits of related companies	x
Profit before tax and extraordinary items	£x
Extraordinary items	(x)
Tax	(x)
Net profit	£x
Fixed assets	£x
Stock	x
Creditors *less* debtors	(x)
Bank	x
	£x
Long-term creditors	(x)
Assets employed	£x

Company B

Turnover	£x
Profit before tax	£x
Profit after tax but before extraordinary items	£x
Earnings per share	xp
Dividend per share	xp

Company B fares poorly compared to Company A even though it gives this information for the past six years whereas Company A gave the information over a five-year period only.

The usefulness of financial summaries must depend on the quantity and quality of information summarized. In the above two cases, Company A does give sufficient information for conclusions to be fairly drawn. It is doubtful if Company B provides anything that could be used.

Financial summaries which contain an abundance of data still have to be approached with caution since they are still dealing with historic cost. For example, consider the following summary of turnover:

	19x9	x8	x7	x6	x5	x4
Turnover (£000s)	12,500	12,017	11,900	11,225	11,005	10,190

At face value, this may seem impressive. The firm's sales have increased by £2,310,000 or by 22.6% over the period. However, if inflation had been running at 6% over this period, sales should have increased to £13,636,000 not £12,500,000. Despite a 22.6% increase, the firm has not kept pace with inflation and is, in fact, poorer in 19x9 than in 19x4!

Inflation adjusted accounts

The above illustration shows the effect of inflation on historic accounts – it makes a comparison between years virtually impossible. The basic problem is that the comparison is not 'like with like'.

To compare one year's results with those of another, it is essential that the underlying bases are similar. This is not the case in times of inflation, as £1 at the start of a year is not worth the same as £1 at the end. Financial accounts deal in monetary units and give the spurious impression of stability, a pound seeming always to be worth a pound, but, as the above example shows, that is not so. Of course, not only are sales values affected by inflation, but every financial aspect of a firm is. Inflation can also affect the definition of profit.

Consider the following example. A firm buys and sells shirts. On 1/1/19x1 it buys 100 shirts at £10 each. During the year, it sells them all at £15 each. Under historic cost accounting, its profit is defined as:

Sales (100 @ £15)	£1,500
Costs (100 @ £10)	1,000
Profit	£ 500

The owner of the business may feel that he has £500 to spend on personal items, but when he goes to replace the 100 shirts he finds that they now cost £13 each. To replace the 100 shirts he will have to spend £1,300; that is, he has to use £300 of his 'personal' profit, which leaves him only £200 for personal use. If profit is excess income, what is this firm's excess – £500 or £200?

Unfortunately, as in most areas, there are different ways of measuring the impact of inflation on firms. To a large extent, the method adopted depends on what the inflation adjusted accounts are trying to show. In the recent past, the accountancy profession has considered two approaches:

- Current purchasing power.
- Current cost accounting.

CURRENT PURCHASING POWER

This method considers the changes in the general purchasing ability of money over time. Thus assets would be adjusted to show the current purchasing power of money used to buy assets in the past. CPP accounts show how much would have to be paid now for assets which the firm currently owns.

CPP is concerned with the changing general purchasing power of money – how much more things are costing on average. As a measure of inflation, it would use the Retail Price Index (published monthly by the government), and firms' assets are adjusted by this index.

For example, if the RPI showed:

19x1	100
19x2	108
19x3	119

this would assume that 19x1 was the base year against which everything else is compared. Thus 19x2 is 8 points higher than 19x1, and 19x3 is 19 points higher than 19x1. In terms of an asset which cost £100 in 19x1, it would be shown as £100 in 19x1, £108 in 19x2, and £119 in 19x3. An asset bought for £120 in 19x2 would be shown in 19x3 at:

$$£120 \times \frac{119}{108} = £132$$

Gains can be made in times of inflation if money is borrowed. Suppose the firm borrowed £60 to help buy the £100 asset in 19x1 and had repaid nothing by 19x3. At the end of 19x3 the purchasing power of that £60 would be:

$$£60 \times \frac{119}{100} = £71.40$$

But it just owes £60. By borrowing, it has made an apparent gain of £11.40.

CPP, then, is a relatively straightforward way of measuring the impact of inflation on a firm's balance sheet. It merely converts everything into terms of how much would have to be spent now for what it has obtained in the past.

Historic profit is also affected. Consider again the 19x1 asset which cost £100, £60 of which was borrowed. By 19x3, that asset had been adjusted to £119 (an additional £19), so the historic cost profits would have to be reduced by that £19 to make good the increased 'value' of the asset. However, there was the gain of £11.40 on the borrowing. This would be set off against the £19 reduction in profit. The actual reduction in profit would be only £7.60 (£19 − £11.40).

This method of accounting for inflation was the first to be recommended by the accountancy profession but has since been rejected. The main criticism is the use of the RPI. The RPI is a general consumer inflation index covering consumer expenditure – it includes, *inter alia*, mortgage interest rates. It is doubtful if such a consumer index has much relevance to business assets and expenditure. Businesses ought to use business specific inflation indices.

CURRENT COST ACCOUNTING

This method has the advantage over CPP in that it does not employ a general inflation index but uses, instead, industry-specific indices – specific to different business assets. It is also the method most recently favoured by the accounting profession and is embodied in SSAP No. 16.

CCA requires certain adjustments to be made to historic cost accounts, notably:

(a)   Fixed assets are shown at their 'value to the business'.
(b)   Depreciation is calculated on assets' 'values to the business' – not on historic cost.
(c)   Stock is valued at its 'value to the business'.
(d)   Cost of sales is calculated on the basis of the 'value to the business' of the goods sold, at the date of sale.

'Value to the business' is obviously an important feature of this method and requires definition. Normally this is taken to mean how much the business would have to pay to replace the asset in question if the firm was deprived of it. Thus, in the case of fixed assets, 'value to the business' would be the cost that the firm would incur if it had to replace those assets with exactly similar assets. With stock it would also mean the replacement cost of that stock. To be able to do this, specific inflation indices must be available for every asset that a firm owns.

Consider a firm which has two assets at the end of 19x3 as follows:

	Cost	Depre-ciation	Net
Asset 1	£10,000	£4,000	£6,000
Asset 2	5,000	3,000	2,000
			£8,000

Both assets were bought in 19x2. The relevant indices are:

	Asset 1	Asset 2
19x2	100	100
19x3	115	125

The adjustments for asset 1 would be:

cost	x	factor	= value
£10,000	x	$\frac{115}{100}$	= £11,500

depreciation	x	factor	
£4,000	x	$\frac{115}{100}$	= £4,600

And for asset 2;

	Historic value		Factor	Value
Cost	£6,000	x	$\frac{125}{100}$	= £6,250
Depreciation	£3,000	x	$\frac{125}{100}$	= £3,750

The revised balance sheet would show:

	Value	Depreciation	Net
Asset 1	£11,500	£4,600	£6,900
Asset 2	6,250	3,750	2,500
			£9,400

that is, an increase of £1,400 over historic cost. This £1,400 would be credited to a special *revaluation reserve account.*

The profit and loss account would be adjusted for an increase in the annual depreciation charge and for an increase in the cost of sales. Other adjustments would be made to reflect the gains (and losses) which are possible from borrowing money (or being due money), similar to that described in CPP.

It can be seen that CCA, although accounting for inflation in a very specific way, will be very complicated in practice since each class of asset must be individually adjusted. This, to a large extent, caused much resistance in firms to adopting this method. In addition, the new accounts were framed in terms of 'value to the business' – a term and concept unknown to most business owners. This, too, caused firms to resist this method.

CURRENT REQUIREMENTS

When SSAP No. 16 was introduced, all large firms were required to produce current cost accounts. However, with inflation running at relatively low and moderate rates, the perceived need for inflation adjusted accounts has diminished. Companies are now no longer required to abide by SSAP No. 16, although they are encouraged to do so.

The encouragement has not met with much success. Production of CCA accounts costs extra money, and their usefulness in times of relative stability has been questioned. Furthermore, few people really know what inflation adjusted accounts are supposed to be saying. It is, therefore, perhaps not too surprising to find that very few firms do still produce CCA accounts.

It would seem realistic to assume that firms will not be required to produce any form of inflation adjusted accounts in the future – at least not unless high levels of inflation have returned.

Questions

6.1   Why is the concept of 'cost' important in the preparation of a firm's annual accounts? What consequences flow from the adoption of this concept?

6.2   To what extent is a firm's reported profit the result of subjective assessment rather than an objective statement of fact?

6.3   What are *value added statements*? What do they contain? Are they more effective at conveying financial information than standard profit and loss accounts?

6.4   Clydecare Ltd has produced the following draft profit and loss account for the year ended 31/12/19xx:

Turnover		£22,000,000
Cost of sales		12,500,000
Gross Profit		£9,500,000
less Costs		
Wages	£4,100,000	
Administration	500,000	
Interest	100,000	
Depreciation	750,000	
Other costs	250,000	
		5,700,000
Profit before taxation		£ 3,800,000
Taxation		1,100,000
Profit after taxation		£ 2,700,000
Dividends paid and proposed		1,200,000
Retained profits		£ 1,500,000

Required: prepare a value added statement for Clydecare Ltd.

6.5   In what ways can financial statements be made to be more easily understood by non-accountants?

6.6   Should firms be required to produce inflation adjusted financial accounts? Why?

6.7   If a firm's financial accounts must be adjusted to reflect inflation, should the adjustment be made on the basis of the general purchasing power of money or on the basis of the specific impact of inflation on the firm? Why?

6.8   Why, in times of inflation, can firms make gains from borrowing money?

6.9   Outline the main adjstments which are required under current cost accounting. What is meant by 'value to the business'?

6.10   Do financial summaries covering a number of past years have any real value in assessing a firm's performance? What information would you include in such summaries?

7 Interpretation of financial statements

Introduction

A set of accounts is a concise summary of many varied transactions and will be used in different ways to fulfil different needs. To do so, they will have to be interpreted. This can be likened to a newspaper report on a football match. Such a report will summarize what happened in the match, the standard of play, the score, the scorers and perhaps how some players behaved. As an interested reader you may want to know only certain points – What are the prospects for promotion now? Has the new striker lived up to his purchase price? Are improvements still needed in the defence? To answer these points you will have to interpret the report. Other users may have other questions and will, therefore, have to interpret the same report in other ways.

Similarly, different users of accounts will use the same set of accounts but, with different needs, will have to interpret them differently. Chapter 1 examined in some detail who the users of accounts are; the following Exhibit summarizes their needs.

EXHIBIT 7.1

User	Requirements
Owners/shareholders	Profitability, financial stability, prospects for growth, efficient use of assets
Management	Long-term stability, use of assets, profitability
Employees	Long-term stability (are their jobs secure for the future?), profitability (can the firm afford to pay them more?)
Lenders	Financial stability (will the firm be able to repay the loans and interest?)
Creditors	Short-term viability
Competitors	Profitability (does the firm earn more profits?), financial stability (can the competition be eliminated?)
Government (Inland Revenue; Customs and Excise)	Profitability (to calculate tax), turnover (to account for VAT)

The above list of users and their requirements is not exhaustive but is meant only to suggest some of the possible uses to which financial accounts can be put and by whom.

The exhibit does show, however, that although there are many users, their requirements can be simplified to a need for knowledge about:

- Profitability.
- Short-term viability – liquidity.
- Long-term stability.
- Efficient use of assets.
- Investor's return.

It is necessary to interpret financial accounts in these various ways simply because the structure of final accounts does not disclose such information. Indeed, final accounts could never disclose this information because, in many ways, interpretation is highly judgemental. For example, you may find that a firm's profits have been rising in the past. To interpret those data and try to say something about the future prospects requires personal judgement. Will profits rise again next year? Past data and trends suggest that they will, but it is not a statement of fact that they will. Final accounts try to be statements of fact – interpretation of these facts can often be very speculative and, as such, has no place alongside the actual accounts.

Financial accounts are also historic in nature, that is, reporting past events. Intepretation of such events must, of necessity, use past data, but the objective is often forward looking – trying to extrapolate into the future. Again, any such extrapolation must be subjective and cannot be placed alongside statements of fact. Nonetheless, such interpretation is necessary as it is the only way in which an outsider, with no access to internal information, can effectively analyse a firm's financial prospects.

Ratio analysis

Interpretation of financial accounts is performed using the technique of ratio analysis, comparing one figure in a set of accounts with another. A ratio is simply the relationship between one number and another; for example, the relationship between 2 and 10 could be said to be:

(a)   1 : 5 – that is, 2 is one-fifth of 10; or
(b)   20% – that is, the first number (2) is 20% of the second number (10).

Applying this to financial accounts, if a firm earns £50,000 profits from a turnover of £1,000,000, this could take the form of the following ratios:

(a)   1 : 20 – that is, £1 of profit is earned from every £20 of sales; or
(b)   5% – that is, the firm makes 5% profit on £1M turnover

In financial analysis, the analyst will be examining the profit and loss account and the balance sheet, and as ratio analysis examines the relationship between any two numbers, ratios can be derived from comparing:

(a)   a profit and loss account figure with another profit and loss account figure; or
(b)   a profit and loss account figure with a balance sheet figure; or
(c)   a balance sheet figure with another balance sheet figure.

As most financial accounts contain about forty individual account items, the number of possible ratios (comparing any one figure with any one other) which can be calculated is 780. Naturally a large percentage of such ratios will be quite meaningless – for example, the relationship between distribution costs and intangible assets. A minority are capable, however, of supplying useful insights into the company – for example, the relationship between net profit and sales. The skill of the analyst lies not in calculating ratios but in knowing which ratios and relationships are significant and in then analysing the results.

Generally, the relationships and hence the ratios which can be signficant are between those figures which are affected by each other.

The main ratios

The following profit and loss account and balance sheet will be used as a basis for illustrating the ratios.

EXHIBIT 7.2

The Easy Go Co. Ltd
Profit and loss account
for the year ended 31/12/19xx

Turnover		£1,500,000
Cost of sales		1,290,000
Gross profit		£ 210,000
Distribution costs	£45,000	
Administration expenses	50,000	95,000
		£ 115,000
Other income		5,000
		£ 120,000
Interest payable		27,000
Profit on ordinary activities before tax		£ 93,000
Tax on profit on ordinary activities		35,000
Profit on ordinary activites after tax		£ 58,000
Preference dividend paid	£ 4,500	
Proposed ordinary dividend	28,500	33,000
Undistributed profit for year		£25,000

The Easy Go Co. Ltd
(Abridged) balance sheet
as at 31/12/19xx

Fixed assets			
Premises			£400,000
Plant and machinery			100,000
			£500,000
Current assets			
Stock		£180,000	
Debtors		150,000	
Bank		20,000	
		£350,000	
Less Creditors due for payment in less than 1 year			
Trade creditors	£25,000		
Overdrafts	40,000		
Taxation	35,000		
Proposed dividend	28,500	128,500	
			221,500
			£721,500
Creditors due for payment in more than 1 year			
10% debentures (19xx)			£250,000
Capital and reserves			
Called-up share capital			
Ordinary shares of £1		£350,000	
9% preference shares of £1		50,000	
			400,000
Revenue reserves			71,500
			£721,500

Note: the market price of 1 ordinary share is £1.10.

Profitability

Profits expressed in absolute figures can be highly misleading. For example, a firm makes a profit of £100,000. Is that good or bad? Naturally, the answer is that it all depends. It depends on the level of sales needed to generate that profit – if it is £10m then £100,000 represents only 1% of that level of sales which is significantly worse than if turnover was only £1m. Also, comparing profits between firms would be impossible without also taking into account, for example, the level of sales made to generate those profits.

For example, Company A earns £100,000 profit, and Company B earns £100,000 profit. Which company has performed better? Would it help if you knew that Company A had turnover of £1,000,000 and that the turnover of Company B was £10,000,000?

The main profitability ratios are usually expressed as percentages, referring either to turnover (how well the firm was able to convert sales into profits) or to capital employed (how well the firm used capital to earn profits).

Net profit to sales

This ratio expresses net profit as a percentage of sales thus:

$$\frac{\text{net profit (after tax)}}{\text{total sales}} \times 100$$

From Exhibit 7.2, this would be:

$$\frac{58,000}{1,500,000} \times 100 = 3.6\%$$

Although the 3.6% cannot be considered on its own to be satisfactory or otherwise – it would have to be compared with something else such as last year's ratio or that of a competitor – it does indicate the percentage of sales which are converted into profits. Basically, the higher the percentage, the better the company's performance, especially if it is higher than that of competitors.

Gross profit percentage

This ratio expresses gross profit as a percentage of sales and is often regarded as a prime indicator of management's ability to perform the basic activity of buying/manufacturing and selling. It is found thus:

$$\frac{\text{gross profit}}{\text{sales}} \times 100$$

and in terms of the example:

$$\frac{210,000}{1,500,000} \times 100 = 14\%$$

As with the net profit : sales ratio, it is impossible to say if 14% on its own is good or bad. Rather, it should be compared with a standard such as predictions, competitors, and so on, and assessed on that basis.

However, this ratio is essentially looking at sales and cost of sales, and a firm should expect its gross profit ratio to be at least as good as the industrial average and/or in line with previous years' ratios. If there is a significant negative difference, it could mean poorer management. In comparison with the industrial average, all firms in the industry will be selling at roughly the same price and paying roughly the same unit price for raw materials and production labour. Therefore all firms should have about the same gross profit ratio. If not, then one firm is selling at a lower price than the average or it is paying more for its raw materials.

Return on capital employed (ROCE)

This ratio examines the level of investment made by a company and the return that it produces. In some ways it can be likened to an investment in a building society. If a depositor has £100 in a building society then that is his/her investment or capital employed. If he/she receives £8 interest then that is his/her return, and this return expressed as a percentage of his/her investment would be:

$$\frac{8}{100} \frac{\text{(return)}}{\text{(capital)}} \times 100 = 8\%$$

The analogy between the rate of return from a building society and ROCE cannot be taken too far, as there many differences between a firm's return and that of the depositor, and between a firm's capital and that of the depositor. Indeed, there is no certain agreement in finance as to how ROCE should be calculated, the main areas of disagreement being:

(a) Should the return (that is, profit) be before or after tax? It can be argued that tax is not a cost such as wages in that the firm has to pay tax and has no control over how much has to be paid. The cost of wages, however, is under management control. Any costs which are imposed on the firm should not be considered when defining the profit earned by management, therefore profit should be before tax.

An alternative view is that tax is as much a cost as wages in that if a profit is to be earned then both have to be paid. Furthermore, the amount of tax could be under management control to some degree in that management could plan ahead and adopt policies which could mitigate the tax burden. Therefore profit should be after tax.

(b) What is *capital employed* in a firm? It could be argued that as the return (profit) belongs to the shareholders then capital employed should only be that contributed by the shareholders. Again, an alternative point of view is that the return is only made because of all the capital in the firm and that the comparison should only be made with all funds available to the firm.

With the above points in mind, one of the more common ratios for expressing return on capital employed is:

$$\frac{\text{profit after tax}}{\text{fixed assets + current assets}} \times 100$$

and in terms of Exhibit 7.2:

$$\frac{58,000}{500,000 + 350,000} \times 100 = 6.82\%$$

The ROCE of firms could be compared with similar competing firms, the industrial average or other 'safe' investments (such as the building society). However, if comparisons are to be made, then it is essential that all comparators have been calculated on the same assumptions as to what is meant by 'return' and 'capital employed'. If different assumptions have been made then there can be no valid comparison.

Liquidity

The principal liquidity ratios are used by analysts to assess a firm's ability to remain solvent in the short term. The balance sheet will provide the basic data in the form of current assets and current liabilities (or creditors due for payment in less than one year). Current assets will show the resources owned by a firm which should produce cash in the near future, and current liabilities will show the calls on this cash in the near future. The liquidity ratios effectively attempt to assess the sufficiency of a firm's working capital.

Current ratio

This ratio is simply a comparison between current assets and current liabilities and is found by:

$$\frac{\text{current assets}}{\text{current liabilities}}, \text{ that is, } \frac{350,000}{128,500} = 2.72$$

This means that for the Easy Go Co., its current assets are 2.72 times greater than its current liabilities. The ratio can also be expressed as:

$$\begin{array}{ccc} 2.72 & : & 1 \\ \text{(current assets)} & & \text{(current liabilities)} \end{array}$$

The second expression says that for every £1 that the firm will have to pay in the near future to creditors, it can expect to receive £2.72 when its current assets are converted into cash.

Being prudent, most analysts would be concerned if a manufacturing firm's current ratio fell below 2 : 1 although a lower ratio is considered acceptable in firms with little or no stock.

Acid test ratio

A major problem with the current ratio is that it includes stock, which, in a manufacturing firm, could take a substantial period of time to pass through the financial process before being converted into sales and cash – perhaps much longer than the time in which current liabilities must be paid. If this is the case then the current ratio is invalid, as it is no longer comparing short-term debts with the resources available to meet those debts.

The *acid test* ratio (sometimes called the *liquidity* ratio) circumvents this problem by removing stock, thus:

$$\frac{\text{current assets} - \text{stock, work in progress}}{\text{current liabilities}}$$

In so doing, this ratio compares genuine short-term resources with short-term indebtedness and gives an indication of a firm's immediate liquidity. In terms of Exhibit 7.2:

$$\frac{350,000 - 180,000}{128,500} = 1.32 \text{ (or } 1.32 : 1)$$

It is generally accepted that this ratio should not fall below 1 in most firms. As it is concerned with very short-term resources and debts, a ratio of 1 (or

1 :1) implies just sufficient resources to cover immediate debts. Less than 1 implies not enough resources, and a figure substantially higher than 1 may be a sign of management inefficiency in that too much money will be tied up in unproductive assets such as debtors and cash.

Long-term stability

If a firm is to be financially stable in the longer term then its long-term financing will have to be judged efficient and sufficient by both the owners (shareholders) and suppliers of long-term loan capital. In the case of lenders, they will also have to be satisfied that they are not being asked to bear an undue element of risk and that the firm is capable of paying interest and capital repayments on time.

Net worth : total assets

This ratio examines the relationship between the owners' capital (both share capital and reserves) and assets and will show the proportion of all assets which have been financed by the shareholders. It is found by:

$$\frac{\text{share capital} + \text{reserves}}{\text{fixed assets} + \text{current assets}}$$

and in terms of Exhibit 7.2:

$$\frac{350,000 + 50,000 + 71,500}{500,000 + 350,000} = 0.55$$

As a general rule of thumb, this ratio should not be seen to fall below 0.5, as to do so would indicate that shareholders contribute less than 50% of the book value of the firm's assets. Potentially, that could be seen as the shareholders being unwilling to accept the greater risk in the enterprise.

Gearing ratio

This ratio considers the proportion of total capital which is contributed by long-term lenders. For most firms it is unlikely that lenders would be willing to contribute more than 50% (and often considerably less), as to do so would mean that they would be taking a bigger share of the inherent risk associated with any business than the owners. The ratio is found by:

$$\frac{\text{long-term loans}}{\text{total capital}}, \text{ that is, } \frac{250,000}{721,500} = 0.346$$

(Note: there is no uniform agreement as to what ought to constitute this ratio. For example, some authorities maintain that preference shares should be included in the numerator since they, like loans, have a fixed annual cost. Other authorities, however, maintain that preference shares are still equity capital and should not appear in the numerator. In examinations, a word of explanation should be given on your understanding of the ratio. The illustration above includes preference shares, as in doing so the ratio clearly highlights the proportion of loan capital to equity capital.)

A ratio of more than 0.5 would indicate that lenders are contributing more capital than the owners, and in the eyes of lenders, that would generally be unacceptable. Also, the closer the ratio comes to 0.5, the less likely a firm is to raise further long-term loans.

Cover for interest

If lenders are to have confidence in a firm, then they must feel reasonably assured that they will receive their interest when it becomes due. If lenders are uncertain, they will either refuse to lend money or, if they do, charge very high rates of interest in compensation for the additional risks they believe they are taking.

This ratio tries to measure how secure payment of interest is by comparing interest payable with the source from which it will come, that is profits, thus:

$$\frac{\text{profits (before tax and interest)}}{\text{interest payable}}, \text{ that is, } \frac{120,000}{25,000} = 4.8$$

(Note: profits are before tax since any interest payable will reduce the firm's tax liability. Interest in the denominator is only the interest on long-term loans and debentures. The balance is interest charged on overdrafts and other short-term loans, the suppliers of which will have different criteria for assessing the suitability of the firm – usually short-term liquidity assessments.)

The figure of 4.8 indicates that the firm is earning profits 4.8 times greater than the interest which has to be paid. The higher the figure, the more confidence lenders will have.

Use of assets

It is management's responsibility to ensure that the assets which are entrusted to it by the firm's owners are being used as efficiently as possible and that, consequently, the finances which were used to acquire the assets were not abused. There are a number of ratios which can be used to measure how well assets are used and how efficient management is in the use of the firm's funds.

Sales : fixed asset

This ratio will show how much sales a firm earns from every £1 invested in fixed assets, thus:

$$\frac{\text{sales}}{\text{fixed assets}}, \text{ that is, } \frac{1,500,000}{500,000} = 3 : 1$$

This ratio shows that £3 of sales are generated from every £1 of fixed assets owned by the firm. This could be compared with a competitor's ratio to see how efficient management is in using fixed assets to make sales. For example, if a competitor achieved a ratio of 5 : 1 (that is, £5 of sales for every £1 of fixed assets) then 3 : 1 is distinctly inefficient and may indicate that management has invested too much in fixed assets. Care should be taken in interpreting this ratio, however, since it is very easy for the comparison to be invalid.

To be valid, the fixed assets in the comparator firm should be very similar to those used in the firm being compared. Yet it is usually impossible to ascertain that fact from a firm's annual accounts. Similarly, the age and condition of the fixed assets in both firms should be comparable, as should each firm's depreciation policies.

Debtors turnover

This ratio estimates the number of weeks' sales which are represented by a firm's debtors. This should be as low as possible while still being consistent with business reality. If it is too high then it could indicate inefficient investment by management in unproductive current assets; that is the firm's managers are not ensuring that the firm's debtors settle their debts quickly. The debtors turnover ratio is found thus:

$$\frac{\text{average debtors}}{\text{sales}} \times 52$$

where 'average debtors' is:

$$\frac{\text{opening debtors} + \text{closing debtors}}{2}$$

and in terms of Exhibit 7.2:

$$\frac{150,000}{1,500,000} \times 52 = 5.2 \text{ weeks}$$

This means that the debtors figure of £150,000 represents 5.2 weeks' worth of sales for the Easy Go Co., or that, on average, the firm has to wait 5.2 weeks before it receives payment for sales which it made on credit. Generally, the lower this ratio is, the better, as that could mean that the firm has good control over debtors. Ideally, there should be no debtors, thus giving a ratio of zero, but that would be unrealistic for most businesses.

Stock : Cost of sales

This ratio is similar to the debtors turnover ratio in that it indicates the number of weeks' purchases of raw materials which are represented by the level of stock carried by a firm. It is found thus:

$$\frac{\text{average stock}}{\text{cost of sales}} \times 52, \text{ that is, } \frac{180,000}{1,290,000} \times 52 = 7.28 \text{ weeks}$$

The firm, therefore, has sufficient stock to service 7.28 weeks' worth of production. Analysts may also say that stock is turned over – that is, completely replaced with new stock – every 7.28 weeks. Generally, the lower this figure is, the better, as it means that less capital is tied up in what is, in effect, a non-earning asset. However, it cannot be too low, as a very low level of stock could result in a firm running out of stock. If that happened, the firm would not be able to produce its products, and with no products manufactured, it will not be able to make sales.

Investors' return

One of the functions of management is to ensure the best possible return is made to the firm's investors. If investors are not happy with the return they are earning on their investment, the consequence is that they will be unlikely to invest more capital in the firm. This may not be of much immediate importance but could be critical should the firm require additional risk capital in the future. Existing investors, unhappy with their current return, would be unlikely to provide this extra finance, and it would be equally unlikely that new investors would be encouraged to invest their money. Investors, therefore, must be kept 'happy' by providing them with an acceptable level of return.

Most of the ratios which measure investors' return compare a firm's earnings with the price of its shares. Earnings are examined as that is what the shareholders, as a body, have earned; and share price is considered since that is what the investor has, in fact, had to pay to become a participant in the firm's earnings. The common ratios are:

Earnings per share

This was considered in Chapter 5, but as a reminder, it is found by:

$$\frac{\text{profit after tax and preference dividends}}{\text{number of ordinary shares}},$$

$$\text{that is, } \frac{58,000 - 4,500}{350,000} = 15.28\text{p}$$

This means that each share is earning its owner 15.28p and so can be easily compared with the earnings from other possible investments.

Earnings yield

A major drawback with the EPS is that it is not related to how much the investor has actually to pay to earn that return. Consider two firms which each show an EPS of 25p. They may appear to be identical, but if the price of a share is £1 in Firm A and £2 in Firm B, then Firm A is obviously the better. In Firm A the investor has only to pay £1 to earn 25p, but in Firm B he/she has to pay £2 to earn the same amount.

The *earnings yield* overcomes the deficiency in the EPS by expressing earnings as a percentage of the cost of the share, thus:

$$\frac{\text{EPS}}{\text{cost of 1 share}} \times 100 = \frac{0.1528}{1.10} \times 100 = 13.89\%$$

Again, this 13.89% can be compared with other firms to see which is the best. Obviously, the higher this percentage is, the better is the firm from an investor's point of view.

Price earnings ratio (P/E ratio)

A slight variation on the earnings yield is the *P/E ratio*. This tries to show the number of years an investor must wait until his/her investment (the cost of one share) is recovered by the earnings made in one year. It is found by:

$$\frac{\text{cost per share}}{\text{EPS}} = \frac{1.10}{0.1528} = 7.2$$

This means that if an investor waits for 7.2 years, the original cost of the share will have been recovered by the earnings it has made. The lower this ratio is, the better, as it means that the cost of the share is recovered more quickly.

Dividend yield

It could be argued that using earnings is misleading since it implies that shareholders actually receive all of the earnings of a company. Very few, if any, in fact do, since most companies retain profits for internal investment – it is only dividends which the owners of shares actually receive. The *dividend yield* ratio examines the real, personal earnings of a share to its owner and is found by:

$$\frac{\text{dividend per share}}{\text{cost of 1 share}} \times 100$$

where 'dividend per share' is found by:

$$\frac{\text{total ordinary shares}}{\text{number of ordinary shares}} \text{, that is, } \frac{28,500}{350,000} = \text{£0.081}$$

and the dividend yield is:

$$\frac{0.081}{1.10} \times 100 = 7.36\%$$

Thus the owner of one share actually receives a return of 7.36%. Again, the higher this ratio is, the better, as it means that the investor is actually receiving a higher return.

Ratio analysis – a comparative analysis

Shown below are the abridged accounts of Easy Go Co. Ltd (taken from pages 106–7) and its main competitor, Good Fortune Ltd, for the year ended 31/12/19xx. The directors of Easy Go wish to know how their company has performed in comparison with Good Fortune.

Profit and loss accounts

		Easy Go		Good Fortune
Turnover		£1,500,000		£2,000,000
Cost of sales		1,290,000		1,660,000
Gross profit		£ 210,000		£ 340,000
Distribution	£45,000		£75,000	
Administration	50,000		90,000	
		95,000		165,000
		£ 115,000		£ 175,000
Other income		5,000		—
		£ 120,000		£ 175,000
Interest payable		27,000		40,000
		£ 93,000		£ 135,000
Taxation		35,000		45,000
Net profit		£ 58,000		£ 90,000

Balance sheets

		Easy Go		Good Fortune
Fixed assets		£500,000		£650,000
Current assets				
Stock	£180,000		£130,000	
Debtors	150,000		140,000	
Bank	20,000		—	
	£350,000		£270,000	
less				
Current liabilities	128,500		174,000	
		221,500		96,000
		£721,500		£746,000
less				
Creditors due in more than one year				
10% debentures		250,000		350,000
		£471,500		£396,000

Capital and reserves

Ordinary shares	£350,000	£330,000
Preference shares	50,000	—
Revenue reserves	71,500	66,000
	£471,500	£396,000

Market price		
per share	£1.50	£2.75

Summary of main ratios

	Easy go	Good fortune
Profitability		
Net profit : sales	3.86%	4.50%
Gross profit	14.00%	17.00%
ROCE	6.82%	9.78%
Liquidity		
Current ratio	2.72 : 1	1.55 : 1
Acid test	1.32 : 1	0.80 : 1
Stability		
Net worth : total assets	0.55	0.43
Gearing	0.346	0.47
Cover for interest	4.8	5.0
Use of assets		
Sales : fixed assets	3 : 1	3 : 1
Debtors turnover	5.20 wks	3.46 wks
Stock turnover	7.28 wks	4.16 wks
Investor ratios		
EPS	15.14p	27.27p
Earnings yield	10.09%	9.91%
P/E ratio	9.91	10.08
Dividend yield	5.71%	4.96%

(Note: the ratios for the two companies have been calculated on the bases explained earlier in this chapter. If you are uncertain as to their meaning or how they are calculated, you are advised to re-read the appropriate preceding pages.)

Analysis

All three profitability ratios of Good Fortune are better than those of Easy Go. Net profit : sales and the gross profit percentage indicate that Good Fortune is better at converting sales into profits than Easy go. An obvious question is, why? The better gross profit ratio suggests either that Good Fortune can achieve a higher unit sales price or that its unit cost of raw materials is lower. In either case, the management of Easy Go should try to emulate Good Fortune.

Easy Go is spending a lower percentage of sales on *other costs* (distribution and administration) than Good Fortune, indicating, perhaps, tighter control over such costs by Easy Go.

The higher ROCE earned by Good Fortune suggests better management by that firm of the finances entrusted to it by its shareholders.

Liquidity must be a real concern to the managers of Good Fortune, as both ratios are lower than what would be expected in a trading/manufacturing firm. Such low ratios could be tolerated in the short run but they are clear indicators that the management of Good Fortune must inject more funds into working capital. The liquidity position of Easy Go appears satisfactory.

The shareholders of Good Fortune have a lower commitment to their firm than those of Easy Go as seen by the lower net worth and higher gearing ratios. The latter suggests that the long-term borrowing capacity of Good Fortune may be approaching its maximum level. Even although Easy Go still has a relatively low gearing level, it too may be approaching its maximum borrowing level, since the cover for interest is roughly the same in both firms. If Easy Go borrowed more, it would have to pay more interest, which could reduce its cover for interest to an unacceptable level for lenders.

Both firms are using fixed assets to generate the same value of sales but Easy Go does appear to have a higher level of investment in current assets. The low values for debtors turnover and stock turnover in Good Fortune would have been expected given that firm's previously observed low liquidity ratios. Nonetheless, the managers of Easy Go will have to decide if Good Fortune has the 'correct' level by considering:

(a)   Good Fortune has a lower debtors turnover ratio. This could be because it insists on a higher proportion of cash sales or has a tighter debtor control policy. If Good Fortune can do it, why not Easy Go? If Easy Go did adopt similar policies then it too would have a lower debtors turnover ratio and so release some working capital for investment elsewhere.

(b)   Good Fortune's lower stock turnover ratio is the result of carrying lower stock levels. Does Easy Go need the higher levels? If so, why does Good Fortune not? If it does not, why is Easy Go carrying excess stock and wasting funds in unnecessary working capital?

Despite the higher earnings per share shown by Good Fortune, Easy Go has the better investor ratios, although the difference is fairly marginal. Since the three ratios which show Easy Go to be the better firm are all related to the market price of the firms' shares, this may indicate that the price of Easy Go is too low (or that of Good Fortune is too high!).

Summary of comparative analysis

Good Fortune is better than Easy Go at creating profits, but it may be facing a liquidity problem in the near future. Good Fortune's high borrowing strategy is a risk. Money for future expansion will probably have to be self-financed or supplied by shareholders. Policies on the use of current assets are radically different in the two firms, and the question must be, which is right? If Easy Go is right, then Good Fortune is probably losing sales by adopting too tight a debtor control policy and may also run into stock shortages in the near future. If Good Fortune is right, then Easy Go is tying up too much capital in 'dead' assets, and this could be taken to be a sign of poor managerial control.

Limitations of ratio analysis

The calculation of ratios is objective and accurate but that does not mean that financial analysis is similarly objective. Once calculated, the ratios have to be interpreted and this interpretation must involve an individual's subjective assessment and judgement. In addition, it would be wrong to assume that any company could be analysed simply by the calculation of a few ratios (or even many ratios). Some of the main limitations would be:

(a) Ratio analysis usually uses information obtained from published accounts. Such accounts are historic and, by definition, must be out of date. Thus any analysis performed on published data will also be out of date. Before coming to any conclusions, the analyst should be aware that the firm could have changed its policies since the date of its last accounts, and any assessment would have to be made with that borne in mind.

(b) Successive Companies Acts have required firms to supply more and more detailed information in their annual accounts. Nonetheless, such accounts do not yet give full disclosure of all information and almost all figures are little more than summaries. Ratio analysis must therefore be an analysis of incomplete, summarized information. Even internally produced management accounts are summaries, and so their analysis is similarly hindered.

(c) As previously noted, companies are not required to adhere to a strict code of accounting principles and bases. Considerable discretion is given to firms in interpreting and applying underlying principles. Thus, in comparing two companies, the analyst should be aware that the two firms may have adopted different bases and that he/she may not be comparing like with like. Similarly, an intra-firm comparison may also be invalid if the firm has changed its accounting policies and the analysis has not taken that into account.

(d) The calculation of ratios is not an end in itself, nor does a single ratio produce any answers. At best, ratios begin to show where a firm is performing comparatively well, or badly, and indicate areas where management should start asking questions and taking action.

(c) Ratio analysis is only an analysis of the financial affairs of a company; it is not an analysis of the company itself. It cannot analyse subjective elements or non-financial matters such as improving customer relations, potential labour difficulties, and so on. Comparative ratios may pick up the financial consequences of such matters, if they are affecting the firm's financial performance, but they will never show why they are arising or, if they are negative, how they can be cured.

(f) Finally, because ratios are invariably calculated from past data, they will only analyse how well a firm has performed. They may be used to indicate what might happen in the future but they are not crystal balls.

Summary

This chapter was concerned with the interpretation of financial accounts by means of ratio analysis. The main ratios considered were:

Profitability

(a) Net profit to sales $\quad = \quad \dfrac{\text{net profit after tax}}{\text{sales}} \times 100$

(b) Gross profit percentage $\quad = \quad \dfrac{\text{gross profit}}{\text{sales}} \times 100$

(a) ROCE $\quad = \quad \dfrac{\text{profit after tax}}{\text{total assets}} \times 100$

Liquidity

(a) Current ratio $\quad = \quad \dfrac{\text{current assets}}{\text{current liabilities}}$

(b) Acid test (liquidity) ratio $\quad = \quad \dfrac{\text{current assets} - \text{stock}}{\text{current liabilities}}$

Long-term stability

(a) Net worth $\quad = \quad \dfrac{\text{share capital} + \text{reserves}}{\text{fixed} + \text{current assets}}$

(b) Gearing ratio $\quad = \quad \dfrac{\text{long-term loans}}{\text{total capital}}$

(c) Cover for interest $\quad = \quad \dfrac{\text{profit before tax and interest}}{\text{interest payable}}$

Use of assets

(a) Sales to fixed assets $\quad = \quad \dfrac{\text{sales}}{\text{fixed assets}}$

(b) Debtors turnover $\quad = \quad \dfrac{\text{average debtors}}{\text{sales}} \times 52$

(c) Stock turnover $\quad = \quad \dfrac{\text{average stock}}{\text{cost of sales}} \times 52$

Investors return

(a) Earnings per share $\quad = \quad \dfrac{\text{profit after tax and pref. div.}}{\text{number of ordinary shares}}$

(b) Earnings yield $\quad = \quad \dfrac{\text{EPS}}{\text{cost per share}} \times 100$

(c) $\qquad$ P/E ratio $\quad = \quad \dfrac{\text{cost per share}}{\text{EPS}}$

(d) Dividend yield $\quad = \quad \dfrac{\text{dividend per share}}{\text{cost per share}} \times 100$

Although there is no one correct way to analyse accounts, the following technique may be a helpful guide:

(1) Establish the sources of data (such as annual accounts, Stock Exchange, and so on).
(2) Identify the question being posed. For example, if the question is about liquidity, consider only liquidity ratios – do not be concerned with the other types.
(3) Calculate the appropriate ratios and make any required comparisons.

(4) Remember that the calculation of ratios is only part of the answer – you then have to make sense of them.

Questions

7.1 With what reservations should a ratio analysis of a company's financial position be viewed?

7.2 Discuss how financial ratio analysis can be used in assessing the liquidity of a business.

7.3 What are the main financial ratios which assess a firm's profitability? How are they calculated? What do they mean?

7.4 What are the main factors which potential long-term lenders consider when deciding on how much, if anything, to lend to a business? How can ratio analysis assist in such a decision?

7.5 In the year to 31/12/19xx, a firm noticed that its following financial ratios had all decreased from those from the previous year:

- Net profit : sales.
- Current ratio.
- Gearing ratio.

What are the implications for the company as a consequence of these ratios falling? What other ratios do you think may also be affected? Why?

7.6 John Smith Ltd, a manufacturer of decorative ceramic wall plates, has produced the following ratios from its annual accounts:

	19x1	19x2
Current ratio	1.75:1	1.81:1
Acid test	0.98:1	0.64:1
Debtors turnover	10 weeks	13 weeks
Stock turnover	4.2x	3.4x
Gross profit	40%	42%
Net profit : sales	11.5%	11.5%

How has the firm performed in 19x2 compared with 19x1? What possible reasons could there be for the fluctuations?

7.7 Using the accounting information below, construct appropriate ratios and compare the performance of these two fountain pen manufacturers in terms of:

(a) profitability;
(b) liquidity;
(c) financial stability.

Profit and loss accounts for the year ended 31/12/19xx

	Scribble Ltd	Scrawl Ltd
Sales	£3,000	£750
Cost of goods sold	£2,330	£250
Wages and expenses	575	385
Depreciation	30	35
Interest	5	20
Total costs	£2,940	£690
Net profit	£ 60	£ 60

Balance sheets as at 31/12/19xx

	Scribble Ltd	Scrawl Ltd
Fixed assets (net of depreciation)	£ 320	£200
Stock	180	340
Debtors	40	190
Bank	60	0
	£ 600	£730
Share capital	£ 250	£200
Retained profit	50	100
8% debentures	0	150
Bank overdraft	0	60
Creditors	300	220
	£ 600	£730

7.8 Two individuals, Eddie Brow and Adie Laide, each carry on business as wholesalers of the same product. Their respective accounts for the year to 31/3/19xx are as follows:

Profit and loss accounts

		Eddie		Adie
Sales		£144,000		£140,000
less cost of sales		120,000		120,000
Gross profit		£ 24,000		£ 20,000
Selling costs	£7,200		£2,800	
Administration costs	8,160		9,500	
		15,360		12,300
Net profit		£ 8,640		£ 7,700

Balance sheets

	Eddie	Adie
Fixed assets		
Property	£ 20,000	£14,000
Equipment	21,750	13,840
Vehicles	12,000	6,000
	£ 53,750	£33,840

Current assets			
Stock	£32,000		£ 4,800
Debtors	28,800		11,200
Bank	8,950		11,360
	£69,750		£27,360
less Creditors	15,500		30,400
		54,250	(3,040)
		£108,000	£30,800
Share capital		£ 75,000	£20,000
Revenue reserves		33,000	10,800
		£108,000	£30,800

Compare the profitability and financial position of the two businesses using at least eight suitable ratios for each firm. Who do think has the better firm from a financial point of view?

7.9   Bookworm Ltd, a firm of booksellers, has produced the following statistics from its annual accounts over the past four years:

	19x9	19x8	19x7	19x6
Turnover	£9,109,000	£8,344,000	£7,629,000	£7,296,000
Sales per employee	£52,515	£51,826	£51,200	£48,000
ROCE	10%	(5%)	15%	11%
Gross profit	31.7%	29.0%	31.6%	31.4%
Net profit : sales	1.4%	(0.8%)	2.6%	1.9%
Profit per employee	£737	£(410)	£1,335	£934
Stock turnover	7.2 wks	7.4 wks	7.3 wks	7.4 wks
Debtors turnover	4.5 wks	5.2 wks	3.6 wks	4.7 wks
Current ratio	1.15	1.39	1.68	1.24
Acid test	0.56	0.60	0.67	0.59

What is your assessment of the financial performance of this company over the past four years?

8 The management of working capital

Introduction

As we have seen in previous chapters, before trading all firms have to make often substantial investments. Much of this investment is in fixed assets, the plant, machinery, and so on, but a large amount must also be invested in working capital.

Working capital is the term used to identify that investment which allows the firm to trade on a day-to-day basis. Fixed assets are needed to allow the firm to get started, but, on their own, nothing can happen. For example, a firm may have all the equipment necessary to start business but without some investment in raw materials that equipment can produce nothing.

Working capital is also needed to finance the results of trading. If a firm sells its products on credit, it will not receive the cash for some time. Working capital is needed to pay for all the firm's costs until that money comes in.

Content of working capital

Working capital, then, is no more than short-term assets, and these are clearly identified in a firm's balance sheet as current assets. The balance sheet also identifies the other component part of working capital – the current liabilities. A firm does not have to finance all of its current assets on its own. It can purchase on credit, in which case the firm only has to finance that aspect of current assets which it cannot obtain on credit.

The working capital shown in the balance sheet (current assets less current liabilities) need not be a firm's true working capital requirements. The balance sheet is a 'moment in time' document, showing the financial position of the firm at an exact date. The working capital shown in the balance sheet is, therefore, the requirements on that date. At other times, it could be different.

Nonetheless, the balance sheet does show what types of working capital a firm needs and also gives an indication of the amount required. Consider the following extract from a firm's balance sheet:

Current assets

Stock	£15,000
Work in progress	10,000
Finished goods	25,000
Debtors	40,000
Bank	5,000
	£95,000
less Current liabilities	
Creditors	35,000
Working capital	£60,000

This shows that the firm needs working capital for stock, work in progress, finished goods and debtors, and to hold in the bank. It also shows that it has used creditors to part-finance this working capital requirement, and that the firm has to invest only £60,000.

Working capital cycle

Working capital revolves round inside a business. A firm starts with cash. This cash is used to buy stock which is then converted into finished goods which are then sold on credit. The debtors then pay their bills, and the money is used to pay the firm's creditors. We are then back at square one, the firm has cash which it uses to buy stock, and so on. This could be shown in the form of a diagram – see Figure 8.1.

Although working capital revolves inside a firm, it is important that management effectively control the level of investment in working capital. There is no profit to be earned in investing in working capital – it is all 'dead' money.

Figure 8.1

Having mountains of stock or millions of pounds owed to the firm does not produce one penny of profit. The opposite is true; investing in working capital costs the firm money.

The costs can be seen in two ways:

● Investing in non-profitable assets means that money cannot then be invested in profitable assets.
● The firm will probably have to pay interest on borrowed money to finance the investment.

There could be a third, non-financial cost. If a firm is investing in excessive working capital, it is probably being poorly managed. If a firm is being poorly managed in this respect, it will probably be poorly managed in other areas of the business.

Calculation of the working capital cycle

If a firm is to manage its working capital efficiently, it is important that it knows how long its working capital cycle is, that is, how long it has to wait between receiving raw materials and receiving cash from the sale of finished goods.

The shorter this period is, the less working capital is required, as sales income will produce most of the cash needed to refinance stock. In addition, since profit comes from making sales, the faster a firm can buy in and then sell, the more profits can be earned.

The calculation of the working capital cycle (also known as the *operating cycle* or the *trading cycle*) is based on ratios which were introduced in the previous chapter. For example, it was seen that the *debtors turnover* ratio expressed the average length of time taken by debtors to pay their debts. As debtors are part of working capital, the debtors turnover ratio will show how long one part of the working capital cycle is.

EXAMPLE

The financial accounts of Iona Ltd for the year to 31/12/19x9 are summarized below:

Iona Ltd
Summary profit and loss account

Sales	£10,000,000
less Cost of sales	5,000,000
Gross profit	£ 5,000,000
less Other costs	4,000,000
Net profit	£ 1,000,000

Iona Ltd
Summary balance sheet

Fixed assets		£ 2,000,000
Current assets		
Raw materials	£ 500,000	
Work in progress	400,000	
Finished goods	300,000	
Debtors	1,500,000	
Bank	100,000	
	£2,800,000	
less Current liabilities		
Creditors	500,000	2,300,000
		£ 4,300,000
Shareholders' funds		£ 4,300,000

The working capital cycle (the length of time taken for raw materials to produce cash) would be:

		Days
Raw materials	$\dfrac{500,000}{5,000,000} \times 365 =$	36.5
Work in progress	$\dfrac{400,000}{5,000,000} \times 365 =$	29.2
Finished goods	$\dfrac{300,000}{5,000,000} \times 365 =$	21.9
Debtors	$\dfrac{1,500,000}{10,000,000} \times 365 =$	54.75
		142.35
less Creditors	$\dfrac{500,000}{10,000,000} \times 365 =$	36.5
Working capital cycle		105.85 days

Note that you have met all the above ratios in Chapter 6. In that chapter, they were used to analyse company performance. Here they are being used to measure how long it takes a firm to convert the receipt of raw material into cash from sales.

If the firm could reduce this period, there would also be a reduction in the level of investment in working capital and a consequent saving in costs. The firm would certainly not like to see the period increase.

Factors influencing working capital

There are a number of factors which combine to determine how much working capital ought to be invested by firms:

● The nature of the business.

- The length of the operating cycle.
- The seasonality of the business.
- Availability of credit

Nature of the business

Some firms need little, if any, working capital. For example, a fruit stall owner will buy his produce daily for cash. He will, therefore, have no stock to carry, and as he will sell only for cash, he will have no debtors to finance. With no stock, debtors or creditors, the only working capital he will need will be sufficient cash to re-stock at the start of each day. At the other extreme, steel stock holders will have large volumes of expensive stock. They will also have many customers who will expect, and take, credit. Such firms will, therefore, require a large investment in working capital.

As a broad rule of thumb, most manufacturing firms will require large levels of working capital, whereas service businesses will require relatively low levels (even lower if they deal only in cash or require advance payment).

Length of cycle

The length of the operating cycle is often determined by the type of business. Manufacturers tend to have long cycles because of the need to stock raw materials, actually manufacture goods, and then sell on credit. Shops will have fairly short cycles since there is no period of manufacture and it is unlikely that there will be any debtors.

The shorter the cycle, the faster money is received, which means either that less money has to be invested in working capital or that investment is turned over much faster, resulting in higher profits.

Seasonality

Businesses which are seasonal – that is, where the level of activity is determined by the time of year – have special problems regarding the level of working capital.

Consider a toy manufacturer who knows that about 80% of his sales will be for the Christmas period. In terms of manufacturing policy, should that firm:

(a)   manufacture only when there is demand; or
(b)   manufacture steadily throughout the year?

If policy (a) is adopted, there will be large parts of the year when there will be little need for working capital, since manufacture will be virtually at a standstill. Conversely, other months will require large sums of working capital when large stocks must be bought and extra labour has to be hired.

If policy (b) is adopted, the level of investment in working capital is evened out throughout the year, but it may be higher than the average level of investment required if manufacturing only to demand. The reason is that it would be necessary to finance the build-up of stocks of finished goods in times when demand is very low.

Efficient financial management will determine which policy is best for individual firms. Indeed, it may be found to be more efficient to adopt a policy somewhere between even manufacture and manufacturing to demand.

Availability of credit

Buying goods and services on credit means that the buying firm does not have immediately to finance that purchase. This, in turn, means that the firm does not have to introduce so much working capital itself. Although a good way of reducing working capital requirements, it does depend on suppliers being willing to give credit.

Firms which have just started generally find it difficult to obtain credit because they have no track record which suppliers can use to assess credit-worthiness. No credit means that most young firms have to inject larger sums into working capital than existing firms. Similarly, firms which are slow at paying their debts, perhaps because they are having cash flow problems, may find that they too are denied credit and find that they need more working capital (which is a pity since they were denied credit because they did not have enough working capital in the first place).

Working capital control

Controlling the level of working capital is not easy. Working capital has, as we have seen, a number of constituent parts each of which has to be controlled. Unfortunately the skills needed for stock control, debtor control and credit management are quite different and each requires the work of a specialist. This section will examine some of the techniques required in the efficient management of the more obvious parts of working capital.

Stock control

Ideally, firms should carry no stock. If there is no stock, there is no need for an investment in working capital in this important area of business. As it is, most firms have to carry levels of stock, particularly manufacturing firms and especially retail firms.

If firms must carry stock then they should aim to carry the least possible amount, thus minimizing the working capital requirements.

Unfortunately, there is a very thin dividing line between the correct minimum stock levels and too little stock. Too little stock will have serious consequences on firms. As a simple illustration, consider the effect that running out of stock will have on a petrol station! On the other hand, too much stock is bad management as it will tie up too much capital in a non-profit-earning asset. If a firm has too much stock it also runs the risk that some of the stock will deteriorate before it can be used – an obvious waste of money and extra, avoidable, costs to the firm.

Effective stock control usually starts by recognizing that in most firms the

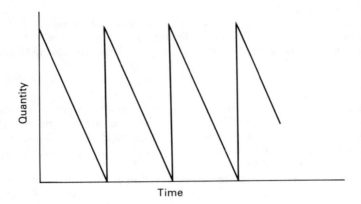

Figure 8.2

'80 : 20' rule applies (that 80% of the stock has only 20% of the value). This is not meant to be a statement of fact, rather that in most firms most stock will have little value and that a few items will account for a disproportionate amount of value. If management skills are at a premium, firms would be well advised to identify their low-volume, high-cost items of stock and use their limited resources to manage these items effectively.

How much stock should be carried will depend on a number of factors. But first consider stock usage in a firm (assuming even production). The firm will buy in stock, use it until there is none left and then have to buy in more. This could be shown in the form of a graph, as in Figure 8.2.

However, it would be most unwise for firms to wait until they have reached nil stock before they buy in more. It takes time to actually place an order for more stock and, more important, it will take time for the supplier to deliver. If a firm waits until it has no stock before ordering, it will have no stock (and no production) during the time it takes to order more and have it delivered.

This time delay is known as the *lead-time*. Firms should identify the lead-time for their stock, convert that into units of stock (how much stock is needed in that time period) and reorder when that level is reached. For example, if a firm uses 100 units of stock per week, and its lead-time is two weeks, then it should order more stock when existing levels fall to 200 units.

In stock control most firms find that they need to carry 'safety', or minimum, stock, that is, a bit extra over and above what they would normally require just in case their suppliers are slow in fulfilling stock reorders. Determining the level of safety stock required is an art in itself.

The reorder level, then, is the safety stock level plus the lead-time. This can be shown graphically again, as in Figure 8.3.

The actual amount and value of stock which should be ordered to bring the level of stock up to maximum will depend on what that maximum should be. This is the subject of some specialized mathematical techniques, but

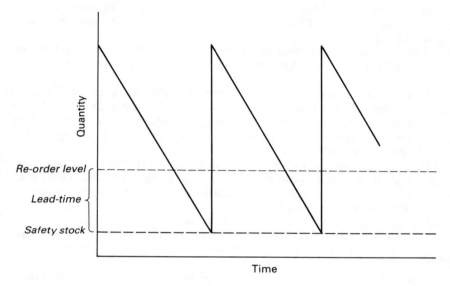

Figure 8.3

briefly it should be the level which minimizes the costs incurred in reordering and holding stock. It should also be a level which ensures that all stock will be used before it starts to deteriorate.

Good stock control also requires good store-keeping. If stock is not accounted for then it is as good as lost. For example, in producing an article, the cost of production will be the total of all the inputs required for production. If some inputs are not accounted for, then the total cost will be wrong, and the firm may end up charging too low a price – a price which may not even cover all the real costs.

Good store-keeping, and stock control, will ensure that all issued stock is properly charged to products. It will also ensure that any unused stock is returned to stores and is not incorrectly charged to production. Since many items of stock are easily converted into cash, good stock control will also ensure that the scope for theft and fraud is kept to a minimum. Many firms find that pilferage is a big problem, particularly retail outlets. Such theft does no more than increase a firm's costs and increase its stock-holding requirements.

Debtor control

Selling on credit means that firms will have to wait for payment. In the meantime, such firms will have to pay their own bills, such as wages and suppliers. If a firm sells on credit, it must also, therefore, inject large sums of working capital into the firm to cover the time delay between making sales and receiving cash. Ideally, firms should insist on cash payment either in advance or at point of sale. Doing so eliminates debtors and so reduces working capital requirements.

Unfortunately, most firms find that they must sell on credit and cannot insist on cash sales only. Among the main reasons why this is so are:

(a)   Competitors sell on credit. If a firm did not offer credit when all its competitors did, customers would buy from those firms which did offer credit – customers realize that taking credit reduces their working capital requirements. Why increase it unnecessarily? By failing to offer credit, many firms would lose trade.

(b)   Customers expect credit. Similar to point (a), in that if customers are used to receiving credit they will only buy from suppliers which offer credit and ignore those firms which insist on cash. Most firms which are also customers expect credit.

(c)   Many large firms and organizations do not have accounting systems which permit cash payments, especially for large sums. By insisting on cash, firms would be denying themselves certain large customers.

Whatever the reason, firms which deal with other firms will be almost forced into offering credit.

Cost of credit

Firms which offer credit ought to be aware that in doing so they will increase their costs in a number of ways, the most notable being:

(a)   Increased administrative costs. At the very least, there will be increased costs because the selling firm will now have to prepare invoices and send them out – a cost which is avoided if cash is received at the point of sale. Inevitably, additional employees will be required to maintain the debtors ledgers, to invoice customers and to chase up slow payers.

(b)   Interest charges. If a firm sells on credit it may have to borrow additional working capital to finance those debtors, and interest will have to be paid on that borrowing. Even if the firm did not have to borrow, there would still be a cost in the form of lost interest. For example, suppose a firm could sell a product for £1,000 and either sell for cash or give two months' credit. If it sold for cash, that money could be deposited in a bank account for two months and receive interest of about £13. This may not be much, but it is £13 more than if it had given the two months' credit, and it would certainly build up if the firm expected to make hundreds or thousands of similar sales in a year.

(c)   Bad debts. Every time a firm sells on credit it is taking a chance, a chance that the buyer will not ultimately pay its debt. If that happens, the seller suffers a real and not inconsiderable cost. Suppose a firm sells a product for £1,000. Its total costs are £900, so the sale nets the firm £100 profit. If the debt goes bad, the firm does not just lose the £100 profit, it loses the whole £1,000. In fact, the profits on the next nine sales of £1,000 are needed simply to recover the costs incurred in the original bad debt.

Debtor control

The best way of minimizing the working capital requirements of a firm which sells on credit is to institute good and effective credit control policies. This will ensure, as far as possible, that customers pay their debts when due and that there will be few, if any, bad debts. Credit control has four distinct steps:

- Customer assessment.
- Customer billing.
- Accounting procedures.
- Follow up.

CUSTOMER ASSESSMENT

The best way of avoiding slow payers and bad debts is not to sell to them in the first place. The objective of customer assessment is to try to eliminate bad risks before they receive any credit. Firms should adopt a policy of cash only unless credit is asked for. Once a customer asks for credit then the customer's credit-worthiness should be assessed. References should be taken up at all times and, if there is uncertainty, a report should be sought from a private credit investigating agency.

If a potential customer passes this initial screening, a credit limit should be imposed.

Customer screening should be continuous, not just a once-and-for-all assessment. Companies which were once prosperous can quickly become very risky and if the seller is unaware of this, excessive credit may be being granted.

CUSTOMER BILLING

A common reason for customers being slow in paying their debts, particularly in the smaller company, is either delay in invoicing or incomplete information being given on the invoice.

If the seller is slow in sending out an invoice, that is not much of an encouragement to the buyer to settle quickly. In addition, if sparse information is given on the invoice, some buyers' payments systems may not be able to handle the invoice. For example, many large firms require to have quoted on an invoice their own order number. The bill will only be paid once it has been matched to the copy of the original order. If the seller omits the order number, then the invoice remains unpaid.

Firms should, therefore, ensure that full and complete invoices are submitted as quickly as possible after completion of the work or delivery of the goods to which they relate.

ACCOUNTING PROCEDURES

The seller will have to install good accounting procedures to keep track of all its debtors. These accounting procedures will have to cope with recording all sales on credit and all payments received, and show the outstanding balances on each customer's account. If the accounting system is incapable of identifying individual debtors and the amounts owed by each, then there is no basis for control.

Experience suggests that the longer a debt remains unpaid, the less likely it is that it will ever be paid. Firms should, therefore, prepare an aged-debt analysis; that is, overdue debts should be ranked into groups of:

(1)   Up to one month.
(2)   One to three months.
(3)   Three to six months.
(4)   Over six months.

(The actual rankings will depend on the circumstances of each company.)

With this information the firm can spend most of its effort pursuing those debts which are likely to be paid. The analysis will also identify those debts, and debtors, which are either excessively slow or bad. The firm can then make sure that it withdraws further credit from such debtors.

FOLLOW-UP

In good credit control, debts are pursued immediately they go past their 'pay-by' date. This can range from gentle reminders to telephone calls, personal visits or passing the debt on to debt collecting agencies. Reminders usually work, although firms should remember the final possibility of taking a defaulter to court.

Court procedures, however, can be rather expensive, and firms will have to assess whether or not they should incur further costs in pursuing a bad debt. If the defaulter has no money, then suing in the courts cannot produce any, and in addition to losing the debt, the firm will also have lost the legal fees.

Cash control

Cash and money in the bank earn very little, if any, income, yet they are still needed, as bills can only be paid by money. Liquid assets such as cash are, therefore, part of the working capital of a firm and, like all other aspects of working capital, ought to be kept to a minimum.

Cash flow and cash control will be examined in greater detail in Chapter 10. At this stage, however, it should be appreciated that cash control is a fine art. Financial managers must always have sufficient cash to meet all debts when they become due but never have too much (since the excess will be earning the firm nothing). Knowing how much cash to hold requires firms to forecast their future cash expenditure and cash income. Excess cash can then be transferred into interest-earning accounts, and deficits can, hopefully, be overcome.

Creditor control

As previously mentioned, creditors are an important element of working capital. They keep down the level of investment required by the firm in working capital. As a simple illustration, a firm may be showing the following working capital structure in its annual accounts:

Stock	£ 75,000
Debtors	115,000
Bank	10,000
	200,000
less Creditors	80,000
Working capital	£120,000

Thus, although the firm has £200,000 of current assets it has not had to find that amount of money – it is effectively using the money it owes creditors to finance £80,000 of the investment.

Using creditors' money is an obviously very cheap way to finance current assets, and the longer a firm takes to pay its creditors, the more of that money is available. The result is that the firm needs less and less of its own money to invest in current assets. The obvious extension of that argument is that firms should take as much credit as they can possibly get away with – delay paying bills until the last possible moment.

The equally obvious outcome of such a course of action is that creditors will become very anxious about the lack of payment and may either refuse to supply further credit or take legal action for the recovery of their money (probably both at the same time).

Firms should adopt good creditor control policies. This will involve identifying the due dates for payment of all creditors and paying them when they are due. Thus the firm will be able to take all the credit to which it is entitled, but no more, and so will not expose itself to the possibility of credit being cut off, being blacklisted as a credit risk or being sued by creditors.

Use of computers

Packages can be bought which can help in the management of working control. The main areas are in:

- Debtor control.
- Creditor control.
- Stock control.

Most accounting packages (discussed in Chapters 2 and 4) contain a function which will provide an aged-debt analysis – literally at the touch of a button on the computer. This will produce a listing of all debtors according to how old their debt is and so allow managers to identify slow payers and doubtful debts. Even the more basic packages allow users to input credit limits against individual debtors; and should a debtor place an order which would exceed his/her credit limit, the machine will 'flag' or warn the user. A decision will then have to be made about whether or not to fulfil the order, but at least the information will be available.

Not only will packages produce a debtors aged listing, but they will normally also produce a creditors aged listing. This will produce a print-out of all bills which have still to be paid and also show how long they have remained unpaid – a useful tool if the firm has decided to improve cash flow by delaying payment of creditors. Users will be able to see which of their creditors are 'non-crucial' and can wait for payment.

Effective stock control packages have to be bought separately from the normal accounting packages. Most use either FIFO or AVCO although other stock valuation methods are available. They operate in basically the same way as the manual methods, inputing receipts and prices as well as usage so giving resultant balances and values but with the added advantage of fast and accurate calculations.

Fixed asset control

This chapter has been concerned with the management of working capital. That is the day-to-day work of management, largely because working capital changes from day to day. Control needs to be exercised over the investment in fixed assets also, however.

In many manufacturing companies there will be a high level of investment in fixed assets – the assets actually needed to manufacture the firm's products. If this investment is not carefully monitored, the firm could find that the level of investment becomes too small or unnecessarily high. The consequence of too low a level of investment is that the firm will not have the productive capacity to meet the demand for its products; that means less sales than it could otherwise achieve, which means less profits. Too high a level of investment means that the firm has over-capacity, that demand does not warrant the amount of equipment owned by the firm. The investment in over-capacity is wasted. The assets are not being used, which means that no return is being earned on the investment.

The overall assessment of the level of investment in fixed assets is usually made by ratio analysis, the common ratios being:

(a)   Sales : fixed assets.
(b)   Profit : fixed assets.

Other ratios could be used, but normally they will relate the investment in fixed assets to some measure of profitability. If the ratio falls, it may mean that there is too high a level of investment in fixed assets. Care has to be taken, since a firm which introduces a lot of new equipment may find that its ratios will fall. This may not mean too high a level of investment if the investment is for future growth.

On a more day-to-day level, management needs to protect the actual assets which represent the investment. This is normally achieved by maintaining asset registers.

Asset registers

Large firms have many individual assets, many of which will be very valuable. Asset registers are a means of identifying the assets owned by the firm and will normally include details such as:

(a)   description of the asset;
(b)   its location;
(c)   its date of purchase;
(d)   its purchase price/revalued amount;
(e)   depreciation charged to date;
(f)   its current book value.

With this information, the firm will always know what assets it owns, where they all are (or are supposed to be) and their current balance sheet value.

Questions

8.1   What is *working capital* and why is it important to firms?

8.2   What factors should a firm consider when deciding on its working capital requirements? Why?

8.3   When considering a firm's stock-holding requirements, what is meant by *lead-time*? How can lead time be determined?

8.4   What are the costs associated with a firm's stock-holding and level of debtors?

8.5   Outline a suitable debtor control policy for a medium-sized manufacturing firm whose sales are all on 30 days' credit.

8.6   The following data has been extracted from the financial accounts of Alba Ltd as at 31/12/19xx:

Sales	£20,000,000
Cost of sales	£14,000,000
Trade creditors	£ 3,000,000
Trade debtors	£ 2,500,000
Stock – Raw materials	£ 200,000
– Work in progress	£ 1,500,000
– Finished goods	£ 400,000
Bank overdraft	£ 100,000

You are required to calculate the length of Alba's working capital cycle.

8.7   Given the data in question 8.6, if the firm decided that it wanted to reduce its investment in working capital, what procedures would you recommend?

Sources of finance

Introduction

The need for money is an essential feature of all firms. It is needed to start up a new business, to keep an existing business going and to expand. Without money there can be no business.

A problem facing many firms is where to find money, for whatever reason they may need it. This chapter will examine the more common sources of finance available to business, discuss which sources are most suitable for various purposes and finally consider the costs involved in raising finance.

Sources of finance

Finance is available from three broad areas:

- Internally generated finance, that is, money which either is already within the firm or can be earned by it.
- Finance which must be raised from external sources – essentially, money which has to be borrowed.
- Grants which the firm is entitled to – usually from central government.

Internal sources

Normally it is wisest for a firm to make use of money which it theoretically already owns. If for no other reason, internally generated finance will almost certainly be the cheapest source of finance available to firms. Unfortunately, there are not too many sources of internally generated finance. The most common are:

- Retained profits.
- Taxation.
- Depreciation.
- Good stock and debtor control.

Retained profits

As a source of finance, retained profits are an obvious choice of finance for any firm. Every firm is in business to make profits and there can be no easier way of raising money for expansion than to plough back into the firm profits which have previously been earned. Firms which are highly profitable can finance steady expansion this way although rapid expansion normally requires more finance than even the most profitable firms can earn.

The principal drawback to the use of retained profits as a means of financing is normally shareholder resistance. The more profits that are retained by a company, the less there is available for distribution to the owners by dividend. As many shareholders want and expect a dividend, firms are often restricted in how much profit they can retain by shareholders' demands for good and improving dividends.

Taxation

The Inland Revenue can contribute to the financing of a firm in an indirect way, if the firm is due to pay tax on profits.

Corporation tax is payable nine months after a company's year end, which means that for those nine months the company has the use of money which, legally, belongs to the Revenue. Consider the following extract from a firm's profit and loss account for the year to 31/12/19x8:

Profit before tax	£270,000
less Taxation	100,000
Retained Profit	£170,000

The company obviously has immediate use of the retained profits of £170,000, but it also has the use of the £100,000 tax until 30/9/19x9 (the date when the tax must be paid).

Firms which are registered for value added tax can make short-term use of this tax. VAT is charged and collected by the seller, but the firm only has to account to Customs and Excise (the government body responsible for VAT) every three months. The firm has the use of VAT collected during that period. The two most common exceptions are non-registered traders and exporters, neither of whom charge VAT.

Tax is not strictly an internal source of finance, since the company is using money which really belongs to someone else – the Inland Revenue. However, since the company earned this money by trading in the first place, it is frequently referred to as internal financing.

Depreciation

Depreciation provides funds because it is a non-cash expense in the profit and loss account. It is a book entry which reduces the amount of profits available for distribution to shareholders and retention in the firm. Consider the following:

Profit before depreciation	£210,000
less Depreciation	40,000
Net profit after depreciation	£170,000
less Dividends paid	70,000
Retained profits	£100,000

Assume for simplicity that the business deals only in cash. At the year end the firm made profits of £170,000, of which it paid out £70,000 in dividends and retained £100,000 for future growth. The cash actually available will, in fact, be £140,000, since depreciation has been deducted to arrive at net profit. The firm will not have written a cheque for depreciation – that cost involved no money going out of the business; it is still inside the firm.

If there is no inflation and if the firm conscientiously 'saves up' the depreciation charge, it will always be able to refinance its assets when they wear out (assuming that the estimate for useful lives in the depreciation calculation is correct).

Stock and debtor control

To acquire stock, a firm has to spend money. However, once the money is spent it is tied up in an asset which does not earn the firm anything – the stock simply lies in a store room waiting to be used. If it were possible, a firm could release some of that money by reducing its level of stock-holding, and that money could be used for more profitable purposes.

It is not possible for most firms to reduce their levels of stock to zero, but introducing tight stock control policies may mean that the correct level only is held. Excess stock can then be converted into cash. The benefit of this method of raising finance is that, not only is money raised, but the firm becomes a much fitter and better-managed organization.

This method is only available once to firms, for once the stock level is reduced to a minimum, further finance cannot be raised by reducing that minimum further.

The same ideas apply equally to a firm's debtors. Debtors are people who owe a firm money, and if a firm wants to raise finance there can be few better sources than getting those people to pay up. Again, this would involve the introduction of good credit control policies, but their introduction has a double benefit. Not only does the firm receive its money, but it also ends up being a fitter and better-managed firm.

External sources

External financing requires the firm seeking finance from outside itself. This will always result in additional costs, as nobody will give a firm money without expecting some recompense.

External financing comes in two forms:

- Debt.
- Equity.

Debt is simply the firm borrowing finance, whereas equity refers to the firm raising finance by issuing shares. Which type of source ought to be chosen depends on a number of factors including:

(a)   The period of time that finance is needed.
(b)   The cost of finance.
(c)   The retention of control of the firm.
(d)   The level of risk.
(e)   Capital gearing.

Period of time

Debt is usually described as being short-term, medium-term or long-term. What each means often depends on each business, but as a broad classification:

- Short-term debt is less than one year.
- Medium-term ranges from more than 1 year to about five years.
- Long-term would be any period of time more than five years.

External finance should be sought for only the length of time that the money is needed. This may seem self-evident but, unfortunately, it is not so for many firms.

   If finance is required for long-term expansion, then long-term sources should be sought. Similarly, if a firm is suffering from a very temporary shortage of cash, then only short-term sources of finance should be sought.

Cost

Since all firms want to make as much profit as possible, they will want to reduce their costs. Since external sources of finance have an inherent cost, firms may well want to select the cheapest source. The cost of finance will be examined in more detail in a later section of this chapter.

Retention of control

This can be particularly important if a firm decides to raise more finance by issuing further shares. Each new share will normally have a new vote and if many shares are being issued, it is possible that the new shareholders will have more votes than existing shareholders. In such circumstances, effective control of the company may be lost. The existing shareholders have to assess whether or not the potential loss of control is surpassed by their ultimately being part of a much larger company.

Level of risk

Lenders of money are usually very cautious people who do not like risking their money unduly. If they do perceive a high level of risk, they will almost certainly charge higher rates of interest and ask for good quality collateral. They may even ask for some say in the management of the firm.

If finance is required for projects which have high levels of risk, it is accepted practice to seek such finance from the ultimate risk-takers in businesses – the owners – rather than from lenders.

Capital gearing

The ratio between equity and long-term capital is referred to as a firm's capital gearing. In selecting between equity and debt, firms should be aware of the effect that choice will have on their capital gearing. Normally, lenders would not like to see this ratio exceeding 0.5, that is, debt should not exceed equity financing. The ratio of debt to equity can have a profound effect on the amount of profits available to the shareholders. The higher the gearing ratio, the more susceptible the profits available to shareholders are to severe variations.

Consider two firms with the same capital financing and earning the same levels of profits. The only difference is that one firm has a low capital gearing ratio whereas the other has a high gearing ratio. For example:

	Company A	*Company B*
Shareholder funds	£100,000	£400,000
15% Debentures	400,000	100,000
Total financing	£500,000	£500,000
Profits before interest	£100,000	£100,000
less Interest (on debentures)	60,000	15,000
Profits (for shareholders)	£ 40,000	£ 85,000

Note: Company A has a gearing ratio of 0.8, and Company B has 0.2. As a return on capital, the shareholders in the two firms are earning:

Company A	*Company B*
$\dfrac{£\ 40,000}{£100,000} \times 100\%$	$\dfrac{£\ 85,000}{£400,000} \times 100\%$
$= 40\%$	$= 21.25\%$

Obviously, the shareholders in Company A are doing better than those in Company B (despite the fact that A's profits are lower than B's).

Suppose profits before interest fall by 50% to £50,000 in each firm. The net profits are now:

	Company A	Company B
Profit before interest	£50,000	£50,000
less Interest	60,000	15,000
Net profit/(loss)	(£10,000)	£35,000

A 50% fall in profits means that the shareholders in A suffer a loss whereas the shareholders in B suffer only a fall in return from 21.25% to 8.75% – perhaps not very high, but considerably better than A's loss.

The dramatic change in A's profitability is also apparent when profits rise. If profits had increased by 50% from £100,000 to £150,000 then the resulting returns would have been:

Company A	90%
Company B	33.75%

(Check it for yourself.)

The moral here is that high gearing is really only suitable for firms with either steady or improving levels of profits. If profits are likely to fall, there will be a disproportionate negative impact on the profits available to shareholders.

Provision of external finance

Short-term sources

The three main sources of short-term external finance are:

- Overdrafts.
- Creditors.
- Factoring.

OVERDRAFTS

Overdrafts are probably the most common and most flexible form of short-term finance available to firms. They operate in the same way as personal overdrafts. The firm agrees an overdraft limit with its bank and can then make use of that facility as and when required. Overdrafts do not provide firms with actual cash – they permit the firm to borrow from the bank.

From the banker's point of view, overdrafts are meant to be temporary, to be used by firms to help them through a temporary cash flow problem. Banks generally prefer to see what is known as the 'whiplash effect' in overdrafts, that is, overdrafts being incurred and repaid, incurred and repaid, and so on. In practice, however, many companies appear to operate a permanent overdraft (somewhat like many individuals!).

CREDITORS

Businesses require finance to enable them to purchase goods and services. Purchasing on credit is a way to raise finance except that it misses out the middle stage of actually borrowing money.

There are very few firms which do not make use of this facility, most firms in the UK buy their goods and services on credit. Those firms which do not are normally brand new (in which case suppliers do not know if the firm is credit-worthy), or else they have been 'blacklisted' (in which case suppliers know not to trust the firm to pay its debts).

As a means of raising very short-term finance, there is no easier way than to stop paying creditors. Money still comes in from sales, but that cash remains in the firm and is not used to pay debts. This must be a very short-term measure, since most firms do not take too kindly to not receiving money due to them.

FACTORING

As mentioned previously, many firms have a lot of money tied up in debtors. Should a firm require finance, a prime target is the money owed to the firm. One way of releasing that money is for a firm to try and get its debtors to pay their bills. Another solution is to 'factor' those debts. There are two ways in which this can be done:

(a)   The firm can sell its debts to someone else (the 'factor'). In this way the firm receives the money it is owed from the factor who then recovers all the debts.
(b)   The firm can borrow money from the factor, offering, as security, the debts that are owed to the firm.

In both cases, factors will only be interested in 'good' debts and will refuse to buy, or lend on, bad or doubtful debts.

Medium-term sources

The three common sources of medium-term finance which will be examined are:

● Bank loans.
● Hire purchase.
● Leasing.

BANK LOANS

In addition to overdrafts, banks also make term loans. Unlike overdrafts, which are repayable on demand by the bank manager, loans are for a fixed period of time and are repaid either by instalments or at the end of the agreed period.

Bank loans should be used to finance the acquisition of specific assets rather than the entire financial restructuring of firms. As banks are effectively lending their depositors' money, they are generally hesitant about lending for very long periods of time (although nowadays the definition of 'long periods' could be up to about ten years for smaller and medium-sized firms; large firms could borrow for even longer). Most bank loans, however, seem to be for less than five years.

HIRE PURCHASE

Hire purchase can be as useful an option for financing specific assets as it is for individuals. Necessary assets can be acquired for a relatively small initial deposit, the balance being repaid over a number of years. Normally, the repayment period does not exceed three years, and the initial deposit is about 20% of the total price.

Strictly legally, ownership of assets bought on hire purchase does not pass until the final payment has been made. This should not be much of a problem for firms, as ownership is not normally essential. What does matter is the use of assets, and hire purchase does allow that. Since ownership does not immediately pass, firms may find that there are some restrictions attached to the asset, for example the firm may not be allowed to resell the asset until all instalments have been paid.

LEASING

As an alternative to outright purchase of assets, leasing may be seen as a useful means of acquiring the use of specific assets. Leasing is little more than renting an asset. Virtually any kind of asset can be leased, ranging from small machine tools to entire factory complexes. Similarly, the length of time which an asset can be leased for can range from a few hours to many years. Leasing is often seen as a suitable means of financing assets when the firm does not require either ownership or permanent use of the asset. There are a number of reasons for this:

(a)   The firm does not have to spend much money if it only requires the asset for occasional use.
(b)   There is no large capital outlay needed at the start.
(c)   The firm only incurs costs as and when the asset is being used.

Long-term sources

Long-term debt finance is usually in the form of either mortgages or debentures. Both sources can provide fairly large sums of finance for long periods of time although such finance will normally be for projects with a relatively low level of risk.

MORTGAGES

Mortgages for industry are the same as mortgages for individuals wishing to purchase their own homes. To raise finance, a firm will offer its land and buildings as security. The lender will almost certainly hold the title deeds for this property, and should the firm go into liquidation, the lender has first call on the proceeds of its sale.

Mortgages are relatively easy to raise, but it does depend on the firm having suitable property to mortgage in the first place. However, it is obvious that there will be severe restrictions placed on the assets mortgaged. Normally, nothing major can be done with or to the asset without the express permission of the mortgage holder.

DEBENTURES

This form of long-term source of finance has already been described in Chapter 5 and, as such, we shall not be repeating the description again (if you have forgotten, turn back to Chapter 5 and remind yourself!).

Debentures have an important feature. They will have a redemption date when the firm must repay the money borrowed, but before that date firms can buy back debentures on the open market. This could be at a price lower than the face value of the debenture – the firm would have to pay back less than it borrowed

EQUITY (OR SHARES)

Finance can be raised by the issue of shares, either *ordinary* or *preference* (see Chapter 5 for an explanation of the difference, if you have forgotten). This is normally done when the firm is planning long-term expansion, requires capital to undertake a risky venture or is completely restructuring its financial base.

For the larger firm, finance can be obtained by issuing shares through the Stock Exchange. Normally the Stock Exchange will only deal with very large issues of shares and is therefore restricted to the largest of companies. The procedure for the issue of new shares can be very onerous and rather expensive. Companies must produce a *prospectus* (a very formal document outlining the firm's past track record, future prospects and reasons for the issue) and hire accountants, lawyers and share dealers before an issue can be made.

Smaller firms can make use of the Unlisted Securities Market to issue new shares. This market does not require the same degree of preparation that is needed for a full listing on the Stock Exchange but it is seen as a much riskier option for investors. Normally, only those investors willing to take relatively large levels of risk buy here.

A small company can sell shares in private deals, but it has to find the investors itself (an advantage of the Stock Exchange and the USM being that potential investors are already there). This is an even riskier option for the investor. The government has tried to reduce the risk of private share dealing (and, hence, encouraging people to invest in the shares of smaller firms) through the Business Expansion Scheme. In certain circumstances, individuals can obtain tax relief on the investment they make in smaller firms, thereby reducing the real cost to them of the investment.

Grants

Central and local government is actively encouraging the creation of new businesses and the growth of existing firms. To this end, government bodies are prepared to give assistance in the form of grants in certain circumstances. Normally, the grants are for the purchase of specific assets or come as a result of the creation of jobs. The grants do not cover the full cost of an asset or the cost of a new job but are restricted to a percentage of the total cost – the balance having to be funded from other sources or by the business itself.

Central government grants are selective in terms of both location and type of business seeking a grant. Normally they are available only to firms which are in areas which are seen to be in need of economic revival.

The obvious benefit of grants, assuming a firm can receive one, is that they are free. They do not have to be repaid, nor is interest charged on them.

Costs of finance

The cost of finance will vary from source to source and is a major aspect to be considered by firms which are seeking finance. This section will examine the costs of the previously described sources. However, it is worth remembering that in times of volatile interest rates, costs of finance can change rapidly.

Internal sources

There is no immediate cash cost involved in using internal sources of finance since they are all generated by the firm itself, none has to be repaid, no interest has to be paid, and they are all readily available to the company. However, there could be an opportunity cost: by using internal sources for one project the firm cannot then use these same sources for another possibly more profitable venture.

There is also a possibility of cost in respect of reducing stock levels and forcing debtors to pay more quickly although the costs are not direct monetary costs. If a firm prunes its stock level too far, it runs the risk of running out of stock. With no stock there could be no production and no sales. With no sales, there would be no income, which in itself is a severe 'cost'. If a firm pursues its debtors too vigorously, these customers may decide to buy from elsewhere in the future. Again, reduced sales will be a real 'cost' to any firm.

External sources

OVERDRAFT

The cost of the overdraft is simply the rate charged by the bank. For smaller firms, this could be about 5 or 6 points above the current bank rate, although for large major customers, banks could reduce this to as low as 1 point above base rate.

Over the past few years, bank base rates have been very volatile, which means that overdraft interest rates have also been very volatile. Nonetheless, overdrafts (if properly used) can be relatively cheap. The reason is that interest is charged on a daily basis, which means that interest is only charged so long as an overdraft exists. If a £10,000 overdraft is repaid evenly over one year, that means that the average loan over the year is only £5,000. If interest rates are, say, 18%, then the cost of the overdraft over the year is the equivalent of 18% on the £5,000, not on the original £10,000. This would be cheaper than a £10,000 one-year loan at 10%!

CREDITORS

Normally there are no costs involved in taking credit so long as the debts are paid by the due date. If the debt is paid after the due date, then, so long as the contract permits it, interest may be due on the debt.

There is also a cost to be paid if a discount is offered for cash payment and this is not taken up. For example, consider a firm which buys something for £100 and can take one month's credit. If cash is paid, then a £2 discount is offered. By taking the credit the firm is paying an extra £2 over the cash cost of £98, that is, an eqivalent interest rate of about 25%.

FACTORING

If a firm raises a loan by offering its debtors as security, then the cost is simply the rate of interest charged by the factor on that loan.

If, by factoring its debts, the firm sells its debts to a factor, then the cost to the firm for finance can be rather high. Factors pay less than the full face value of debts bought, paying about 80% of the value of the debt. Thus, if a firm sells a £100 debt, it may only receive £80 immediately, the balance being received when payment is made to the factor. A factor would charge interest on the 80%, plus an administrative fee for its debt collection services. This system absolves companies from keeping a sales ledger, which must be offset against the factor's charges.

BANK LOANS

The cost of a bank loan is basically just the rate of interest charged. As with overdrafts, the rate charged will be some points above the prevailing bank rate at the time of the loan. In addition, some banks may charge an arrangement fee for loans made by them.

Some loans may have a fixed rate of interest; that is, the same interest is charged throughout the term of the loan. This means that financial planning is easier, since the firm knows precisely how much it will have to pay. Most loans, however, have variable rates of interest attached, and these rates could rise during the term of the loan (or fall).

Care has to be taken in ensuring that the firm understands the basis on which interest will be charged. Interest can be either *flat rate* or *APR* (*annual percentage rate*, or *true rate*).

The *flat rate* is the rate which will be charged on the original sum borrowed and will be applied to the original loan even if it is being repaid. The *APR* is the rate charged on the average loan held by the firm.

For example, assume a firm borrows £1,000 at 10% per annum flat rate over two years. The capital has to be repaid by monthly instalments. The firm will only actually borrow £1,000 for one month, for, after that, the loan is being repaid. After one year, half the loan will have been repaid and only £500 will be outstanding. The rate of interest, however, will remain at 10% and will still be based on the original sum of £1,000. The average loan over the two years is only £500, yet the firm still has to pay £200 interest, that is, an average rate of 20% per annum. The APR, however, is the rate which is applied on the average loan over the period borrowed. In the above example, it is the 20%.

If a firm is offered a loan of £1,000 over two years at either 10% flat rate or 15% APR, it would be cheaper to accept the 15% APR despite the fact that it may appear at first glance to be more expensive.

HIRE PURCHASE

The cost of HP is only the interest charged by the financing company, bearing in mind that some finance firms may quote flat rate and others may quote APR. There may be non-monetary costs imposed on the firm by way of restrictions placed on the use of assets being bought.

LEASING

Since leasing is little different from renting, the cost will be the rental (or leasing) charge made by the leasing firm. Since the firm does not own the asset, there will be restrictions placed on the use of the asset. However, since the firm does not own the asset, it will make savings in that the firm will not have to depreciate any assets which are leased.

Money can also be released by means of sale and leaseback. In such cases, a firm will sell its assets to a finance firm and then immediately lease them back from the finance company. This has the advantage of the firm having continual use of required assets and releasing the capital tied up in those assets. Of course, this method of raising finance does require a firm to actually own assets in the first place.

MORTGAGES AND DEBENTURES

The costs of mortgages and debentures are the rates of interest agreed at the time of raising the mortgage or issuing the debentures. The rate of interest depends on many factors including:

(a)   Prevailing interest charges at the time of issue.
(b)   The level and quality of security offered.
(c)   The ratio of equity finance to long-term debt finance. Being essentially cautious, lenders will normally want to reduce their exposure to risk by ensuring that the owners contribute as much capital as possible. The higher the ratio of debt to equity, the higher the level of risk that lenders are taking and, consequently, the higher will be the rate of interest they will charge.

In addition, there will almost certainly be fees to be paid in arranging a mortgage or debenture issue.

EQUITY (SHARES)

Theoretically, there is no cost associated with equity, since there is no legal necessity for firms to pay dividends. In practice, however, a firm will only be able to sell shares if it can convince investors that it will pay good dividends. The cost of equity is therefore the amount of dividends which the firm must pay in the future to attract new investors. This can be very expensive, since once shares are sold the firm will have to pay dividends for ever. Equity financing is permanent, whereas all other forms of finance are limited in time. All other forms of finance will eventually be repaid, and the associated costs will stop – equity finance is permanent, and the firm will have continually to pay dividends.

In addition, there are fairly substantial costs associated with the issue of new shares on either the Stock Exchange or the Unlisted Securities Market.

Questions

9.1   Why does a reduction in *net current assets* release funds?

9.2   What factors should a firm consider before deciding on which source of finance is most appropriate for its needs?

9.3   Explain, briefly, the following forms of finance:

a)   Preference shares.
b)   Debentures.
c)   Working capital.
d)   Depreciation.
e)   Leasing.

9.4   What are the main sources of long-term finance available to limited liability companies?

9.5   What are the costs associated with internal sources of finance?

9.6   What is meant by the term *capital gearing*? In what circumstances would it be advantageous for a firm to be highly geared? (Explain your answer using figures.)

9.7   What are the main sources of external short-term finance? What costs are associated with these sources?

9.8   Delta Ltd is considering expanding its currently profitable operations and has identified the following additional assets which it needs if it is to expand:

a)	New premises	£4,000,000
b)	Additional machinery	750,000
c)	Additional stock	100,000
d)	Extra debtors (this is not needed but will result from extra sales)	90,000
e)	A new Daimler for the chairman	45,000

You are required to write a memo to the chief accountant suggesting the most appropriate sources of funds for each of the above assets.

9.9   Mary Matthews sells her products on 30 days' credit although most of her customers take considerably longer than that to settle their accounts. In the year ended 31/12/19xx, her financial accounts showed:

Sales	£80,000
Net profit before tax	8,000
Debtors	10,000
Bank overdraft	2,000
(she pays interest at 20%)	

During the year, Mary posted 450 invoices, 250 reminders and 300 statements of account, each posting costing her 17p. Two debtors went bad in the year owing a total of £650. 19xx was a typical year for Mary in all respects.

One of Mary's competitors sells only for cash. However, Mary is reluctant to adopt this policy as she feels that to demand cash with an order would result in sales falling by 5% and net profit by 8%. Her net profit would then be only £7,360.

Would you recommend that Mary carry on selling on credit, or should she adopt a 'cash only' policy? Why?

10 Cash flow forecasts and financial plans

Introduction

Previous chapters have concentrated on the work of the financial accountant, the production of financial accounts, their interpretation and their implications for firms. This work is necessary but it is backward looking – it reports on what a firm has achieved. Firms must, however, also look forward – to see where they are going – and quantify in monetary terms the outcome of current decisions. This emphasis on the future and on the results of decision making falls into the realm of management accounting which is concerned with the management of firms, with costs, budgets and the appraisal of internal performance.

There is no neat dividing line between management and financial accounting; they frequently call on each other's expertise. This chapter will examine one particular area where the two types of accounting merge – cash flow forecasting and the use of cash flow forecasts to plan the financial performance of small businesses. The use of both types of accounting is evident because:

- projections deal with the future – normally seen as a function of management accounting; and
- the end result will be projected financial accounts, and financial accounts are normally the preserve of financial accountants.

What is a cash flow forecast?

A cash flow forecast is simply a statement of expected cash coming into a firm from any source and going out of the firm for any reason. It is an extremely important statement, since it forecasts how much cash a firm can expect to have available over the planning period, and cash is a very important commodity for any firm.

Firms can make use of credit to finance some costs, such as the purchase of raw materials, but cash is required for others. Credit cannot be used to pay wages, for example, nor to repay loans or interest or tax, and so on. Only cash will do. The cash flow forecast will show if there will be sufficient cash available when it is needed.

There are at least five benefits to be gained by firms in cash forecasting:

(a) Cash is not profit. Firms can survive in the relatively short term without making profits – many firms make temporary losses but carry on and eventually become profitable. Firms which run out of cash cannot pay their bills and cannot survive.

You will remember that profit is the excess of revenue income over revenue expenditure and that it ignores non-revenue income such as loans or capital injections by the owners. If revenue expenditure exceeds revenue income (that is, losses are being made) the firm can carry on so long as it has sufficient non-revenue income coming in to cover those losses.

(b) Cash flow forecasts will identify potential cash shortages during the planning period and give the firm time to do something about those shortages before they arise. The firm could arrange overdraft facilities or try to encourage debtors to pay faster or do something else. The point is that the firm has time to consider the alternatives and select the best one. Waiting until the shortage is upon the firm may force it into accepting the easiest (and probably most expensive) option, assuming that there will be one available at the time.

(c) The forecast may identify excess cash. Having excess cash is not the aim of management, since it will not be earning the firm any profit. The cash flow forecast will identify how much excess cash there is and for how long it will be excess to the firm's needs. The management can then think about how best that cash could be used in other profitable areas.

(d) A carefully prepared cash flow forecast will show a firm's ability to repay loan capital and interest. This would be useful if the firm were seeking a loan from some source, as it could lessen the perceived risks that the lenders would be taking. This may make the likelihood of receiving a loan that much greater. (In fact, many bankers now will not even consider a loan request from smaller firms without first seeing a cash flow forecast.)

(e) Cash flow forecasts will also indicate when new projects should be started, as the availability of sufficient cash is normally required before any capital-intensive project can be undertaken.

Action to be taken

Having prepared a cash flow forecast, if a firm finds that it is going to run short of cash, there are a number of courses of action which it could consider. But first, it will have to decide if the shortage is temporary or long-term.

If the shortage is temporary the normal response is to obtain an overdraft – that is what they are for, to help overcome temporary cash shortages. If the shortage is going to be long-term, then the firm will have to consider borrowing in the form of loans or, if severe, the injection of new capital.

There are a number of other options available to most firms which fall short of borrowing:

(a) Shorten the credit period given to debtors.
(b) Delay payment of creditors.

(c) Sell off stock.
(d) Lease new assets instead of buying them.
(e) Sell off under-utilized fixed assets.
(f) Reduce costs.
(g) Sale and leaseback

(The subjects of *working capital control* and *sources of finance* have already been covered. If you have forgotten, refer back to Chapters 8 and 9.)

Construction of cash flow forecasts

Cash flow forecasts are little more than estimates of future bank balances, showing how much ready cash a firm thinks that it will have at the end of, and during, a planning period. Consequently, only cash movements will be considered in a cash flow forecast. Any non-cash adjustments, such as depreciation, will be ignored as far as cash flow forecasting is concerned (no firm writes an annual or monthly cheque for 'depreciation'). All cash income and expenditure will be included in the cash flow forecast no matter where the money came from or where it went to – the important fact being that there is a movement in cash.

Timing of cash movements

Most cash flow forecasts are prepared in series of months, showing cash receipts and expenditure in each month over the required planning period. It is therefore important to allocate the cash movement to the appropriate period and not to the period when the movement was incurred.

For example, imagine a firm which sells its products on one month's credit. In month 1 it may sell £1,000 worth of products, but the cash will not be included in the cash flow forecast until the firm expects to receive the cash, that is, month 2.

Problems which require consideration of timing will almost certainly arise in firms which buy and sell on credit. Before constructing a cash flow forecast, schedules showing the receipt of cash from sales and the expenditure on purchases should be prepared.

EXAMPLE

John Smith is planning a new business. He will sell his goods for cash and on one month's credit (40% will be for cash and 60% will be on one month's credit). His purchases will all be on one month's credit and will be bought in as required by each month's expected level of sales. His sales price will be £10 per unit, and the purchase price will be £6 per unit. His expected volume of sales over the first six months is forecast to be:

		Months				
	1	2	3	4	5	6
	100	150	150	200	250	200

Sales schedule

	Months					
	1	2	3	4	5	6
Value	£1,000	1,500	1,500	2,000	2,500	2,000
Cash (40%)	£400	600	600	800	1,000	800
Credit (60%)	—	600	900	900	1,200	1,500
Cash received	£400	1,200	1,500	1,700	2,200	2,300

Points to note:

(1) Since sales for cash mean that cash is immediately received, the value of such sales is accounted for in the month of the sale.

(2) Sales which are on one month's credit will produce cash one month after the sale has actually been made. Thus, in month 1, £1,000 worth of sales were made, 60% being on one month's credit (£600). That cash will not actually be received until month 2 when it will be accounted for.

(3) Since this is a new business, there is no income from credit sales in month 1 (as shown in point 2 above, this will be received in month 2). If this had been an existing business, then the debtors from the previous period would have paid, and be shown to have been paid, in this month.

(4) 60% of month 6's sales will not be received until month 7, which is outside this planning period. If accounts were to be drawn up at the end of month 6, this figure would represent the firm's debtors.

(5) The *cash received* row shows the important figures for cash flow planning as it shows the expected cash receipts for each month which, because of the credit sales, are quite different from the value of sales earned in each month.

Purchases Schedule

	Months					
	1	2	3	4	5	6
Value	£600	900	900	1,200	1,500	1,200
Cash paid	£—	600	900	900	1,200	1,500

Points to note:

(1) The value of purchases is each month's volume times the unit purchase price.

(2) Payment is made one month after the month of purchase. Thus the value of purchases in month 1 is £600, but this will not be paid until month 2.

(3) Payment for the purchases made in month 6 will not be made until the following month, which is outside the planning period. These will form part of the firm's creditors at the end of month 6.

Example of cash flow construction

Patricia King is planning her new business venture. She plans to sell leather clothes to the general public and has supplied the following information:

(a) She will introduce £10,000 of her own money, and will raise a £12,000 loan. This loan is repayable over five years and interest is at 10% per annum, flat rate. Interest and capital are payable monthly.
(b) The cost of her shop's fittings and other equipment will be £18,000. All of this cost must be paid in her first month in business.
(c) Her expected sales, in value, over the first six months are:

			Month		
1	2	3	4	5	6
£6,000	2,500	4,000	5,000	3,000	3,500

70% of sales will be for cash, the balance on one month's credit.
(d) She will buy her opening stock at the start of month 1 for cash and this will cost her £5,000. The cost of replacing stock sold will be 40% of the retail value. Orders for replacement will be made in the middle of each month and will be paid one month later.
(e) The rent and rates for the shop will be £6,000 per annum, payable monthly.
(f) Wages will be £400 per month, and she will pay herself £500 per month.
(g) The cost for heat and light will be £350 every second month, payable one month in arrears.
(h) Other costs will amount to £250 per month.
(i) Depreciation will be at 20% straight line per annum.

WORKING NOTES

(1) *Interest on loans:* Loan £12,000; rate of interest 10%; therefore, interest per annum = £1,200; interest per month = £100.
(2) Capital repayments: repayment period = 5 years × 12 = 60 months; monthly repayment = £12,000 ÷ 60 = £200.
(3) Sales schedule:

	1	2	3	4	5	6	Total
Value	£6,000	2,500	4,000	5,000	3,000	3,500	£24,000
Cash (70%)	4,200	1,750	2,800	3,500	2,100	2,450	16,800
Credit	—	1,800	750	1,200	1,500	900	6,150
Cash in	£4,200	3,550	3,550	4,700	3,600	3,350	£22,950

(4) *Stock purchases:*

	1	2	3	4	5	6	Total
Value	£2,400	1,000	1,600	2,000	1,200	1,400	£9,600
Due + initial stock	£ —	2,400	1,000	1,600	2,000	1,200	8,200
	5,000						
Cash out	£5,000	2,400	1,000	1,600	2,000	1,200	£13,200

Note that although the stock is ordered and bought in one month, the payment is not actually made until the following month.

(5) Depreciation is a 'red herring' at this stage. It does not involve cash expenditure and so will not appear in a cash flow forecast.

Patricia King
Cash flow forecast

	Months						Total
	1	2	3	4	5	6	
Cash in							
Own capital	10,000						10,000
Loan	12,000						12,000
Sales	4,200	3,550	3,550	4,700	3,600	3,350	22,950
Total in	26,200	3,550	3,550	4,700	3,600	3,350	44,950
Cash out							
Loan interest	100	100	100	100	100	100	600
Loan repaid	200	200	200	200	200	200	1,200
Fittings	18,000						18,000
Stock	5,000	2,400	1,000	1,600	2,000	1,200	13,200
Rent/rates	500	500	500	500	500	500	3,000
Wages	400	400	400	400	400	400	2,400
Personal	500	500	500	500	500	500	3,000
Power			350		350		700
Other	250	250	250	250	250	250	1,500
	24,950	4,350	3,300	3,550	4,300	3,150	43,600
Difference	1,250	(800)	250	1,150	(700)	200	
Balance b/f	—	1,250	450	700	1,850	1,150	
Balance	1,250	450	700	1,850	1,150	1,350	1,350

Points to note:

(1) All *cash in* and *cash out* refer to the expected movements in cash in each of the six months. Thus, income from sales is as calculated in the sales schedule (workings 3), and payments for stock are as shown in the stock schedule (workings 4). The figures for heat and light also reflect the time delay in payment.

(2) There is no *balance brought forward* in month 1 since this is a new venture. If it had been an existing business then there would have been a 'brought forward' figure from the preceding period.

(3) From a planning point of view, the end balance is the interesting figure since this shows the expected cash, or bank, balance at the end of each month.

Projected accounts

Cash flow forecasts consider only one aspect of a firm's financial future. Although cash is of paramount importance for the immediate survival of any firm, profits have still to be earned and financial stability must be assured. This can be assessed by producing a projected profit and loss account and balance sheet.

The basic rules for the construction of these statements still apply even though they will be projections rather than historical statements as considered in previous chapters. In particular, the statements will be concerned with value. For example, 'sales' in a cash flow forecast predict the cash that will be received over a planning period, whereas the projected profit and loss account will show the expected level of sales which will be earned.

The data for the construction of the projected profit and loss account and projected balance sheet will be the 'total' figures in the cash flow forecast – they will, in effect, act as a projected *trial balance*. These figures will, of course, be subject to some adjustments, such as for debtors, creditors and depreciation.

The following example uses the data from Patricia King's cash flow forecast.

Projected profit and loss account

WORKINGS

(1) *Sales*:

Value per cash flow forecast	£22,950
add Debtors outstanding	1,050
Total value of sales	£24,000

Note that this figure is the same, and must be the same, as the value of sales in the *sales schedule*.

(2) *Cost of sales*:

Value per cash flow forecast	£13,200
add Creditors outstanding	1,400
Total value of purchases	£14,600
less Closing stock	5,000
	9,600

(3)   *Power*:

Value per cash flow forecast	£700
add Creditor outstanding	350
	£1,050

(4)   *Depreciation*:

Cost of fittings per cash flow	£18,000
less Depreciation at 20% for half a year	1,800
Closing book value	£16,200

(5)   *Loans outstanding*:

Loan received	£12,000
less Repaid	1,200
Balance	£10,800

Patricia King
Projected profit and loss account
for first six months

Sales		£24,000	(workings 1)
less Cost of sales		9,600	(workings 2)
Gross profit		£14,400	
less Expenses			
Rent and rates	£3,000		
Wages	2,400		
Power	1,050		(workings 3)
Other costs	1,500		
Loan interest	600		
Depreciation	1,800		(workings 4)
		10,350	
Net profit		£ 4,050	

Patricia King
Projected balance sheet
as at end of first six months

Fixed assets (net)			£16,200	(workings 4)
Current assets				
Stock		£5,000		(workings 2)
Debtors		1,050		(workings 1)
Bank		1,350		
		£7,400		
less Current liabilities				
Purchases	£1,400			(workings 2)
Power	350	1,750		(workings 3)
			5,650	
			£21,850	
as financed by:				
Capital introduced			£10,000	
add Profit			4,050	
			£14,050	
less Personal drawings			3,000	
			£11,050	
add Loans outstanding			10,800	(workings 5)
			£21,850	

A fuller example

Donald MacRae is thinking about starting a driving school and has produced the following information:

(a)   He will buy three cars, each costing £5,300.
(b)   Each car will be used for 1,000 hours per annum, each hour's lesson being charged at £11 per hour. Donald believes that months 5, 6, 7 and 8 will each account for 10% of annual fee income. The remaining months of the year will produce an equal level of income.
(c)   60% of lessons will be on a cash basis, the balance being on one month's credit.
(d)   The three cars will use, in total, 2,000 gallons of petrol per annum. Petrol will be used in direct proportion to car usage. Donald will buy his petrol from a local garage which will invoice him on the 30th of each month. Each month's invoice must be paid within seven days of the date of the invoice. Petrol costs £1.50 per gallon.
(e)   He will rent an office for £1,200 per annum, payable quarterly, at the start of each quarter.
(f)   Office equipment, which must be bought immediately, will cost £1,000.
(g)   He will employ two instructors and pay each of them £6,000 per annum. He will also employ a part-time receptionist at a cost to him of £3,360 per annum. Payment will be at the end of each month.

Donald Macrae
Sales schedule

	1	2	3	4	5	6	7	8	9	10	11	12	Total
Value	£2,475	2,475	2,475	2,475	3,300	3,300	3,300	3,300	2,475	2,475	2,475	2,475	£33,000
Cash(60%)	£1,485	1,485	1,485	1,485	1,980	1,980	1,980	1,980	1,485	1,485	1,485	1,485	19,800
Credit (40%)	—	990	990	990	990	1,320	1,320	1,320	1,320	990	990	990	12,210
Cash in	£1,485	2,475	2,475	2,475	2,970	3,300	3,300	3,300	2,805	2,475	2,475	2,475	£32,010

Purchases of petrol schedule

	1	2	3	4	5	6	7	8	9	10	11	12	Total
Value	£225	225	225	225	300	300	300	300	225	225	225	225	£3,000
Cash paid	£—	225	225	225	225	300	300	300	300	225	225	225	£2,775

Donald Macrae
Cash flow forecast

	1	2	3	4	5	6	7	8	9	10	11	12	Total
Cash in													
Own cash	£12,000												£12,000
Loans	9,000												9,000
Sales	1,485	2,475	2,475	2,475	2,970	3,300	3,300	3,300	2,805	2,745	2,745	2,745	£32,010
Total in	£22,485	2,475	2,475	2,475	2,970	3,300	3,300	3,300	2,805	2,745	2,745	2,745	£53,010
Cash out													
Cars	£15,900												
Petrol	—	225	225	225	225	300	300	300	300	225	225	225	2,775
Rent and rates	300			300			300			300			1,200
Equipment	1,000												1,000
Wages	1,280	1,280	1,280	1,280	1,280	1,280	1,280	1,280	1,280	1,280	1,280	1,280	15,360
Car tax and ins.	1,650												1,650
Heat and light			125		125		125		125		125		625
Telephone	100			250			250			250			850
Personal	550	550	550	550	550	550	550	550	550	550	550	550	6,660
Loan interest	—	90	90	90	90	90	90	90	90	90	90	90	990
Loan repays	—	150	150	150	150	150	150	150	150	150	150	150	1,650
Total out	£20,780	2,295	2,420	2,845	2,420	2,370	3,045	2,370	2,495	2,845	2,420	2,295	48,600
Difference	£1,705	180	55	(370)	550	930	255	930	310	(370)	55	180	
Balance b/f	—	1,705	1,885	1,940	1,570	2,120	3,050	3,305	4,235	4,545	4,175	4,230	
Balance	£1,705	1,885	1,940	1,570	2,120	3,050	3,305	4,235	4,545	4,175	4,230	4,410	4,410

(h)   Car tax will be £100 on each car. Car insurance will be £1,350 per annum. Both costs will be paid annually.
(i)   Office heat and light will cost £125 every two months, payable one month in arrears.
(j)   He will have to pay £100 immediately for the installation of a telephone. His quarterly phone bill, payable one month in arrears, will be £250.
(k)   His personal drawings will be £550 per month.
(l)   Depreciation will be on the straight line basis over three years for the cars and at 20% reducing balance for the office equipment.
(m)   Donald intends putting £12,000 of his own money into the venture and has arranged a £9,000 bank loan at 12% per annum repayable over five years. Interest and capital must be paid monthly, one month in arrears.

Donald now requires his financial projections to be prepared.

Donald Macrae
Projected profit and loss account
for first year of business

	Notes		
Sales	(1)		£33,000
less Costs			
Petrol	(2)	£3,000	
Rent and rates		1,200	
Wages		15,360	
Car tax & insurance		1,650	
Heat and light	(3)	750	
Telephone	(4)	1,100	
Interest	(5)	1,080	
Depreciation	(6)	5,500	
			29,640
Net profit			£3,360

Donald Macrae
Projected balance sheet
as at the end of first year in business

	Notes		
Fixed assets	(6)		
Motor cars			£10,600
Office equipment			800
			£11,400
Current assets			
Debtors	(7)	£ 990	
Bank	(8)	4,410	
		£5,400	
less Current liabilities			
Creditors for:	(9)		
Petrol		£225	
Heat and light		125	
Telephone		250	
Interest		90	
		690	
			4,710
			£16,110

as financed by

Capital introduced	£12,000
add Profits earned	3,360
	£15,360
less Personal drawings	6,600
	£8,760
add Loans outstanding (10)	7,350
	£16,110

Points to note:

(1) Sales are the total value of income, that is:

$$3 \text{ (cars)} \times 1,000 \text{ (hours)} \times £11 = £33,000.$$

(2) Petrol is also the total value, that is:

$$2,000 \text{ gallons} \times £1.50 = £3,000.$$

(3) The heat and light value is made up of:

Cash paid per the cash flow forecast	£625
add Sum due in month 12 but unpaid	125
	£750

(4) The telephone cost consists of:

cash paid	£850
add Bill outstanding for month 12	250
	£1,100

(5) The interest cost is for the full year, that is:

$$£9,000 @ 12\% = £1,080.$$

(6) Depreciation has been calculated thus:

	Cars	Equipment	
Cost	£15,900	£1,000	
Depreciation	5,300	200	= £5,500
Book value	£10,600	£800	

(7) Debtors are found thus:

Total income	£33,000	
less Cash received	32,010	
Balance due at year end		£990

(8)   The bank balance is the final balance in the cash flow forecast.
(9)   Creditors are found thus:

	Total Cost −	cash paid =	Balance due
Petrol	£3,000	£2,775	£225
Heat and light	750	625	125
Telephone	1,100	850	250
Interest	1,080	990	90
			£690

(10) The loan outstanding is:

Total loan	£9,000
less repaid	1,650
Balance outstanding	£7,350

Use of computers

Once a cash flow forecast and financial plan have been prepared, managers will know where they think the firm is going. Unfortunately, since the plan is a projection of the future, it depends on the outcome of many variables. It is full of assumptions such as the expected volume of sales, selling price, cost of materials and labour, and so on. It would be unreasonable to assume that managers can forecast everything accurately and what would be useful would be a plan which could be altered to show the effect of a change in some, or many, variables.

Consider Donald MacRae's driving school. What would happen if the cost of petrol went up by 10% in month 4 and Donald then increased his fees by 7%? To find out, a new plan would have to be prepared from scratch. Once a manual plan has been prepared, it is a very time-consuming process to alter any of the assumptions which went into its preparation.

Fortunately, computer packages have been written which make the manipulation of numerical variables very easy, and the result of changes in assumptions can be seen within seconds (if not more quickly). There are many such packages – spreadsheets – the more common probably being SuperCalc, Lotus 1–2–3, and Symphony. They all operate in essentially the same way; that is, with a grid made up of rows and columns creating individual cells such as

```
    A    B    C    D    E    ...
1
2
3
4
5
```

Thus, there are individual cells for A1, A2, A3, B1, B2, B3, and so on. Each cell can contain text, a number or (more importantly) a formula which can make use of numbers in other cells. For example, suppose in cell A1 there was the number 50, and in cell B1 there was the number 25. Cell C1 could then contain a formula to add the contents of A1 and B1 and would then show the answer – 75. (The formula could be any arithmetic function.) Changing the content in A1 would automatically result in C1 changing, since C1 is dependent on the content of A1.

Cash flow forecasts and financial plans are no more than numbers in cells or arithmetic calculations of various cells and, so, are ideal for computer spreadsheets. With a financial plan on computer, users can ask many 'what if' questions (such as 'What happens if the cost of materials increases by 10% halfway through the year and we increase our prices by only 4%?') and find the answer simply by changing the numeric value of the variables. All cells which contain reference to those variables will then be altered.

Appendix III contains a list of commands for a cash flow forecast and financial plan using SuperCalc 4 (or SuperCalc 3). It shows the variables upon which the whole plan depends, and a change in any variable will be reflected in the cash flow forecast, projected profit and loss account and balance sheet. If you have access to SuperCalc, you may wish to enter the commands and then find out what happens when you change the variables.

Questions

10.1   What is a *cash flow forecast*? Why should firms prepare one?

10.2   'The most important business objective is to survive and survival depends on firms having sufficient cash to pay their debts when they become due. Therefore, cash flow forecasts are more important to firms than projected profit and loss accounts.' Comment on this statement.

10.3   Explain why cash in the bank at a year-end is seldom, if ever, the same as profits earned in that year.

10.4   To what extent is the cash flow forecast underpinned by a realistic sales forecast?

10.5   The owner of Alpha Electrics, a small manufacturer of electrical equipment, is concerned that the firm's cash flow forecast for the coming year indicates cash deficits for the first nine months. Outline the courses of action which could be considered to alleviate this potential problem.

10.6   John Smith plans to sell a single product at £10 each. His expected volume of sales for his first six months in business from January to June 19xx is as follows:

	Jan.	Feb.	March	April	May	June
Volume	200	400	500	900	800	700

He will sell his product for both cash and credit and expects 80% of all sales to be on credit.
Research has shown that debtors will settle their debts as follows:
(a)   60% in the month following the month of sale;

(b)   30% in the second month following the month of sale; and
(c)   10% in the third month following the month of sale.

Required: produce Mr Smith's sales schedule for his first six months in business, showing how much cash he can expect to receive in each month.

10.7   Megan Roberts has been in business for some time. She has asked you to prepare her cash flow forecast for the first six months of 19x9 and has supplied the following information:

(a)   Her debtors on 31/12/19x8 totalled £15,700. Of this, £7,500 is due in January 19x9, and the balance one month later.
(b)   Her bank balance on 31/12/19x8 was £1,500.
(c)   Expected monthly sales are:

Jan.	Feb.	March	April	May	June
£25,000	30,000	30,000	40,000	50,000	40,000

(d)   20% of sales are for cash, 50% on one month's credit and the rest on two months' credit.
(e)   Purchases cost 60% of the retail price. Stock is replaced at the end of each month and must be paid seven days later. She has sufficient stock to last through January but owes £15,000 for it.
(f)   Rent is £12,000 per annum. This is due in six equal instalments, starting in January.
(g)   Other costs amount to £5,000 per month, payable in cash.
Required: prepare Ms Robert's cash flow forecast.

10.8   Mr I. B. Good has decided to start up his own business. He has £5,000 to invest and will borrow a further £3,600, repayable over three years. Interest will be charged at 12% per annum and must be paid monthly in arrears. Capital repayments of the loan are also to be made monthly in arrears. Mr Good has asked you to prepare a financial plan for his first six months and has supplied the following additional information:

(a)   Fixed assets (equipment) will cost £4,500, payable in cash.
(b)   He will buy a van for cash costing £3,000. All fixed assets will be bought in January.
(c)   His sales volume will be:

Jan.	Feb.	March	April	May	June
£600	750	1,150	1,500	1,050	900

The retail price per unit will be £4, and receipts will be 45% in cash, 40% on one month's credit and 15% on two months' credit.

(d)   Raw materials will cost £1.30 per unit. Materials are ordered in the month of manufacture and sale but are paid the following month.
(e)   Labour is paid monthly and is based on the number of units made and sold in each month. The rate of payment is £0.80 per unit.
(f)   Heat and light costs £435 every second month, payable one month in arrears.
(g)   Rates are £3,000 per annum, paid annually in arrears.
(h)   Personal drawings will be £500 each month.
(i)   Depreciation on all assets is 20% straight line.
(j)   In January he will buy, for cash, £350 worth of 'safety stock'. He will always have this stock on hand at the end of every month.

Required: prepare Mr Good's cash flow forecast, projected profit and loss account and projected balance sheet as at the end of June.

(Note: this question forms the basis of the example of forecasting in Appendix III. That example shows the input commands to create the financial plan on a microcomputer using SuperCalc 3 or 4. It is fully integrated in that the effect of a change in any variable will be seen throughout the whole plan.)

10.9   You are given the following information about a firm which will start trading at the start of the spring:

(a)   sales for the first two years will be £500,000 per annum. All sales will be for cash.

(b)   Sales are seasonal, and each annual quarter will account for the following proportions of total annual sales:

Spring	20%
Summer	50%
Autumn	20%
Winter	10%

(c)   Sales will provide a gross profit of 20%.

(d)   The cost of goods for resale in the first spring will have to be paid for in cash at the start of the business. Thereafter, goods for resale in any one quarter are bought in the middle of the previous quarter and paid for two months later.

(e)   Wages and other overheads cost £15,000 per quarter, paid by cash.

(f)   The owners will inject an initial £200,000 capital at the start of trading.

(g)   Capital equipment will cost £220,000 and will be depreciated over ten years on the straight line basis.

Required: prepare the cash flow forecasts, profit and loss accounts, and balance sheets for the firm's first two years.

10.10   Ivor Payne has decided to start up a business as a manufacturer of specialist glass. He has asked you to prepare a cash flow forecast, projected profit and loss account and projected balance sheet for him and has supplied the following information:

(a)   He will put £25,000 of his own money into the venture.

(b)   He will raise a £10,000 loan at 12% repayable over five years. Interest and capital are to be paid monthly, although for the first six months interest only will have to be paid.

(c)   The value of sales in each of the first four months will be £16,000, rising by 10% in month 5. This new monthly sales value will continue for three months after which an extra £3,000 will be earned.

(d)   Payne expects 10% of sales to be for cash, the balance being on one month's credit.

(e)   The sales price has been arrived at after adding 25% on to the purchase price of raw materials.

(f)   He will receive one month's credit from his suppliers of raw materials, all of which he orders and receives in the month of sale.

(g)   He has to have equipment costing £12,000 and vehicles costing £8,000 in place by the end of his first month. No credit will be allowed.

(h)   Three employees will be recruited at the start of the business at an average cost of £1,000 per employee.

(i)   Rent is £3,600 per annum, payable monthly in advance.

(j)   Rates are £5,000 per annum. He will pay them annually in arrears.
(k)   The phone will cost £250 each quarter, payable one month in arrears.
(l)   Motoring costs will be £150 each month, payable in cash.
(m) Payne will pay himself £600 each month.
(n)   Depreciation will be charged at 15% on equipment and at 25% on vehicles.
(o)   There will be no stock at the end of any one month.

Required:

(1)   Prepare Mr Payne's financial plan, as requested, for his first nine months in business.
(2)   Comment on the figures produced in your financial statements.

10.11   Ms Mel Bourne has gathered the following information in respect of her proposed business of jewellery manufacture:

(a)   The first year's sales, in units, will be:

					Month						
1	2	3	4	5	6	7	8	9	10	11	12
Volume 50	60	100	110	300	20	45	65	90	120	180	450

(b)   Her average unit selling price will be £50. 25% of all sales will be for cash; 40% will be on one month's credit; and the balance will be on two months' credit.
(c)   Purchases of raw material will be made as required and will give her a 30% gross profit. Cash payments are required for the first two months, after which purchases will be on one month's credit.
(d)   Equipment costing £5,000 must be bought and paid for at the start of month 1.
(e)   The rent of premises is £2,000 per annum, payable every third month. Ms Bourne expects to be one month late in paying her rent.
(f)   Power and telephone costs will be £90 and £250 per quarter respectively, each payable one month in arrears.
(g)   Delivery charges are £1 per item sold, payable by Ms Bourne at the time of sale.
(h)   Her total wage bill is £800 per month including personal wages of £450. (Ms Bourne will start up as a sole trader.)
(i)   Other cash costs amount to £160 per month.
(j)   Ms Bourne will put £5,000 cash into the business together with her own car, currently valued at £4,000. She has raised a £6,000 bank loan repayable monthly over five years together with interest at 20% flat rate. Interest, however, must be paid one month in advance.
(k)   Depreciation will be charged at 25% per annum on the car and at 10% per annum on the equipment.
(l)   She will have minimal stock at the end of each month, valued at £50.

Required:

(1)   Prepare Ms Bourne's cash flow forecast, profit and loss account and balance sheet for her first year in business.
(2)   From your forecasts, does Ms Bourne have a financially viable business proposition? Why?

11 Budgets – principles and preparation

Principles

Planning is essential in most areas of human enterprise. Managers and others in positions of responsibility must plan on a daily, weekly, monthly or annual basis if they are to operate efficiently.

Because of the importance of money to businesses, and because of the fact that it is the common denominator in all departments, the vast majority of enterprises produce *budgets* as an aid to planning. A budget may be defined as 'a coordinated financial plan reflecting the agreed policy and detailed intentions of an enterprise for a future period'. The budgetary process has the following advantages:

- All departments of a business are compelled to consider the effects of a common set of assumptions on their operations over an agreed time period, thereby coordinating all departmental plans.
- One outcome of the exercise is the production of a series of departmental financial targets. Each subdivision of the enterprise is expected to strive to achieve, or improve upon, these targets inasmuch as circumstances allow.
- The detailed financial targets will be combined to produce a budget for the enterprise as a whole, the *master budget*. If the resultant profits, cash flows and other key figures are not acceptable, appropriate cuts or changes can be made in the supporting budgets prior to finalization.
- The budget can be used as a yardstick of performance throughout the period. As deviations from the budget (*variances*) occur, management will discuss them at specially convened meetings, in order to establish what action, if any, needs to be taken. In this way, budgets provide enterprises with a vital means of *control*.

While short-term cash flow forecasts act as a basic form of financial control in the smaller firm, the sophistication of a budgetary system is indispensable for larger enterprises, where the organization is complex and the resources required are considerable. It is no surprise, therefore, that preparing the annual budget is the most time-consuming planning activity carried out by large businesses. The budgetary process also plays a vital educative role; senior managements acquire a deeper understanding of the detailed workings of their companies as they deal with the budget submissions and reports of subordinates.

Budget preparation – preliminaries

Budget preparation in the larger organization is a huge exercise in coordination. The coordinator will normally be the management accountant, reporting directly to the financial controller or finance director. Sometimes the coordinator is given the title of 'budget officer'. Budgeting activities will depend to a great extent on the size and structure of an organization. Matters will be relatively straightforward in a single site company, whereas a complex company structure which involves 'divisions', 'product groups' and multiple sites calls for a number of budget officers and a central budget structure. Complex interchanges of information will also be necessary as a result of the trading taking place between the different parts of the organization. Purchases made by one subsidiary company from another will form part of the supplying company's budgeted sales as well as part of the purchasing company's budgeted costs. There must therefore be complete agreement on the volume and selling price figures that are to be used, or the budget will not be soundly based.

Certain fundamental questions have to be dealt with at the outset. Are individual sites/groups of sites to be held accountable for their budgeted expenditure levels alone, that is, treated as 'cost centres', or are they to be held accountable for the achievement of budgeted profit levels, that is, treated as 'profit centres'? This decision is usually related to the location of the sales and marketing and sales accounting functions either at site/group level or at head office; it is not generally logical to separate a function geographically from the senior management to whom it is accountable.

The arguments for and against cost-centre accountability can be summarized as follows:

COST-CENTRE ACCOUNTABILITY

'For'	'Against'
Senior management can concentrate on those factors over which they have complete control, such as labour, material costs, localized overheads.	Profit responsibility gives a senior executive a sense of accountability, independence and motivation.
Since the sales or marketing functions are often centralized, sales prices and the completion of contracts are largely outside management's control.	Responsibility for production and the achievement of delivery schedules usually lies with site/group management, so, to a large extent they 'achieve' sales. They should therefore be accountable for profit.
Cost-centre accountability reduces inter-site/group rivalries over profitability, which can be a distraction.	Inter-site/group rivalry can be healthy, since it is a microcosm of the external world.
Some products generate a greater margin than others, and therefore executives responsible for low-profit-earning goods or services have less opportunity to do well as profit centres.	The absolute profit made is not the yardstick of success. It is the achievement of the target that is important.

In the last analysis the choice of accountability basis is a matter of opinion but will be linked to the corporate management style and culture.

A question closely related to accountability is that of 'transfer pricing' policy. Should goods and services transferred between sites or divisions of the same company be transferred at cost, or should the prices contain an agreed profit margin? Transfer pricing at cost matches cost-centre-based accountability, while the incorporation of profit matches profit-centre accountability.

Given that these questions are already decided, a budget timetable or calendar will be drawn up. The budget period usually corresponds with the enterprise's financial year, and also with the accounting periods within that year. Where appropriate, target dates will be set for the submission of individual cost-centre or profit-centre budgets to central staff, and backed up by dates for the provision of key information to and from head office. In many organizations, preparations for the forthcoming budget year can begin as much as eight or nine months before its commencement.

One of the earliest events in the budget calendar is the provision of budget assumptions to cost or profit centres by head office. These assumptions are issued to ensure that each centre is planning in harmony with the others. Long-term company policy will have been translated into specific events intended to happen in the budget year, such as:

(a)   New products to be introduced.
(b)   Old products to be phased out.
(c)   New plants or departments coming onstream.
(d)   Changes to the management structure.
(e)   Operations/plants to be phased out.

In addition, central guidelines will be supplied regarding economic factors such as:

(a)   The timing and amount of wage and salary increases, by negotiating group, if applicable.
(b)   The timing and amount of price increases, by product or service.
(c)   The timing and amount of inflation factors such as direct material cost increases and overhead increases.

The final, and perhaps the most important budget assumption is *sales volume*. All concerns are constrained by limitations on the amounts that they can produce or sell, called 'limiting factors'. For example, a market garden might find that it has sales inquiries for 50% more goods than it can produce, and is unable to acquire more land to take advantage of the extra sales. Land is therefore the limiting factor, since it restricts production.

In practice, many enterprises are in the position of being able to produce more than they can sell, and sales are therefore the constraint. In these cases, sales volume will help to determine production and manning levels, shift patterns and supporting assumptions; in fact, it will 'drive' the budget. It will be assumed throughout this chapter that sales are the limiting factor.

The following matters will be taken into account in settling the budgeted sales volume:

- *Economic forecasts.* What are the leading forecasters predicting about the economy in the budget year? Is expansion or contraction of sales likely?
- *Competitor activity.* What is known about the product and pricing intentions of competitors over the budgeted period, and what are the anticipated effects on prices and sales?
- *Market shares.* What trends are emerging in terms of market shares?
- *Pricing policy.* Would suitable levels of concession on a selective or blanket basis increase volume and/or profit?
- *Marketing strategy.* What are the anticipated effects of the changes planned?
- *Export territories.* Is the economic/political situation in key export markets likely to alter in the budgeted year, and how will it affect sales? How are exchange rates moving, and what are the implications?

Senior sales and marketing management will consider factors such as these alongside detailed knowledge of customers and markets before deciding on the budget volumes. When their deliberations are complete, the volumes will be discussed at the highest levels in the organization, and the resultant budgeted sales levels will be added to the budget assumptions.

The budgeting process

The example which follows will demonstrate a typical chain of practical activities involved in preparing a budget for a manufacturing unit on a single site.

Delta Ltd is an engineering company with the organizational structure shown in Figure 11.1. The following details are relevant:

(a) Delta is a wholly owned subsidiary of the Epsilon Group Plc.
(b) Comprehensive budget assumptions have been received from the parent company, ranging from monthly sales volumes of Delta's sole product, an electric motor, to inflation factors which are expected to apply to costs and sales in the budget year.

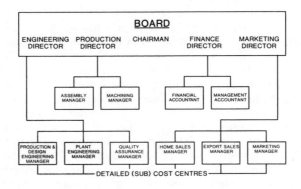

Figure 11.1

(c) The management accountant has been nominated as the company's budget officer.
(d) The parent company has set a deadline for preliminary submission of Delta's budget to head office. It is to be provided by 30 June. Thereafter revisions may arise from the Epsilon Group Plc review of the Delta budget.
(e) Delta is a profit centre, negotiating purchase prices of the components it buys from fellow subsidiaries of Epsilon on an 'arm's length', or commercial, basis.

PROCEDURE

The budget officer, together with his staff, will prepare budget files for each *internal* cost centre at the plant. While the plant as a unit is a profit centre, it contains a number of cost centres which will together account for its total expenditure in the budget year.

Looking at the organization chart, you will see that there are ten management positions overseeing distinct departments below directoral level. While each is a cost centre in its own right, there are also sections or work groups within each managed by senior staff or foremen. These are large enough to be treated as sub-cost centres and to have their own budgets. Each of the ten managers will have overall responsibility for the sub-cost centres, but the foremen and senior staff responsible for the sections or work groups will be accountable to the managers for budget performance in their individual cost centres.

The cost-centre files will be grouped together in accordance with managerial responsibility. Given that there are ten managers below directoral level in Delta, each will receive a bundle of files.

In addition to the list of assumptions referred to above, each file will contain a statement of:

● Year to date expenditure by account heading to each cost centre.
● Forecast total year expenditure by account heading for the *current* year, again by cost centre.
● Existing manpower levels, broken down by category of staff and wage negotiation group if relevant.

(1) The foreman or supervisor, together with the manager responsible, will be asked to return the file to the budget officer, complete with expenditure and manpower requests for the budget year. These should incorporate lateness, absence and overtime forecasts.
(2) Each director will then arrange to review the budget requests of his/her managers, making alterations where necessary and returning the completed files to the budget officer by the time required.
(3) The budget officer and his staff will check the files for completeness and accuracy, and will aggregate all budget request figures by account heading. Manpower requests will be aggregated and grossed up at the appropriate wage and salary rates, after which employment costs (such as National Insurance) will be calculated. Any other figures required to complete the overhead (expense) total, such as depreciation, will be calculated.

(4) At the same time the *capital budget* will be prepared to reflect the capital expenditure required within the budget year to support the production and sales budget. Renewals and replacements of existing capital stock will be requested as well as outright purchases of new items. The collection of capital expenditure requests may be treated as a separate exercise, or can be done through the budget files.

(5) Direct material and direct labour costs for the budget year will be computed with reference to current unit costs and budget volumes. The direct labour costs will then be reconciled with the requests for direct labour manpower made by the two production managers and their staff. sales volumes will be multiplied by current sales price and, together with the rest of the figures, will be uplifted in line with the inflation and pricing assumptions received from head office. A preliminary figure of budgeted profit will thus be produced.

(6) At this point the finance director will brief the chairman on the salient features of the budget requests and their effects on profit. The process of review can now begin in earnest, with each director attending review meetings to justify his/her figures. Those attending will include the directors affected, the finance director, the chairman and the budget officer, who will take a note of any alterations resulting from the discussion so that the figures affected can be amended.

(7) The finalized figures, which will include a budget for cash flow and budgeted final accounts, will be sent to head office by 30 June. The budget staff there will aggregate the budget submissions from each location, producing a total group picture. This will then be reviewed by the main board, together with the finance director and chairman of each subsidiary, Delta included, who will then advise site staffs of any final changes to their submissions. The budgets, which have now been agreed at all levels within the company, are ready for 'calendarization' (subdivision by accounting period) and issue to the various departments.

Budgets in the smaller firm

The smaller firm is free from the complexities of communication, coordination and review which characterize the budget process in larger firms. The assumptions, decisions and perhaps even the calculations may all be made by the proprietor him-/herself, or by a suitably qualified member of staff. The following example illustrates the straightforward calculations involved.

Kitsch Products

Kitsch makes two types of garden furniture, A and B. The following budget information for the forthcoming financial year has been developed by the proprietor:

(a) Budget sales volume:
    A – l00 per month; B – 200 per month

(b)   Financial information (current):

	A	B
Direct material cost	£50	£30
Direct labour cost	£10	£5
Sales value	£100	£60

(c)   Overheads and indirect manpower levels budget information are as under:

(i)   Administration – two clerks required.
(ii)   Quality/dispatch – two inspectors/dispatchers required.
(iii)   Miscellaneous overheads – £1,000 per month.
(iv)   Employment costs – 30% of all salaries and wages.
(v)   Inspectors/dispatchers earn £500 month; clerks earn £400 month.
(vi)   Prices are to be increased on 1 June by 5%. Wages/salaries are to be increased by 3% on 1 September. Material costs are expected to remain static.

The budgets would be developed as follows.

BUDGETARY CONTROL EXERCISE

Sales

	Jan.	Feb.	Mar.	April	May	June	July	Aug.	Sept.	Oct.	Nov.	Dec.	Total
A.	10	10	10	10	10	10	10	10	10	10	10	10	120,000
						0.5	0.5	0.5	0.5	0.5	0.5	0.5	3,500
	10	10	10	10	10	10.5	10.5	10.5	10.5	10.5	10.5	10.5	123,500
B.	12	12	12	12	12	12	12	12	12	12	12	12	144,000
						0.6	0.6	0.6	0.6	0.6	0.6	0.6	4,200
	12	12	12	12	12	12.6	12.6	12.6	12.6	12.6	12.6	12.6	148,200
Total	22	22	22	22	22	23.1	23.1	23.1	23.1	23.1	23.1	23.1	271,700

Direct material costs

	Jan.	Feb.	Mar.	April	May	June	July	Aug.	Sept.	Oct.	Nov.	Dec.	Total
A	5	5	5	5	5	5	5	5	5	5	5	5	60,000
B	6	6	6	6	6	6	6	6	6	6	6	6	72,000
Total	11	11	11	11	11	11	11	11	11	11	11	11	132,000

Direct labour costs

	Jan.	Feb.	Mar.	April	May	June	July	Aug.	Sept.	Oct.	Nov.	Dec.	Total
A	1	1	1	1	1	1	1	1	1	1	1	1	12,000
B	1	1	1	1	1	1	1	1	1	1	1	1	12,000
	2	2	2	2	2	2	2	2	2	2	2	2	24,000
									0.06	0.06	0.06	0.06	240
Total	2	2	2	2	2	2	2	2	2.06	2.06	2.06	2.06	24,240

Labour overheads

	Jan.	Feb.	Mar.	April	May	June	July	Aug.	Sept.	Oct.	Nov.	Dec.	Total
Clerks	0.8	0.8	0.8	0.8	0.8	0.8	0.8	0.8	0.8	0.8	0.8	0.8	9,600
Insp	1	1	1	1	1	1	1	1	1	1	1	1	12,000
	1.8	1.8	1.8	1.8	1.8	1.8	1.8	1.8	1.8	1.8	1.8	1.8	21,600
									0.054	0.054	0.054	0.054	216
Total	1.8	1.8	1.8	1.8	1.8	1.8	1.8	1.8	1.854	1.854	1.854	1.854	21,816

Employment costs

Total Wage Cost ×	3.8	3.8	3.8	3.8	3.8	3.8	3.8	3.8	3.914	3.914	3.914	3.914	46,05◖
.30	1.140	1.140	1.140	1.140	1.140	1.140	1.140	1.1742	1.1742	1.1742	1.1742	1.1742	13.816◖

Misc.

OHD	1	1	1	1	1	1	1	1	1	1	1	1	12,00◖

Sales	271,700
Direct mat. costs	132,000
Direct lab. costs	24,240
Overheads	47,633
Profit	67,827

Notes:

(1) *Price increases.* These have been phased in at the appropriate times, based on the assumptions supplied. In the case of products A and B, the calculations have been carried out separately, so that there is a sales budget for each product each period.

(2) *Cost increases.* The increases on costs have been calculated on a total basis only, since it is unlikely that further analysis would be required in a small business.

(3) *Employment costs.* Employment costs are the overheads associated with the employment of staff, and might include:

● Employer's contribution to National Insurance.
● Employer's contribution to pension/superannuation schemes.
● Employer's provision for holiday pay.

It is the practice in many firms to treat all employment costs as overheads, although an argument can be raised which states that those associated with production workers are direct, or prime, costs. In the above example we have assumed that *all* employment costs are overheads, and it was therefore necessary to bring direct (production) labour costs into the calculation.

(4) *Direct labour costs.* These costs have been worked up from the unit cost information supplied, and it was not therefore necessary to know the numbers or wages of production employees.

(5) *Stocks.* It has been assumed that there is no opening stock and that all production will be sold.

In many cases it will be possible to make calculations such as these using computer spreadsheet software. The formulas connecting the calculations can be fed in at the outset, and when changes in the assumptions are made, the figures can be altered at the touch of a key. The above example, reworked on the microcomputer, can be found in Appendix III.

Production, sales and cash budgeting

In the simplified example just given, the various detailed budgets were expressed in a few lines and combined into a total budget (the master budget) on a single page. In the larger organization, matters would be more complicated. The sales budget, for example, would involve a multiplicity of products, sales of which would have to be worked out on an individual basis, with volumes of each perhaps fluctuating from month to month at different rates. It would be customary for production and sales levels to differ from period to period, and the production and sales budgets would involve increases and reductions in stock.

EXAMPLE

Sales of a product made by John Frew Ltd will be as follows in the budget year:

				Period								
	1	2	3	4	5	6	7	8	9	10	11	12
Units	100	100	150	175	150	150	150	150	150	300	250	450

If the production budget is to be 200 units per month, and the opening stock at the beginning of the budget year is 175 units, calculate the budgeted stock level at the end of each of the first six budget periods.

SOLUTION

	Period					
	1	2	3	4	5	6
Opening stock	175	275	375	425	450	500
Production	200	200	200	200	200	200
	375	475	575	625	650	700
Sales	100	100	150	175	175	150
Closing stock	275	375	425	450	500	550

This pattern will be reflected in the purchases budget and on the balance sheet in the master budget, which will contain budgeted stock figures.

Cash budgets differ from the cash flow forecasts discussed in Chapter 10. The latter are short-term forecasts, while the cash budget is prepared as a yardstick against which comparisons are made throughout the year. It too must interlock with other budget figures, including budgeted debtors and creditors as they move from month to month, and with the capital budget, which contains the budgeted expenditure on fixed assets. By bringing all projected cash earnings and expenditure together, a budget for the cash and bank balance can be worked out. This can be done either by using the techniques discussed earlier or by inference from other budget figures.

EXAMPLE

Work out the cash budget of Clegg Ltd from the following:

Forecast balance sheet at beginning of budget year	£000		Budget balance sheet at end period 12		£000
Fixed assets		1,000	Fixed assets		2,900
Current assets			Current assets		
Stock	2,000		Stock	3,000	
Debtors	3,000		Debtors	2,500	
Cash/bank	2,000		Cash/bank	?	
	7,000			?	
Creditors	3,000		Creditors	2,500	
		4,000			?
		5,000			?
			Opening capital and reserves		5,000
			Budget profit		2,000
					7,000
			Budget dividends and tax		500
					6,500

The missing figures can be worked out by subtraction as follows:

(a)   Total net assets £6,500 (from closing capital).
(b)   Working capital £3,600 (£6,500 – fixed assets £2,900).
(c)   Current assets £6,100 (£3,600 + £2,500 creditors).
(d)   Cash/bank £600 (£6,100 – £5,500 stock/debtors).

The budgeted fixed assets figure would have been worked out from the capital budget; the stock figure from the purchases and sales budgets; and debtors and creditors figures on an assumed week's supply basis, using budgeted purchases and sales. Monthly budgets for cash/bank could be derived in the same way.

Zero-based budgeting

As was seen earlier, budgets in most businesses are based on existing levels of manpower, resources and expenditure levels. These are augmented or reduced in line with increased or decreased sales and production, or because of other factors which will take effect during the budget year, such as the introduction of new technology or increased administrative workload. The future is projected from the present. This methodology is open to the criticism that inefficiencies can be perpetuated by assuming that current practices and resources are effective.

To counter this possibility, zero-based budgeting was devised. Under zero-based budgeting, managers with budget accountability are expected to justify their resource requirements from first principles. What is the function of the department? Is it really necessary? What resources are required to fulfil the department's objectives at minimum cost? It is claimed that, by asking these questions, decision makers arrive at more realistic budgets and halt the tendency to empire-build.

Because of the depth and stringency of the investigations associated with zero-based budgeting, it is costly and time consuming. The organizations in which it is employed therefore tend to have zero-based reviews at five- or six-yearly intervals. The technique has been used extensively in local government in the USA.

Final points

The discussion of zero-based budgets conveniently raises an important question. How difficult should it be for those managers accountable for budgets to achieve them? It is generally accepted that to impose unachievable budgets will demotivate managers, and that budgets which are 'hard but achievable' are more likely to help in the attainment of an organization's aims and to win the enthusiasm of staff. Coordination of management's efforts is unlikely if this philosophy is not applied.

Secondly, it is obvious that budgets cannot predict the future. The principal advantage of a budgetary system lies, however, in its ability to co-ordinate the planning and operation of a business, and to provide the opportunity for systematic and logical reviews of its progress. Deviations from budget are not necessarily failures; often there are factors completely outside the control of management which can explain variances. Nevertheless, departures from budgets do show that an enterprise has not met its short-term corporate objectives. How, therefore, are variances to be interpreted and used?

This topic will be dealt with in the next chapter.

Questions

11.1   What is the purpose of a system of budgetary control?

11.2   How should firms be organized in order to install and operate systems of budgetary control?

11.3   Describe the practical steps which the management of a profit-making manufacturing enterprise might take in order to prepare a budget for its forthcoming financial year.

11.4   Comment on the following:

(a)   Limiting factors.
(b)   Cost-centre and profit-centre budget accountability.

11.5   Kappa Ltd has made the following forecasts for its budget year, which runs from January to December:

(a) Opening stock – 5,750 units.
(b) Production – 2,850 units per month, January to March inclusive, rising by 10% April to July inclusive, dropping by 20% August to October, rising to 4,000 units per month November and December.
(c) Sales – 3,050 units per month January to May inclusive, 2,565 per month June to September inclusive, 4,000 per month October to December inclusive.

Required:
(1) Work out the budgeted stock levels for each of the twelve months.
(2) If the cost of each unit is £55, what is the closing stock value at the close of the budget year?
(3) What are the implications of the figures you have worked out for other parts of the budget?

11.6 Omicron Ltd's summarized balance sheet forecast for the end of the present financial year shows the following figures:

		£000s
Land		1,200
Buildings		575
		1,775
Stock	1,595	
Debtors	796	
Cash	313	
	2,704	
Creditors	1,716	
Working capital		988
		2,763
Share capital		1,500
Reserves		1,263
		2,763

The following information is available for the budget year:

(a) Sales: £6.1m.
(b) Purchases: £3.3m
(c) Land and buildings will not be increased during the budget year; nor is any depreciation to be charged.
(d) Reserves are to be increased by the amount of the budgeted profit, which is £745,000, by the budget year-end.
(e) No additional capital will be issued.

Required: Complete the budget balance sheet as at the budget year end, using the following guidelines:

● Stock to be calculated on the basis of three months' purchases.
● Debtors to be calculated on the basis of one month's sales.
● Creditors to be calculated on the basis of two months' purchases.

11.7 The Nestor Rest Home, a home for the single elderly, is calculating its budgeted profit and loss account for the total budget year. The following assumptions, information and preliminary calculations have been collected:

(a) Total number of rooms: 40.
(b) Room utilization: 80%.
(c) Weekly rate (full board): £190, to be increased by 10% at the beginning of period 7.
(d) Food costs: £20 per person per week.
(e) Staff costs: matron, £14,500 p.a.; 18 care assistants at £7,450 p.a.; 3 kitchen staff at £6,745 p.a. (Wages/salaries to be increased by 7% at the beginning of period 4.)
(f) Employment costs: 20% of all staff costs.
(g) Mortgage interest: £21,500 p.a.
(h) Rates: £25,000 p.a.
(i) Miscellaneous: £15,750 p.a.

Required: The budgeted profit and loss account.

11.8 The following budget information relates to Cyma Recta Ltd for the forth-coming year:

(a)

	Sales price	Material cost	Labour cost	Budget production
Product 1	23	3	5	3,400 units
Product 2	17	6	4	5,195 units
Product 3	13	4	3	1,900 units

(b) There are three non-production workers who earn £7,090 p.a., and two salaried staff who earn £6,750 p.a. Employment costs run at 20% of *all* wages and salaries.
(c) Depreciation amounts to £5,750 p.a.
(d) Maintenance costs are £3,980 p.a.
(e) Administrative costs are £7,465 p.a.
(f) All wages and salaries are to be increased by 8% from the beginning of month 5. Maintenance and administrative costs are expected to rise gradually at a rate of 12% per annum. Material costs will not alter.
(g) Stock at the start of the budget year is nil. At the close of the budget year, 100 units of product 1 will remain in stock, together with 50 units of product 3.
(h) Sales price of all products will be increased by 8% at the start of period 10.

Required: The budgeted profit and loss account for the year.

12 Controlling through budgets

Budget reporting

Once the new financial year begins, the budget is ready for implementation, which involves the reporting and analysis of variances for each accounting period and for the cumulative period within the year. This will be done at a number of levels, which will usually include:

- Profit and loss account variances.
- Departmental/functional cost variances.
- Unit cost variances.

The budget reports highlighting the above variances will be prepared by the management accountant (by whatever name he/she is called) and presented to senior management as quickly as possible after each period end. In most firms formal reviews of performance against budget are taken seriously enough to be timetabled well in advance. Prior to these sessions, management should examine those variances for which they are responsible, and with the help of the management accountant should attempt to establish the major underlying factors, so that most of the time at the budget performance meeting can be devoted to discussion of remedial action. Since the variance between actual and budget profit is of critical importance, it will perhaps be among the first to be discussed.

EXAMPLE

Profit and loss account for period 1 19xx

£000s	Budget	Actual	Variance fav (unfav.)
Sales	2,500	2,440	(60)
less Cost of sales			
Material	1,056	976	~~26~~ 70
Labour	195	169	26
Gross margin	1,249	1,295	~~46~~
less Overheads			
Maint. wages	247	261	(14)
Salaries	150	152	(2)

Indirect materials	186	140	46
Purchased services	194	198	(4)
Depreciation	40	39	1
	817 —7	790 —7	27
Profit	432	505	73

First, note the way in which the variances have been displayed. In the extreme right-hand column, those variances which compare unfavourably with budget have been bracketed, while those which are favourable have been left unbracketed. This convention is widely used, and is the one we have chosen for this chapter. (In some businesses, variances from budget are shown by pluses or minuses.) It should be noted that *expenditure* in excess of budget is always unfavourable, while *sales* in excess of budget are always favourable. The variances move in opposite directions, since expenditure goes out of the business and sales revenue comes in.

What do the above figures mean? Senior management can see at a glance that profit was £73,000 better than budget (the profit variance), and that this result was achieved by underspending on materials, labour and overheads, which more than offset the lower than budgeted sales revenue. The business has therefore exceeded its short-term profit objectives, and to that extent its directors will probably be satisfied. There is however, a major question which the figures, as presented, do not answer: to what extent do the favourable (unbracketed) cost variances simply reflect lower production costs arising from lower sales, and to what extent do they reflect the efforts of management in controlling expenditure?

This question can be answered by employing a technique called *flexible budgeting*. It is based on the idea that some business costs remain relatively static even if the volume produced and sold fluctuates. Examples of costs behaving in this way are rates, depreciation, office/management salaries and computer hire costs. These are called *fixed costs*, while those which fluctuate in line with production and sales are called *variable costs*. Variable costs include production labour and the materials that go into the finished product as well as those overheads which move in proportion to production. The fuel used to drive machines is a case in point.

Flexible budgeting requires that the budgeted costs for the period be broken into their fixed and variable elements. After this has been done budgeted variable costs are altered in proportion to the volume difference between budget and actual production or sales, producing a revised budget. Variances are then recalculated to show the differences arising from factors other than volume. The process of altering the budget figures in this way is referred to as 'flexing' the budget. The figures given above will now be subjected to this procedure.

STAGE 1 – SPLIT BUDGET OVERHEADS INTO FIXED AND VARIABLE

Maintenance wages relate to non-productive workers whose number does not tend to vary in line with production; this item will therefore be treated as fixed. The same applies to salaries. On examination it is found that the *indirect materials* item is related closely to production and is the cost of consumable stores used in proportion to the volume produced. It will be treated as a variable cost. *Purchased services* contain a number of hire, rental and service costs which do not move in line with volume and are therefore fixed. *Depreciation*, as discussed above, falls into the same category.

STAGE 2 – ALTER (FLEX) VARIABLE BUDGET FIGURES IN PROPORTION TO VOLUME, THEN RECALCULATE VARIANCES

In the absence of any other indicators of volume, sales will be used:

*Profit and loss account
for period 1 19xx*

£000s		Budget	Actual	Variance fav (unfav.)
Sales		2,440	2,440	—
less Cost of sales				
Materials		1,031	976	55
Labour		190	169	21
Gross margin		1,219	1,295	76
less Overheads				
Maint. wages (F)	247	261	(14)	
Salaries (F)	150	152	(2)	
Indirect materials (note 1) (V)	182	140	42	
Purchased services (F)	194	198	(4)	
Depreciation (F)	40	39	1	
		813	790	23
Profit		406	505	99

Note:
(1)   Indirect materials are calculated as follows:

$$(2,440 \times 186) \div 2,556 = 182.$$

The flexed budget produces variances quite different to the unamended 'fixed' budget. We can now see that cost performance was favourable, with the exception of fixed overheads. This category should be investigated to explain the adverse variances, which may arise from inadequate levels of price increases being built into the budget, or from some other relatively uncontrollable factor. There are several possible explanations for the favourable cost variances. Perhaps the mix of products sold was different from the budget mix, and involved a lower material or labour expenditure per unit sold. Perhaps the cost increases for materials and labour built into the budget were more generous than necessary. While underlying factors such as these should be established, management would, however, tend to concentrate on any unfavourable variances (management by exception).

An example of a departmental budget statement will now be given.

EXAMPLE

Plant Engineering Department
Monthly overhead report for period 3, 19XX

£000s	Budget			Actual	Variance B (W)
	F	*V*	*Total*	*Total*	
Maintenance materials	67	33	100	120	(20)
Maintenance services	30	30	60	75	(15)
Coal, coke, fuel	170	30	200	165	35
Maintenance wages	650	350	1,000	1,150	(150)
Salaries	50	—	50	49	1
Electricity	20	30	50	35	15
Gas	5	8	13	9	4
Totals	992	481	1,473	1,603	(130)

Budget production standard hours – 59,352
Actual production standard hours – 39,568

This time the budget will be 'flexed' using standard hours produced, a measure of production which converts components produced into the *target* time allowed for them. This is a good measure of volume, but is only available when sophisticated work measurement systems are in operation. Flexing on this basis, the statement would be altered as follows:

Plant Engineering Department
Monthly overhead report
for period 3 19XX

£000s	Flexed budget (note 1)			Actual	Variance fav. (unfav.)
	F	*V*	*Total*	*Total*	
Maintenance materials	67	22	89	120	(31)
Maintenance services	30	20	50	75	(25)
Coal, coke, fuel	170	20	190	165	25
Maintenance wages	650	233	883	1,150	(267)
Salaries	50	—	50	49	1
Electricity	20	20	40	35	5
Gas	5	6	11	9	2
	992	321	1,313	1,603	(290)

Note:
(1) The variable costs have been factored down by

$$39,560 \div 59,352, \text{ that is, } \frac{2}{3}.$$

Maintenance materials, services and wages are decidedly overspent in a period of low activity. The plant engineering manager would be expected to explain this. Rather than pointing to inefficiency, there might be a perfectly good reason for such figures emerging. If, for example, a major breakdown had occurred in the production area, maintenance activity and cost would rise dramatically, while fuel costs associated with the production process would decline in line with output.

The third level of budget reporting, looking at the performance of individual units of production, will now be shown.

EXAMPLE

Motor car Type A
Monthly cost report,
period 5 19XX

	Budget	Actual	Variance
Sales value	£5,000	4,925	(75)
Material cost	2,100	1,997	103
Labour cost	655	701	(46)
Overhead cost	1,714	1,540	174
Period profit	531	687	156

In this case, it is not necessary to flex the budget, since all figures relate to one unit of production, a motor car. It can be seen that product A, while it is attracting a lower selling price than anticipated, is more profitable than the budget because of lower material and overhead costs. Management would address themselves principally to investigating and rectifying the adverse variances. Can price be increased? Can labour cost be reduced, or is the increase a by-product of the last wage negotiation?

Variance analysis

An alternative approach to the analysis of variances in the profit and loss account will now be examined. Its purpose is to separate those variances related to volume from those related to price and cost. The technique depends on the provision of unit cost and price data as well as total figures.

EXAMPLE
The following information is available for a company:

Profit and loss account
for period 2 19XX

	Budget	Actual	Variance fav. (unfav.)
Sales	£150,000	155,610	5,610
less Cost of sales			
Materials	40,000	42,237	(2,237)
Labour	20,000	23,342	(3,342)
Variable overheads	20,000	21,119	(1,119)
Fixed overheads	20,000	20,000	—
Profit	50,000	48,912	(1,088)

Unit data:

	Budget	Actual
Sales units	10,000	11,115
Selling Price	£15	£14
Material cost	4	3.80
Labour cost	2	2.10
Variable overheads	2	1.90

The *sales variance* will be broken into two components, *sales quantity variance* (the units difference × budgeted selling price) and *sales price variance* (actual units sold × the price difference).

The *material variance* consists of *material usage variance* (the units difference × budget cost) and the *material price variance* (actual units × the cost difference).

The *labour variance* again has two components, *labour efficiency variance* (the units difference × budget cost) and *labour rate variance* (actual units × the cost difference).

The *variable overhead variance* likewise breaks into a volume component (the units difference × budget cost) and a cost component (actual units × the cost difference).

Employing these definitions, the total variance can be analysed as follows:

	Total variance	Volume variances	Price variances
Sales	£ 5,610	16,725	(11,115)
Materials	(2,237)	(4,460)	2,223
Labour	(3,342)	(2,230)	(1,112)
Variable overheads	(1,119)	(2,230)	1,111
Fixed overheads	—	—	—
Profit	£(1,088)	7,805	(8,893)

It will perhaps be appreciated that flexing the budget would give the same result:

	Flexed budget	Actual	Price/cost variances
Sales (11,115 × £15)	£166,725	155,610	(11,115)
Materials (11,115 × £4)	44,460	42,237	2,223
Labour (11,115 × £2)	22,230	23,342	(1,112)
Variable overheads (11,115 × £2)	22,230	21,119	1,111
Fixed overheads	20,000	20,000	—
Profit	57,805	48,912	(8,893)

This latter presentation of the effects of volume on the profit is not so explicit as the first. The 'variance analysis' approach lets management see at a glance that £7,805 has been gained by selling more units than budgeted, and that £8,893 has been lost as a result of inability to achieve budgeted selling prices and cost targets, in spite of good performance against budget on material and variable overhead costs. They are thus in a better position to judge what steps they should take to improve the situation in later periods.

Conclusion

The techniques given above embody the main principles of variance reporting and analysis. In practice, however, many sophistications and variations of approach can be found. It is possible, for example, to isolate the variances arising from differences between budgeted inflation and the levels actually experienced, or to calculate the effects of product mix alterations on variances. These refinements help management to identify and tackle variances caused by internal slackness rather than extraneous factors, although it can be argued that in some cases the latter can also be controlled.

Finally, a good system of budgetary control will satisfy the following criteria:

- Reports, expensive to produce and time consuming to read, should be sufficient in number to highlight all significant variances. The level of analysis should reflect the relative importance of the figures and the accountabilities operating within the management structure. The danger of there being too many reports and too much detail ('paralysis by analysis') should be avoided.
- The reports must also be timely. The fundamental principle involved is the identification of problems at the earliest opportunity so that they can be corrected immediately thereafter. Computerization has been a great help in this respect. It is now easy and relatively cheap to buy proprietary software packages containing budgetary control facilities. As an alternative, software houses can develop tailor-made packages to meet an organization's exact reporting requirements. In both cases, the actual expenditure information comes from computerized financial accounts, usually part of the same software package. It should never be forgotten that the reports are not an end in themselves. Unless the variances are followed up through a system of regular management meetings and corrective action taken, the whole point is lost.

Questions

12.1   Are all unfavourable variances from budget necessarily bad? Discuss.

12.2   Explain the difference between a *fixed* and a *flexible* budget, indicating how each is used.

12.3   What is the purpose of budget review meetings? How should they be run?

12.4   Outline the features of a good system of budgetary control.

12.5   The chief executive of your company is not impressed with your proposal to introduce a system of budgetary control. He argues that 'We seem to have done quite well without it, and I'm reluctant to approve the expenditure necessary to implement such a system.'
In your capacity as company accountant, explain the mechanics and benefits of budgetary control to him, answering the specific points he raises.

12.6   Rework the budget in the undernoted statement by converting it to a 'flexible' basis, and then recalculate the variances.

Schinkel Ltd
Profit and loss account
for period 1, 19xx

£000s	Budget	Actual	Variance
Sales	35,406	32,656	(2,750)
Cost of sales			
Materials	11,595	12,314	(719)
Labour	8,963	7,968	995
Gross margin	14,848	12,374	(2,474)
Expenses			
Indirect labour	998	1,014	(16)
Salaries	1,451	1,427	24
Indirect materials	2,569	2,400	169
Services	1,372	1,395	(23)
Depreciation	550	564	(14)
Profit	7,908	5,574	(2,334)

Notes:
(1) Sales may be taken as the best indicator of volume for flexing purposes.
(2) Indirect labour and salaries are fixed.
(3) 50% of indirect materials relate to planned maintenance activities, while the other 50% fluctuate in proportion to sales.
(4) Services are 80% fixed, 20% variable.
(5) Depreciation is Fixed.

12.7 The production control department manager has received the budget statement given below for period 3 of the budget year. Since the firm produced 20% more than budget during the period, he feels that comparison with a fixed budget does not do his department justice. As the factory accountant, you agree, and undertake to prepare a comparison of his actual expenditure with a flexible budget for discussion. Work out the figures.

Production control department
Budget statement
period 3

	Budget	Actual	Variance
Progress – salaries	£ 5,000	4,650	350
Material control – salaries	3,500	3,908	(408)
Production control – salaries	2,750	2,804	(54)
Overtime premiums	575	907	(332)
Employee benefits	3,950	3,681	269
Computer costs	1,750	1,800	(50)
Miscellaneous costs	750	700	50
	£18,275	18,450	(175)

Notes:
(1) Treat 80% of all salaries as fixed.
(2) Overtime premiums and miscellaneous costs are both variable.

12.8 From the figures given below, calculate the *sales quantity and price variances*, the *material usage and price variances*, the *labour efficiency and rate variances*, and identify the *volume and cost variances* pertaining to overheads.

Trumbauer Ltd
Profit and loss account
for the period to 31 March 19xx

	Budget	Actual	Variance
Sales	£332,500	354,461	21,961
less Cost of sales			
Materials	£147,000	156,327	(9,327)
Labour	43,750	47,262	(3,512)
Variable overheads	40,250	39,991	259
Fixed overheads	75,125	75,125	—
Profit	£ 26,375	35,756	9,381

Unit Data

	Budget	Actual
Sales units	35,000	36,355
Selling price	£9.50	9.75
Material cost	4.20	4.30
Labour cost	1.25	1.30
Variable overheads	1.15	1.10

Note: variances should be rounded to the nearest £.

13 Costing

Definition

Costing, sometimes referred to as *cost finding*, is simply the calculation of the costs of individual units of product or service. It differs from financial accounting and budgetary control in that it does not deal with the finances of whole firms or sections of them; costing looks at the unit of production. It has a multiplicity of uses. In the previous two chapters, unit costs were used for budget calculation and variance analysis. Other uses to which costs can be put include:

- Providing a 'base line' to help establish selling prices for products or services.
- Enabling the profitability of products or services to be measured over time by comparing changing costs with changing selling prices.
- Helping in the search for improved profitability by highlighting potential savings.
- Providing data for financial studies of various kinds, such as the evaluation of capital expenditure proposals.

These will be examined in more detail later.

Technique

As a first step in establishing what products or services actually cost, accountants have found it useful to *classify*, or categorize, the various types of business expense passing through the accounts. This makes the calculation of unit costs easier and ensures that they can be put to maximum use. In manufacturing businesses (the model chosen for this chapter) it is standard practice to break business costs into *direct material*, *direct labour* and *overheads or expenses*. These terms will now be explained.

DIRECT MATERIAL

Direct material is the material which goes into, or becomes part of, the finished product. If a firm manufactures desks, then the wood and metal of which they are made is a *direct material cost*. The term is not applied to retail businesses. The costs of products sold in a shop would simply be referred to as 'cost of goods sold' or 'cost of sales'.

DIRECT LABOUR

Direct labour is the cost of production wages related to the manufacture of a unit of product or service. Again, this term does not apply to retail or non-manufacturing businesses.

OVERHEADS (EXPENSES)

These might simply be defined as those other business costs which do not fit into the above two categories, hence their description as 'indirect costs' in the context of manufacturing firms. It is also common practice to break overheads into at least two categories: *manufacturing overheads* and *selling and administration*. Examples of overheads include depreciation, salaries, maintenance costs, computer hire costs and employee welfare costs.

It should be noted at this stage that the way in which the direct material and labour costs are gathered together will depend on the nature of the manufacturing process being carried out. Some businesses are involved in *job* or *contract* operations, that is, producing a piece of tailor-made work to a customer's special requirements. Examples range from body repair on a motor car to the building of a ship or a large piece of specially designed machinery. Other businesses manufacture *batches* of components, such as metal castings, steel tubes or even loaves of bread, the distinctive characteristic being the simultaneous production of multiple units. Alternatively, some businesses pass raw materials in bulk through a series of *processes* which might involve wastage or loss at various stages. Examples include the manufacture of chemicals and the production of plastics or their derivatives, such as floor covering. It is also perfectly possible to produce a product by means of combinations of the above methods.

In each case, the broad principles of costing will be the same; it will be necessary to establish the direct materials required and the direct labour times relating to the product from internal sources and then find a suitable method of assigning a share of overheads to the product. Fortunately, most products or jobs need to be engineered, planned or estimated prior to production and this generates a variety of documentation which is also useful to the accountant for costing.

Direct materials required will be listed by part number, description and quantity on engineering specifications, drawings or production planning sheets of some kind or another. There is no uniformity in this area, and the documents can be given a variety of names such as specifications, bills of material or more simply, parts lists. In a well-organized firm, the various operations by direct workers will also be listed in detail on internal documentation which will vary in layout and nomenclature depending on the use to which it is being put. Examples include work study forms and bonus sheets. In the more sophisticated firms, both material specifications and labour data will be held in computer files.

Given that this information is available, the costing of direct material or labour will simply amount to multiplying the various parts or operations by the relevant up-to-date costs, with appropriate allowances (usually based on average historical experience) for scrap, wastage or unproductive time. In the exercises which follow later in the chapter, it will normally be taken for granted that these simple mechanical computations have been carried out.

Overheads

The treatment of overheads in the building up of unit costs is not so straight-forward. Relatively few overhead expenses can be directly related to the production of a single unit of output; how much of the depreciation on the office buildings 'belongs' to a single unit produced or to each production department? The exception is job or contract costing, where the sheer size and diversity of the tasks undertaken make this easier. In a shipyard, it will be possible to tie up many of the invoices received for overheads to the individual contracts in progress. The process of assigning costs in their entirety to specific jobs, contracts or departments in this fashion is called *allocation*.

Where this is not possible, it will be necessary to *apportion* overheads, that is, to divide them up between products or departments in proportions that are felt to be reasonably fair. This is done by approximation, sharing overheads out pro rata to floor area, numbers employed or some other indicator of usage. Once allocation and apportionment have been attended to, it is then necessary to devise methods of loading total overheads into product costs. This is again done by approximation through the use of *absorption* rates, which are often developed using budget data.

A number of approaches are possible. Absorption rates can be expressed as a percentage of direct labour cost or direct labour hours. On the other hand, if it were felt that the expenditure on overheads was more dependent on the amount of direct material handled (perfectly possible in a mechanical process industry), then an overhead absorption rate based on direct material could be devised. It is even possible, where it is judged to be appropriate to the business, to develop absorption rates based on prime (direct) cost. In mechanical engineering businesses, overhead absorption rates may even be based on machine hours. The level of sophistication required depends on the amount which a company is prepared to spend on costing. There are no norms. All that is required is that absorption rates are rationally based. The example which follows demonstrates the principles outlined above.

EXAMPLE

The following list of budget overheads is available for XYZ Ltd:

Indirect wages	£25,000
Employee benefits	15,000
Salaries	10,000
Salaried benefits	3,000
Maintenance materials	5,000
Heat, light, power	10,000
Rates	20,000
Depreciation	3,000
Miscellaneous	2,000
Total	£93,000

XYZ has two production departments, Machining and Assembly, for which the following information is available:

	Machining	Assembly
Direct workers	3	2
Indirect workers	3	2
Last year's maintenance costs	70%	30%
Floor area	1,000 sq ft	2,500 sq ft
Asset values	£12,000	£9,000

The proposed expenditure in the 'miscellaneous' category relates to a computer project undertaken to streamline production in the Assembly shop. It has been decided that separate absorption rates are to be established for Machining and Assembly areas, the firm's two 'cost areas'. Apportionment of overheads is to be based on fair methods. Further analysis of the budget overhead figures is not possible. The overheads might be allocated and apportioned as follows:

	Machining	Assembly	Basis chosen
Indirect wages	£15,000	10,000	No. of workers (3/2)
Employee benefits	9,000	6,000	Total workers (6/4)
Salaries	6,000	4,000	Total workers (6/4)
Salaried benefits	1,800	1,200	Total workers (6/4)
Maint. materials	3,500	1,500	Last year
Heat, light, power	2,857	7,143	Floor area
Rates	5,714	14,286	Floor area
Depreciation	1,714	1,286	Asset values
Miscellaneous	—	2,000	
Totals	45,585	47,415	

XYZ must now decide on a basis for *absorption* rates. The following information has been made available for the budget year:

(a)   Direct hours: Machining 5,000, Assembly 3,000.
(b)   Direct wages: Machining £20,000, Assembly £14,000. *(i.e.w.)*
(c)   Machine hours: 40,000.

The possibilities suggesting themselves are therefore:

(1)   Rate per direct labour hour.
(2)   Rate per £1 direct labour cost.
(3)   Machine-hour rate.

(These have been suggested because they can easily be developed from the available information.)

(1)   If a rate per direct labour hour is chosen, the following absorption rates would be calculated:

$$\text{Machining: } \frac{\text{£45,585}}{5,000} = \text{£9.12 per direct labour hour}$$

$$\text{Assembly: } \frac{\text{£47,415}}{3,000} = \text{£15.81 per direct labour hour}$$

(2) If a rate per £1 direct labour cost is chosen, the rates would be as follows:

$$\text{Machining: } \frac{\text{£45,585}}{\text{£20,000}} = 228\%$$

$$\text{Assembly: } \frac{\text{£47,415}}{14,000} = 339\%$$

(3) If a machine-hour rate is chosen (this is only possible for Machining), it would be:

$$\frac{\text{£45,585}}{40,000} = \text{£1.14 per machine-hour}$$

Each of the above are *alternatives*, and it is possible to have permutations – for example, a machine-hour rate for Machining and an Assembly rate based on £1 direct labour cost. A cost will now be built up using these rates

The following information is available for a product currently made by XYZ Ltd:

Direct materials:	£14.40
Direct labour:	30 minutes machine time
	£1 Machine shop wages
	£2 Assembly shop wages
Overheads:	Machine shop overhead is to be calculated on a machine-hour basis, Assembly on each £ of labour cost

Material (M)	14.50
Labour (L)	3.00 . (machine + Assembly shop wages)
Overheads (0)	
M/C (0.5 hr × £1.14)	0.57
Assy (339% × £2)	6.78
Total cost	£24.85

It should be noted that if the basis of the overhead absorption rates were different, then product costs would differ. If the rate were based on direct labour hours, the product would cost:

MATERIAL	£14.50
LABOUR	3.00
OVERHEAD	
M/c $\dfrac{£1}{£20,000/5,000} \times £9.12$	2.28
Assy $\dfrac{£2}{£14,000/3,000} \times £15.81$	6.79
Total cost	£26.57

Similarly, if the overhead absorption rates were based on direct labour cost, the following answer would be given:

M	£14.50
L	3.00
O	
M/c 228% × £1	2.28
Assy 339% × £2	6.78
Total cost	£26.56

It should also be noted that it is not necessary to develop separate overhead absorption rates for Machining and Assembly. A combined or total rate could be developed by dividing total budget overheads by either direct labour cost or hours. Using labour cost, the rate would be:

$$\frac{£93,000}{£34,000} = 274\%$$

The product would then cost:

M	£14.50
L	3.00
O	
£3 × 274%	8.22
Total cost	£25.72

We have now developed *four* different costs using the same information, simply by choosing different types of absorption rates. This has been done to show that the treatment of overheads is the most subjective area in costing, and to emphasize that costing, like accounting itself, is not an exact science. None of the approaches is the 'right' one. However, it should be understood that, whichever type of absorption rate is chosen, the aggregate amount of overheads charged to all products will be the same in each case, even although *individual* product costs will differ under different systems of absorption.

Which methods should a firm choose? There is no easy answer. A range of factors must be taken into account, including the questions of convenience, logic, consistency and cost. Sophistication must be balanced against the 'cost

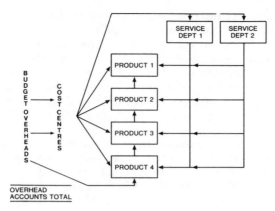

Figure 13.1

of costing', although the two can be reconciled where the computer is used. Costing, with its emphasis on detail and complex arithmetic calculations, is catered for in many of the financial software packages now on offer. Tailor-made systems can also be provided by the software houses if the proprietary systems do not suit.

It will be appreciated that the XYZ example was greatly simplified in order to bring out the principles. In practice, many firms will have more than two cost areas, and within these, a great many cost centres, in order to monitor costs in detail. Allocation/apportionment of overheads might be done by account heading, of which there could easily be several hundred. Where the budgeted overhead accounts are backed up by detailed cost-centre budgets, indicating where, in detail, money is spent, this facilitates the allocation of overheads to cost area or product. Where there are service departments such as the power station or the maintenance department, it will be possible, if required, to apportion some of the overheads to the service department before finally re-apportioning the service department itself to cost area or product so that absorption rates can be built up.

Figure 13.1 shows how budget overheads might be allocated/apportioned in order to produce totals applicable to each of the four products involved. There are two service departments, and the budgeted overheads accounts have been prepared in the first instance from detailed cost-centre budgets. The cost-centre expenditure is allocated to products or to the service departments; any general accounts such as depreciation are allocated/ apportioned to product or service department and the service department itself is allocated to product or cost area.

The resultant totals collected against each product (or cost area) can now be used for the calculation of absorption rates by applying a suitable denominator.

Some final notes on overheads

In the examples above, budgeted overheads were used to devise absorption rates and build up product costs. Other approaches are possible. Historic (actual) overheads from prior years can also be used, provided the structure of the business has not changed radically. Obviously, if it has, then past overheads no longer reflect the present cost structure. It is for this very reason that many businesses prefer to work on a budgeted overheads basis. If they do, then the denominator used in devising the absorption rate must also be based on budget information. It should also be noted that abnormal 'once-off' overhead charges appearing either in historical or budgeted expense totals must be omitted from absorption calculations since they distort costs.

It is inevitable that the total amount of overheads built into product costs will not exactly match the actual overhead expenses incurred in any one period. If the total absorbed into actual units sold is greater than actual overheads incurred, then the firm will have made more profit than antici-pated. In this situation, overheads are said to have been 'over-absorbed'. The reverse is also true. If actual overheads incurred in a period exceed overheads absorbed by those units sold, then overheads are said to be 'under-absorbed' or 'under-recovered'. In this case the firm will have made less profit than anticipated. It is therefore necessary to monitor the position so that adjustments to selling price can if required be made

Costing in action

Firms will develop costs at different times. It is good practice to establish the costs of new products in advance of production to check that they will be profitable. Indeed, it is normal in the motor industry to set maximum cost targets for new models at the design stage, since the market niche they are intended to fill will limit the selling price they are able to command. If necessary, specifications can be altered to reduce costs prior to production. In these circumstances, when a product is at the prototype or pre-production stage, full engineering or price information may not be available, in which case estimates will need to be worked out in conjunction with design, engineering or purchasing staff.

The mainstream use of costing relates to the comparison of *established* product costs, as they increase over time, with selling prices.

In the jobbing or contracting industries, costs will be worked out *before* commencement of production, usually for tendering or quotation purposes. Once the contract is awarded, the costing staff will then compute actual costs as they are incurred, comparing them (for control purposes) with the original estimates. They will also produce accounting statements which show cumu-lative costs to date, expected future costs to complete contracts and a comparison of expected totals with the original estimates. Management will then be in a position to judge the likely profitability of contracts as the projects progress, taking any remedial action thought to be necessary.

Standard costing

In Chapter 12, budgeted unit costs were compared on budget statements with actual costs, for control purposes. These budgeted costs could equally have been described as standard costs. In practice, the terms are virtually interchangeable, although some theorists would argue that the term *budget* is more appropriate for the planned costs of whole companies, functions or departments and the term *standard* for the planned costs of units of product or service.

There are two main approaches in the setting of standard or budget costs. The first of these is the *ideal standard* approach. Under this method, the costs are established on the principle that the target costs for the product should reflect the most efficient working practices and production methods possible in making the product. Comparisons with actual cost during the budget year will reveal how far short of realizing its potential the company is.

The second approach involves the production of *attainable standards*. The underlying principle here is that budget costs should be 'hard but achievable'. Present shop-floor practices and operator efficiency form the starting point for the creation of attainable standards. Those cost and efficiency improvements which are considered to be achievable during the budget year are then incorporated.

EXAMPLE

Nunzio Ltd makes its sole product rather inefficiently. The management are not sure whether to set an ideal standard or an attainable standard for the budget year. The accountant has prepared both, giving the following cost figures:

	Ideal standard	Attainable standard	Current actual
M	£50	52	55
L	7	9	11
VO	14	18	22
FO	20	20	20
Total	£91	99	108

Efficiency improvements are made during the budget year, and the actual cost of the product at period 2 is as follows:

M	£53
L	8
VO	16
FO	20
	£97

If the ideal standard had been chosen, the comparison on the monthly product cost statement would have been:

	Standard cost	Actual cost	Variance
M	£50	53	(3)
L	7	8	(1)
VO	14	16	(2)
FO	20	20	—
Total	£91	97	(6)

If the attainable standard had been set, the comparison would have shown:

	Standard cost	Actual cost	Variance
M	£52	53	(1)
L	9	8	1
VO	18	16	2
FO	20	20	—
Total	£99	97	2

Which is best? Those in favour of ideal standards argue that it is important to stamp out complacency as well as inefficiency, and that the adverse variances are a constant reminder of the task that still lies ahead. Those in favour of attainable standards argue that it is important not to set impossible tasks, since management, faced with adverse variances on their budget reports, will become demotivated and cynical.

The company's managerial culture will have a bearing on the type of standard chosen. In 'task oriented' companies where management emphasize their 'right to manage' and accountability is stressed, the ideal standard might be chosen. In companies which are more 'people-oriented', the attainable standard might be chosen. A third option is chosen in some firms. The budget statement contains both an ideal and an attainable standard. Variances are worked out against the attainable standard, but the ideal standard appears on the page as a reminder that there is still scope for improvement.

When setting standard costs, whichever method is chosen, management should consider some or all of the following questions as they relate to the budget year:

MATERIAL

(a) Can this be purchased from suppliers at a cheaper price either by sourcing it elsewhere or by buying larger, and therefore cheaper, batches?

(b) Can scrappage be reduced or eliminated, perhaps by improving material handling methods or equipment, retraining operators or providing better tools and machinery?

DIRECT LABOUR

(a) Can operators be induced to work more efficiently, either by increasing bonus for more output, or by eliminating waiting time or breakdowns, or by better supervision?

(b) Would more careful quality control of materials bring about the elimination of scrapped work in progress?
(c) Will the industrial engineering/work study team, if any, be able to identify more efficient methods of working?
(d) Will restrictive practices, if any, continue?

OVERHEADS

(a) Can expenses be better controlled through the introduction of requisition systems on the shop-floor, or by improving those already existing?
(b) What can be done to eliminate pilferage?
(c) Is energy (heat, light, power) being used efficiently?
(d) Can in-house services, such as a canteen, be provided by an outsider for a cheaper price? Is the reverse the case?

No system of standards and budgets will improve performance in its own right. It will only help insofar as it generates questions such as these and only then when action follows.

Cost behaviour

In the chapter on budget reporting, the distinction between fixed and variable costs was briefly mentioned. Since this distinction is a most useful tool in business and will feature in some of the techniques introduced in the next chapter, it is appropriate to examine it more closely at this point.

What are fixed costs? As indicated before, these are the costs which tend not to fluctuate in line with increases or decreases in the volume produced. The word 'tend' was deliberately used since matters are not quite so simple. The first qualification to the concept of fixed costs that we must make concerns the range of output over which it can be said that costs do not move. Obviously, a radical change in the level of output will affect fixed costs. If a plant is producing to the limit of its capacity, perhaps 24 hours a day, and making maximum use of its production space, then clearly it could not produce more without an extension of the physical facilities and possibly also the workforce. When this happens there will be more depreciation, more rates to pay, and so on. Conversely, if the volume produced reduces drastically, it will be sensible to decommission facilities and perhaps sell part of the plant. In cases like this, fixed costs clearly drop. This is what is meant by the term *relevant range*. Accountants have long recognized that fixed costs remain static provided the volume of production stays within bands which do not affect the basic fabric of the business. *Relevant range* may be shown graphically, as in Figure 13.2.

As output reaches the top of each relevant range, fixed costs increase.

Even within the relevant range, matters are not straightforward. Mention must be made at this point of *semi-variable* costs. These are costs which are part fixed and part variable. The classic example is the telephone bill, which is made up of fixed hire and rental charges, and a component relating to the cost of calls. As the number of calls increases, the proportions of fixed and variable cost change. Another example is maintenance cost. While some

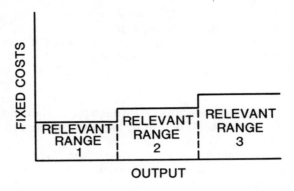

Figure 13.2

parts of maintenance cost alter in line with production (the element related to the repair of machines), other parts will not change (the element relating to planned maintenance). This can be shown graphically, as in Figure 13.3.

Another example of a cost not behaving in a strictly linear fashion is direct or indirect material purchases subject to bulk discounts. In cases where increased quantities qualify for discounts, there might be a slight fall in total cost as quantities increase. Where this coincides with the need to purchase a minimum quantity, the cost behaviour graph would be drawn as in Figure 13.4.

It will be seen in the next chapter that, generally speaking, it still suits businesses to work on the assumption that costs are either *fixed* or *variable*. This distinction lies behind two techniques that will be introduced, *marginal costing* and *breakeven analysis*. These are very useful but not precise techniques, and it would be unrealistic to try and cater for the relatively minor effects of those costs with irregular patterns when operating them.

SEMI-VARIABLE COSTS

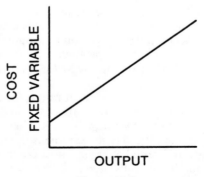

Figure 13.3

"BULK DISCOUNTS" COST BEHAVIOUR

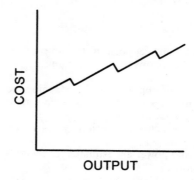

Figure 13.4

Questions

13.1 Distinguish between *allocation*, *apportionment* and *absorption* in relation to costing, stating why these techniques are important.

13.2 It has been argued that there is no such thing as an accurate cost for any product or service. Do you agree? Why might such an assertion have been made, and, if it is true, does it mean that costing is pointless?

13.3 The production manager at your plant has described the standard costs calculated for each of his products as 'completely unrealistic if not impossible to attain'. The standards have been prepared on an 'ideal' basis.

(a) Why might the standard costs have been prepared in this way?
(b) Explain an alternative approach to the setting of standards.

13.4 In establishing budget, or standard, product costs for the forthcoming budget period, where might management look for improvements, and how can they be achieved?

13.5 List four possible methods of absorbing overheads into product costs, explaining in what circumstances each might be appropriate.

13.6 The information given below relates to the budget year of RLT Ltd., a small business:

Machine shop – 10,000 machine hours.
Assembly shop – 15,000 man hours.

Budget overheads

Salaries	£ 7,500
Indirect wages	15,400
Maintenance	3,900
Depreciation machines	2,500
Depreciation assembly	1,000
Heat, light, power	6,000

Computer hire	2,750
Miscellaneous	1,960
	£41,010

Required: allocate and apportion the overheads to Machine shop and Assembly, using the following notes as a guide:

(a)   Salaries are to be apportioned 3/5 Machine shop, 2/5 Assembly shop.

(b)   Indirect employees' wage cost is estimated to relate 9/14 to Machine shop, 5/14 to Assembly shop.

(c)   Maintenance expense in previous years was 80% Machine shop, 20% Assembly.

(d)   Heat, light and power are estimated to relate 60% to Assembly, 40% to Machine shop.

(e)   All computer hire costs relate to a project connected with streamlining production in the Assembly shop.

(f)   'Miscellaneous' is to be apportioned 5/6 Machine shop, 1/6 Assembly shop.

13.7   Product C is made at RLT Ltd, the same company as above, and it has the following costs:

Direct material	£15
Direct labour – machining	6 (12 machine-hours)
Direct labour – Assembly	1 (20 minutes operator time)

Required:

(1)   Calculate the cost of product C. Machine shop overheads are to be recovered on the basis of machine-hours, and Assembly shop on the basis of man-hours. Selling and administration overheads of 150% of prime cost will apply.

(2)   Calculate the selling price of product C, which is to be based on cost plus 25%.

13.8   Blazeaway Fires Ltd manufactures a 1 kW electric fire for which the following information is available:

Material content

2 metres flex at	35p/metre
Sundries	75p
1.5 square metres mild steel sheet at £1.60 square metre	
2 fireclay formers at	£2.05 each
1 switch at	£2.16
Metal finishing (subcontracted)	£1.00 per fire
Wooden trim – 3 linear metres at	40p/metre
1 kw bar at	£1.90

Labour content

Fly press	2 mins at £2.50/hr	(1 minute machine time)
Guillotine	1 min. at £2.50/hr	(1/2 minute machine time)
Assembly	10 mins at £2.25/hr	
Finishing	6 mins at £2.25/hr	

Overhead content

The following additional information has been provided for the development of overhead absorption rates:

Fly press

Budgeted machine-hours	£2,000
Budgeted overheads	£4,000

Guillotine

Budgeted machine-hours	£ 500
Budgeted overheads	£1,150

Assembly

Budgeted direct labour	£10,000
Budgeted overheads	£15,800

Finishing

Budgeted direct labour	£3,000
Budgeted overheads	£6,750

Required: calculate the cost of a 1 kw electric fire, laying out your workings logically and neatly.

13.9 Mies Ltd manufactures high quality metal furniture in three departments, Machining, Assembly and Finishing. The following budgeted information is available for the forthcoming year:

Department	Overheads	Direct wages	Direct labour hours	Machine-hours
Machining	500,000	93,750	18,750	625,000
Assembly	250,000	450,000	100,000	125,000
Finishing	125,000	62,500	15,625	25,000

Finishing department overheads are absorbed over cost units on the basis of a percentage of direct wages, Machining department overheads on the basis of a machine-hour rate and Assembly department overheads on a rate per direct labour hour.

The company wishes to cost and price a new product, details of which are:

(a) Direct material cost: £75.
(b) Direct labour hours required: Machining 2 hrs; Assembly 2 hrs; Finishing 2 hrs.
(c) The estimated number of machine hours required in the Machining department is 15.
(d) An allowance is to be made for administration overheads on the basis of 10% of prime cost.
(e) Selling price is to be obtained by applying a 20% uplift to total costs.

Required: prepare appropriate overhead absorption rates then calculate the cost and selling price of the product.

13.10　Aaron Fire Ltd manufactures a hair drier for which the following information is available:

Material content

2 plastic mouldings at	30p each
1 motor at	£3.71
3 metres flex at	75p/metre
1 rotor at	73p
Sundries	65p

Scrap runs at 5%, for which a surcharge is added to material cost.

Labour content

Sub-assembly – 7 minutes
Final assembly – 5 minutes

Budget overheads

Indirect labour	£50,000
Indirect materials	21,000
Indirect services	19,200
Sundries	7,000
Total for year	£97,200

Overheads have historically been split 80 per cent sub-assembly, and 20 per cent final assembly. Budget information is available as follows for total direct labour costs and hours:

	Cost	Hours
Sub-assembly	£60,000	20,000
Final assembly	£10,000	2,800

Required:
(1)　Draw up a cost sheet and calculate the product cost, after working out the overhead rates, which are to be based on each £ of direct wages in each department.
(2)　What would the cost have been if sub-assembly and final assembly overheads had not been split and a total overhead rate had been calculated instead?
(3)　The selling price is to contain a profit margin of 30%. Work it out, based on your answer for (1).

14 Pricing and cost behaviour

Pricing methods

Businesses establish the prices they will charge for their products or services in a variety of ways, which include:

- 'Cost-plus' pricing.
- Market exploitation.
- Fee basis pricing.
- Marginal-cost-based pricing.

'Cost-plus'

'Cost-plus' pricing involves establishing the total cost of the product or service by the methods already outlined and then adding a profit margin. The profit margin may be expressed as a sum of money, where, for example, a firm may wish to make a specific profit on each unit sold. Alternatively, a percentage uplift, say 10% or 20%, may be added to total cost to give a selling price. The percentage uplift could be established in several ways: a customer might accept that his/her supplier is entitled to recover all costs and a 'reasonable' percentage on top as profit. In other words, the profit percentage may be agreed between the parties at the outset.

As an alternative, the supplier may well establish the percentage him/herself. Given that he/she has access to a figure of budgeted or forecast sales for the next financial year, he/she will be in a position to calculate the proportion of profit that he/she will require in order to receive an appropriate return on capital invested.

EXAMPLE

Average capital invested	£500,000
Forecast/budget annual sales	£1,000,000
Profit required (say 25% on capital invested)	£125,000

$\therefore$ Profit as a percentage of sales $\quad \dfrac{125,000}{£1,000,000} = 12.5\%$

$\therefore$ Profit as a percentage of cost ('mark-up' or 'uplift') $\quad \dfrac{125,000}{£1,000,000 - 125,000} = 14.3\%$

14.3% is therefore added to the estimated or actual costs of products to arrive at a selling price.

'Cost-plus' is normally only practised where the supplier is in a monopolistic position and the purchaser is unable to obtain alternative price quotations. Until recent times it was quite common in the defence industry and for ancillary work after the award of a major contract in the construction industry. It has been criticized along the lines that it encourages inefficiency; if the supplier's workforce or methods of operation are not as efficient as they might be, the extra cost is passed on to the customer, and the mark-up or uplift is proportionately larger.

Market exploitation

Market exploitation simply refers to the practice of charging what the market will stand. Where demand for a product is high and supply is limited, 'price skimming' is often attempted, that is, pushing prices as high as possible. Naturally enough competition will limit what can be charged, and excessive supply will exert downward pressure on prices and margins. Products and services may well have slightly different characteristics which, even in times of tough competition, will tend to ensure that price differentials are not eroded.

While the selling prices of some products will be kept close to costs by market forces, the selling prices of others will compensate by being well in excess of costs. The supplier must, however, ensure that the aggregate profit he/she makes over a period is sufficient for his/her requirements. He/she will therefore keep an eye on the profits yielded by each segment of the market, whether generated by volume sales or by high margins on a small number of units. The age of products must also be taken into account in establishing the price to be charged to the customer. If they are made to old designs and are becoming less competitive, prices will be forced downwards, the reverse applying to new designs. Constant comparisons of unit costs and selling prices, as they increase or decrease, is vital.

Fee basis pricing

In the case of very large engineering or construction projects, it would not be wise to quote the customer a fixed price at the outset. It would almost be impossible to estimate the total costs accurately and consequently difficult to establish a final selling price. The expedient of adding a huge margin to cover contingencies would result in prices which were unacceptable. In view of these difficulties many large contracts are carried out on a 'fee' basis. In essence this means that the contractor promises to carry out the project at whatever cost it takes in return for a fixed fee, or profit, payable at agreed intervals. In these circumstances, either the contractor may pay the bills him/herself and claim reimbursement from his/her client; or alternatively, the client will meet all costs directly and supply all materials directly to the site. Large petrochemical projects are frequently built on this basis, doubly necessary since they are often still being designed as construction proceeds.

Marginal costing

In the chapter on costing, the assumption was made that, in establishing costs of products or services, it was necessary to include *all* costs. This approach is referred to as *absorption costing* or *full costing*. There are, however, situations where it is preferable to exclude part of the total costs in making pricing and other business decisions.

Marginal costing is the term applied to this approach, which involves the omission of fixed costs from unit costs. Fixed costs are not forgotten, but are considered separately. Fixed costs, referred to in Chapters 11 and 12, are those which do not tend to fluctuate with the volume produced or sold, and are invariably overhead costs. In most businesses they are easy to identify: the finance staff can isolate total fixed costs in the profit and loss account or in the budgeted overheads, and the absorption rates can even be split into fixed and variable elements.

The simple idea behind marginal costing is that the difference between the variable cost of a product and its sales revenue is available to make a *contribution* to fixed overheads and profit. In certain circumstances it will be advisable to continue to make and sell products which do not contribute their full share of fixed costs. As long as some contribution, even a fairly small one, is made to fixed costs, the product will be worthwhile. To discontinue production and sales would result in lost contribution, which would reduce profits since fixed overheads would still be incurred at their previous level.

EXAMPLE

Product A sells for £15, and it is expected that 1,000 units will be sold in the financial year. Fixed costs relating to this product are £3,000 per annum and its variable costs are as follows:

Direct materials	£5
Direct labour	2
Variable overheads	2

News has also been received from the sales staff that there has been a sudden increase in overseas competition in product A's market and that it can now only be sold for £11. Should the product be continued?

ANSWER

The product, at £11, still generates a contribution:

SV *value*	£11
less: M ⎫	5 ⎫
L ⎬ *variable costs*	2 ⎬ 9
VO ⎭	2 ⎭
Contribution	£2

Assuming 1,000 can still be sold, total contribution would be £2,000, leaving only £1,000 in fixed overheads to be met. This is preferable to discontinuing the product, which would result in £3,000 in fixed overheads still being incurred. It should therefore be sold at £11.

However, if product A were the only product sold by the company, an absolute loss of £1,000 would appear in the profit and loss account, in which case the proprietors might decide to stop trading. The decision to continue product A would be perfectly sound in normal circumstances, where it was only one of a range of more profitable products which generated enough surplus to offset the absolute loss of £1,000 it still made.

The workings of marginal costing can be illustrated in another way. Suppose a company has three departments, each making a single product, and that the following figures have been abstracted for the financial year:

Product	A	B	C	£000s	Totals
sales	5,000	6,000	5,400		16,400
Materials	1,000	2,000	1,500		4,500
Labour	500	400	600		1,500
Prime cost	1,500	2,400	2,100		6,000
Gross margin	3,500	3,600	3,300		10,400
Variable overheads	700	800	900		2,400
Contribution	2,800	2,800	2,400		8,000
Fixed overheads	1,800	3,300	2,000		7,100
Profit (loss)	1,000	(500)	400		900

The analysis shows clearly that B is making a loss, leading to the conclusion that it is not commercially sensible to keep on producing it. This reasoning is mistaken, since to discontinue the product would result in a lost contribution of £2,800. Fixed overheads would remain, giving the following revised totals:

Profit if product B discontinued

	Contribution	Fixed overheads	Profit (loss)
A	2,800	1,800	1,000
B	—	3,300	(3,300)
C	2,400	2,000	400
	5,200	7,100	(1,900)

The lost contribution from product B, £2,800, takes the profit of £900 down to a loss of (£1,900) because of fixed overheads, and it would therefore make sense to keep product B.

In practice other factors would have to be looked at if B were to be continued. Is there any scope for price increases? Can production costs – that is, direct material, labour or variable overheads – be reduced through the introduction of more economical methods of working such as rationalized work layout, better flow of products, engineering modifications, reduced wastage or greater operator efficiency? If this were possible, contribution would be increased, producing a smaller overall loss for the product and a larger overall profit for the company.

The question of discontinuing a product entirely is seldom made on financial grounds alone. Supposing the three products just discussed were three models of agricultural tractor, small, medium and large. If the firm discontinued a model, the tractor distributors selling this company's products would be at a disadvantage compared with distributors of other manufacturers' products, who would be able to offer a complete range to their customers. Products are often interdependent in this way.

Marginal costing is applied in many circumstances. Restaurants provide cheap 'businessmen's lunches' at little more than variable cost in order to make a contribution to fixed costs such as rent and rates. Cheap tariffs are offered in hotels at weekends for similar reasons, as are standby tickets on airlines. There may also be sound marketing reasons for pricing on a marginal costing basis. Customers may be encouraged to come back at times when the full rates are being charged.

Marginal costing can also be used to choose between alternative courses of action, as in the following example.

EXAMPLE

Company X maintains a production facility at a fixed cost of £50,000 per annum. 2,500 units of product Y are produced there each year. The following details are available for that product:

Sales value	£45
Direct materials	10
Direct labour	5
Variable overheads	3

Company X has been asked by Company Z to make a new component, V, at an annual volume of 5,000 units. Financial information for V has been calculated as follows:

Sales value	£27
Direct materials	4
Direct labour	2
Variable overheads	5

If the contract for the new product is accepted, it will not be possible to produce any units of product Y, since the whole facility will be taken up. Is it more profitable for company X to switch to product V?

ANSWER

	Product Y		*Product V*
Contribution per unit (45 − 18)	= £ 27	(27 − 11)	16
Total contribution (27 × 2500)	= 67,500	(16 × 5000)	= 80,000
less Fixed costs	50,000		50,000
Profit	£17,500		30,000

V is the more profitable option.

A third application of marginal costing lies in the area of 'make vs buy' decisions. Where a component or a complete product can be purchased for a price less than its in-house manufactured cost, it would appear sensible to discontinue its manufacture and purchase it. This takes no account of fixed costs, however, which will continue even if the product is no longer manufactured. How, therefore, is this to be catered for? Once again the idea of contribution comes to the rescue. If the contribution made by the outsourced part is greater than that made by the part produced in-house, then it is wise to outsource it. To meet this condition, the total purchase price of the outsourced part will require to be less than the variable cost of the in-house manufactured product. Only if it is less will it be viable, since the difference between its eventual selling price and its purchased cost will produce a greater contribution.

EXAMPLE

	In-house	Purchased
Selling price	£40	40
Variable cost	20	12 (purchased price)
Contribution	20	28
Fixed costs	10	10
Profit	£10	18

Postscript

The validity of marginal costing can easily be called in question. The most obvious objection is perhaps the fact that the technique depends entirely on the distinction between fixed and variable costs, which, as we have seen in a previous chapter, is not always absolutely clear. Another objection is that the apportionment of costs across products can only ever be an approximation, leading to the possible overstatement or understatement of profitability for individual products or departments, with its consequences for wrong decisions. Another objection is that fixed overheads do not remain in their entirety if a department or product is eliminated. Buildings and plant can be decommissioned, and staff can be paid off, meaning that only a portion of fixed overheads would actually remain in the long term.

On balance, however, most organizations regard it as a useful business tool.

Breakeven analysis

So far, the concept of fixed costs has been used twice; it lies at the heart of flexible budgeting and marginal costing. Its third use is in *breakeven analysis*, a technique employed to indicate the level of sales volume at which a firm makes neither a profit nor a loss. In times of falling sales, it is useful for management to know the level below which a loss will be made. Breakeven analysis is particularly suitable for presentation in chart form, making it easy to read off profit and loss levels at different sales volumes, useful to know

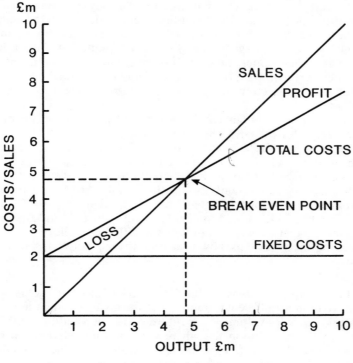

Figure 14.1

when sales are likely to increase. Breakeven charts can be drawn from historical data.

EXAMPLE

The profit and loss account of Amco Ltd reveals the following figures for last year's trading:

	£000s
Sales	7,000
Direct materials costs	2,000
Direct labour costs	1,000
Variable overheads	1,000
Fixed overheads	2,000
Profit	1,000

This can be plotted on a graph – see Figure 14.1.

Notes:

(1)   Fixed costs, at £2m, remain constant at any output level, from nil to £10m or more.

(2)   The sales line is found by plotting a point at, say, £7m on each axis, and by drawing a straight line from the origin of the graph through it.

(3)   The total costs line is found by adding variable costs (£2m + £1m + £1m) to fixed costs, £2m, giving £6m. A point is plotted at £7m on the sales line and, immediately beneath, a point is plotted opposite £6m on the vertical axis, above £7m on the horizontal. A straight line is drawn from the intersection of fixed costs and the vertical axis through this point.

(4)   The profit figure of £1m can be confirmed by reading off the difference between sales and costs from the vertical scale.

(5)   The sales volume at which Amco Ltd would have made no profit (broken even) last year is represented by the intersection of the total costs and sales lines. It can be seen that this occurs at sales of just under £4.7m, which can be confirmed arithmetically. At £4.7m, variable costs would drop proportionately to sales, that is, $(0.57 \times 4.7m =)$ £2,686,000, which added to £2m fixed costs, would total £4,686,000.

(6)   In the same manner, profit or losses at different levels of output can be read off the vertical axis by measuring the gap between sales and total costs.

While breakeven analysis is useful for establishing what profits or losses might have been at different volumes, and for giving a rough indication of what breakeven sales volume is for future years, the validity of the exercise depends on the assumption that there is a constant relationship between variable costs and sales. If, however, the mixture of products sold differs in future years, it is obvious that this relationship will not apply – different products make different contributions.

Another objection to breakeven analysis is that fixed costs levels only hold good provided volumes do not change dramatically. A drop or increase of, say, 50% in production might well result in reduction or increases in fixed costs as production facilities might be either dismantled or extended. Depreciation, rates, maintenance, and so on, or fixed costs, might thus be decreased or increased. Breakeven analysis is not, therefore, a perfect tool, but is invaluable as a rough guide for businesses, as well as a constant reminder of the effect of fixed costs on profits. It is clear from the above chart that the further sales go beyond the breakeven point, the better the return on sales becomes, since each additional unit sold has to bear a progressively smaller share of fixed costs.

In the previous example, the breakeven chart was drawn up from historical profit and loss account information. Current or projected unit cost figures can also be used.

EXAMPLE

The fixed costs for a plant amount to £440,000 per annum. It sells electric motors for £40 each, the costs of which are:

M	£12
L	3
VO	4

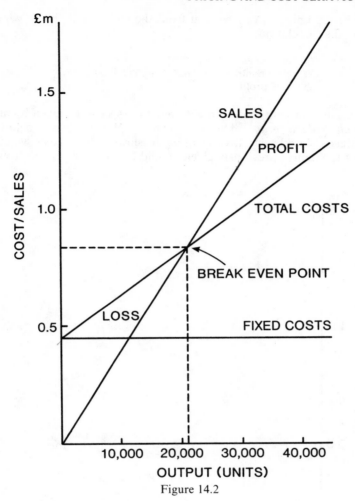

Figure 14.2

Annual sales volume is 25,000 units.

Required: Draw a breakeven chart from the above information, establish the breakeven point by inspecting the chart, then verify it by calculation. What would profit be at 30,000 units?

The first step in drawing the chart is to establish an appropriate scale for both axes. Since the problem involves sales of 30,000 units, then it is sensible to accommodate more on the graph. In the circumstances £1.5m would be an appropriate figure for the vertical axis and output stretching to 40,000 units would be suitable for the horizontal axis – see Figure 14.2.

The breakeven volume can be worked out according to the formula:

$$\frac{\text{Fixed costs}}{\text{sales value} - \text{marginal cost}} = \frac{£440,000}{£40 - (l2 + 3 + 4)}$$

Profit at 30,000 units, as can be seen from the chart, is £190,000, which is verified by the calculation:

$$30,000 \times £[40 - (12 + 3 + 4)]$$
= £630,000 contribution, less £440,000 fixed costs
= £190,000 profit.

An alternative presentation of breakeven analysis can be given by means of the *profit volume graph*. This is drawn by plotting losses below the horizontal axis. At nil sales, losses will be the same as fixed costs, which, in the case of the figures previously given, would be £440,000. By plotting the

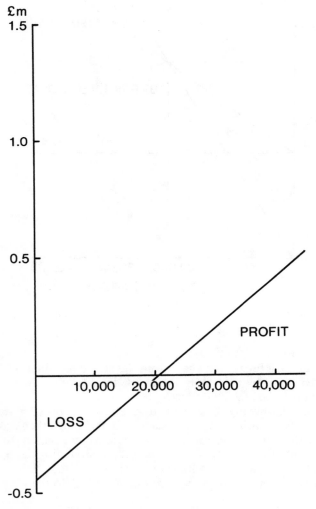

Figure 14.3

loss levels at several output volumes below breakeven level, a straight line can be drawn through the horizontal axis. For example, at 10,000 units, total costs would be £440,000 plus variable costs of (£19 x 10,000), that is, £630,000. The loss would be sales £400,000, less £630,000, £230,000. If this loss is plotted directly below 10,000 units, it provides a second point enabling the profit/loss line to be drawn. This will represent profit at various sales levels, which gives a clearer presentation of profit than in the standard breakeven chart – see Figure 14.3.

Since the profit volume graph has been based on the same information as the breakeven chart just given, its workings can be tested by reading off the profit at 30,000 units of output.

Questions

14.1   It has been suggested that costs are largely irrelevant to the establishment of selling prices. Do you agree? In what situations is this statement true, and in what situations is it not?

14.2   Explain the advantages and disadvantages of *cost plus* pricing from the point of view of the seller *and* the purchaser.

14.3   Why has the *fee basis* contract become so prevalent in large-scale construction projects? How does it work?

14.4   Smith intends investing £175,000 to start a new business, which will make golf clubs. His estimates suggest that he will be able to sell 10,000 clubs in the first year, each of which will cost £16. If he requires a return of 30% on his investment, what must the selling price of each golf club be?

14.5   Sharp is worried that his business is becoming less profitable. Last year, profits of £102,000 were recorded on capital invested of £1.1 million. Sales were £1,457,000. He feels that he could easily obtain 20% return on his investment if it were elsewhere. Calculate the profit/sales percentage required for the forthcoming year to raise his return to this level. He has asked you to make this calculation on the assumption that his investment will remain the same and that sales should be about £1.5 million. What percentage increase on cost does this imply?

14.6   Compare *full (absorption) costing* with *marginal costing*, outlining the circumstances in which each can be meaningful.

14.7   Lord Ltd has decided to undertake a review of the profitability of its four products, A, B, C and D, from which the following has emerged:

Product	A	B	C	D
Selling Price	£25	27	41	17
Material cost	10	8	12	3
Labour cost	3	4	12	2
Variable overheads	4	4	6	2
Fixed overheads	3	5	12	14
Profit (loss)	£ 5	6	(1)	(4)
Annual volume	3,500	2,750	2,000	1,500

Required:
(1) Based on the above, calculate the projected annual profit.
(2) There is a strong feeling that D should be discontinued since it makes a large loss. Explain the effects if this takes place and no use can be made of the vacated facility.
(3) It might be possible to produce and sell another 2,000 units of C if the facility occupied by D were made available. The maximum selling price achievable would be £40. Is it best to do this, or to keep D in production?

14.8   Arodin Ltd manufactures a product with the following cost breakdown:

M	£41
L	19
VO	17

Its selling price is £121. Fixed costs are £26 per unit at an annual volume of 760. Arodin discovers that it can outsource this product from Taiwan at a total cost of £72, delivered.

(1) Should it outsource the product? What are the implications?
(2) What if the exchange rate were to move 10% against the £? (The price of £72 is based on the present £/$ exchange rate.)

14.9   Acroteria Ltd. makes a number of products, one of which has the following cost structure:

Material	£35
Labour	6
Variable overhead	7
Fixed overhead	12
Total cost	60

It has a selling price of £80. The sales manager has advised that equivalent products imported from overseas are selling for as little as £58, and are beginning to seriously affect its sales. The general manager states that Acroteria would be foolish to sell this product for less than £60, and that its production would be discontinued at that price level. The annual sales volume of this product is 50,000 units.

(1) Do you agree with the general manager? Give reasons for your answer.
(2) How low could the price go, and why?
(3) What would happen to the unit cost if annual sales rose to:

(a) 60,000 units,
(b) 75,000 units,
(c) 100,000 units,

and the selling price remained at £80?
(4) What would the *profit* be in each case?

14.10 The following information is available for the Wombat, an electro-mechanical product of Beta Ltd:

Normal annual sales	10,000 units
Fixed costs – Wombat	£95,000 per annum
Sales value	£75
Direct materials	£14
Direct labour	£8
Variable overheads	£10

As a result of import licence difficulties, a major customer of Beta in West Africa has been forced to cancel its orders, which will reduce annual sales volume to half its normal level. The sales director indicates that he can sell the lost 5,000 Wombats in South-East Asia if Beta is prepared to accept a price of £40 each. The other directors feel this is unacceptable, and ask you, the accountant, for advice. Advise along the following lines:

(1)   Compare the profit made in normal circumstances with the profit if the South-East Asian option is ruled out and no other customers are found.
(2)   Raise suitable arguments either supporting or rejecting the South-East Asian option, using figures.
(3)   Indicate the price increase that would have to be obtained on the remaining 5,000 sales to maintain normal profits if the Asian option were rejected.
(4)   Calculate the breakeven point for the Wombat at current price.
(5)   What would the unit profit of the Wombat become if its price were raised to £90 (assuming only 5,000 per annum sold; it *might* be possible to obtain this price in the home market).

14.11   Brunel Ltd has provided the following financial information for your analysis:

£000s	19XX
Sales revenue	4,865
Cost of sales	
Direct materials	923
Direct labour	1,201
Gross margin	2,741
Expenses	
Indirect labour	897
Salaries	336
Employee benefits	706
Maintenance materials	28
Other materials	6
Heat, light, power	37
Rates	44
Depreciation	15
Administration	83
Trading profit	589

Required: working on the assumption that one-third of the material costs in the expenses category move in line with production and that half the heat, light and power costs vary with production, calculate the breakeven point for Brunel, verifying your answer by drawing a chart.

14.12 (1) Why has breakeven analysis been described as inaccurate?
       (2) Outline the detailed differences between a *breakeven chart* and a *profit/volume graph*.

14.13 Chink Martin Ltd, a musical instrument manufacturer, is deciding which of three alternative products to manufacture in its limited production space during the next financial year. The following information has been produced:

	Sousaphone	*Bass saxophone*	*Alto saxophone*
Selling price	£750	1,100	550
Materials	£120	134	79
Labour	£217	278	149
Variable overheads	195	250	119
Annual volume	5,000	2,750	6,050

Fixed overheads are £438,125 per annum.

Required:
(1) Which is the most profitable instrument to produce? Show your workings and draw up a budgeted profit and loss account for that instrument for the year.
(2) Calculate the breakeven volume for this instrument.
(3) What is the profit at breakeven volume plus 10%? (Work to the nearest whole instrument.)
(4) If the variable costs of the most profitable instrument are revised upwards by 8%, and the selling price is revised upwards by 6%, what is the revised total annual contribution for this instrument?

15 Contract accounts

Introduction

So far, this book has divided fairly neatly into two sections. The first nine chapters covered the *financial accounting* area, and were followed by chapters on *management accounting*, including *costing*. Accounting for contracts falls between the financial and cost accounting areas, involving principles from both, and requires a short chapter in its own right.

The *contract account*, a specialized form of account, has been developed to reflect the peculiarities of the contracting industry. In contrast with other types of business, the end product in the contracting industry is a large-scale unit – a stretch of road, a dam, a bridge, a refinery, a factory, a school or perhaps a hospital. The work is mostly carried out on site, as opposed to workshops or retail premises. Contracts are usually awarded after the client, or purchaser, has selected a tender from a number submitted by competing contractors. Various criteria are used to make the selection, ranging from technical capability to completion schedule and price. The contract eventually signed by contractor and client normally makes provision for staged or progress payments at different points in the life of the project. These are necessary to finance the construction over the long period of time that may be involved.

Contractors will usually have a head office where senior management and support functions such as design may be located, and a number of contracts in progress at any one time. Under the terms of the contracts, payments will be sanctioned by a surveyor, architect or engineer working on the client's behalf. Most of the materials involved will be ordered from, and delivered directly to, the site. The employees will operate on the contract until their services are dispensed with, when they may be sent to another site. All expenditure relating to the site is considered part of the contract cost. Examples include:

- Construction wages.
- Plant hire.
- Site salaries, managerial and other.
- Subcontract costs.
- Consumable tools.
- Consumable supplies.
- Hire of buildings, mobile offices.
- Medical and safety supplies.

- Electricity.
- Maintenance costs.
- Computer costs.
- Computer hire.
- Materials delivered to site.

In addition to the above, depreciation of on-site plant will have to be taken into consideration. This is not done through the calculation of depreciation, as in other industries, but by charging all plant delivered to the site at cost, and by revaluing it at the end of each accounting period. As the cost of the plant will be charged (debited) to the contract account when it is sent to site, and since its residual value will be credited to the contract account at period ends, the net effect is to charge the contract with depreciation, but not at a uniform rate. This is entirely appropriate, since the plant will be operated in demanding conditions which will vary from period to period. When work is done or expenditure is incurred on a contract by the contractor's head office, this too is charged to the contract.

Payment arrangements and accounting

As soon as expenditure on a contract begins, the contract account will be opened. All expenditure will be debited to the contract account and credited either to cash/bank or to creditors, as appropriate. As work is certified by the engineer, architect or surveyor responsible, the value certified is credited to the contract account and debited to the client's account. This is equivalent to 'sales'. The value certified will be expressed in terms of the total contract price.

The contracting industry is, however, prone to defects which may only become apparent after work has been certified. Concrete may crack after it has cured, subsidence may take place. To cover eventualities such as these, *retention money* may be deducted from payments for the work certified, provided such a procedure has been agreed in the contract terms. Retention money is usually expressed as a percentage of work certified. No debits or credits are made for this. The client will next pay over the value of work certified, less retention money and cash/bank will be debited, leaving the amount retained outstanding on the client's account. Once the defects have been cleared and the agreed retention period has expired, this balance will be paid over, cash/bank debited and the client's account credited.

At accounting period ends, contracts may well be incomplete, and profit has therefore to be calculated on this basis. The following procedure will be adopted:

(1) Revalue plant on site. Credit the contract account with its value, debiting the relevant asset account.
(2) Quantify and value unused stocks of materials on site, crediting the contract account with their value and debiting stock account
(3) Uncertified expenditure on work done will next be quantified, at cost. This must also be credited to the contract account and debited to work in progress account.

(4)   Once all the debits and credits have been made, a profit or loss can be calculated from the contract account. This will only be an *apparent profit*, since rectification or reworking may be required for the reasons already given.

Since accountants are anxious not to overstate profit, the prudence concept again comes into play. Profit on incomplete contracts has traditionally been worked out using the formula:

$$\frac{2}{3} \times \text{apparent profit} \times \frac{\text{cash received}}{\text{work certified}}$$

This is no more than a rule of thumb intended to ensure that profit is not overstated. Other approaches, based on the actual experience of contractors, are possible, but since the formula is widely used, it will be employed in the examples which follow.

The amount of apparent profit excluded or 'reserved' is shown in the contract account and debited to a reserve account so that it appears in the balance sheet as an asset at period end.

Obviously, if the debits (costs) in the contract account exceed the credits (income), then a loss will ensue and no formula need be applied, since it would be completely wrong to factor a loss down by two-thirds.

EXAMPLE

At the financial year end of Agger Ltd, the following information is available for contract No. 6:

Site wages	£1,500,000
Site salaries	493,000
Employee benefits (site)	594,000
Site consumables	85,000
Materials delivered to site	1,964,000
Work certified	6,250,000
Retention monies	125,000
Cash received	6,125,000
Site subcontract works	96,336
Plant delivered to site	220,000
Plant closing valuation, year end	109,000
Consumable stock, year end	3,500
Head office costs allocated to site	40,000
Site computer costs	19,100
Work in progress not certified	75,000

There are no stocks of unused materials. Profit is taken in line with the custom for the industry.

Required:

(1)   Draw up the contract account.
(2)   Show clearly the profit calculation.

Contract No.6

Site wages	1,500,000	Work in progress	75,000
Site salaries	493,000	Consumables	3,500
Site Benefits	594,000	Plant at	
Site consumables	85,000	valuation	109,000
Materials delivered		Work certified	6,250,000
to site	1,964,368		
Subcontracts	96,366		
Plant delivered			
to site	220,000		
Head office costs	40,000		
Computer costs	19,100		
Profit taken	931,459		
Profit reserve	494,237		
	£6,437,000		£6,250,000

Work in progress b/d	£75,000	Profit reserve b/d	£494,237
Consumable stock b/d	£3,500		
Plant b/d	£109,000		

$$\text{Profit taken} = \frac{2}{3} \times \text{apparent profit} \times \frac{\text{cash received}}{\text{work certified}}$$

$$= \frac{2}{3} \times £1,425,696 \times \frac{£6,125,000}{£6,250,000}$$

$$= \underline{£931,459}$$

In addition, the values shown for work in progress, consumables and plant at valuation would be shown in the balance sheet of Agger Ltd, together with the values of similar items relating to other contracts. The balance sheet will also show profit reserve for this and other contracts, as an asset. The profit and loss account of Agger Ltd would receive the profit of £931,459, together with the profits taken on other contracts. It will also be noticed that the balances on profit reserve, work in progress, consumable stock and plant are brought down into the contract account in the next period, and the relevant asset accounts credited.

Financial control of contracts

Expenditure on contracts will be monitored by both the contractor and the client. The client will prepare accounting statements showing:

(a)   Payments actually made for the period and year to date for each section of the contract.
(b)   Forecast of expenditure for the period and year to date for each section of the contract.

(c)   The variance between (a) and (b). This will reveal the effects of time delays and expenditure on unforeseen modifications to the contract.
(d)   An 'estimate to complete' figure. This will project expenditure forward to the end of the contract, so that a comparison can be made with the total contract price, as signed.

The contractor will prepare similar statements, but the figures will be expressed in his costs, not in terms of the selling price.

Questions

15.1   In what way does a contract account incorporate elements of both costing and financial accounting techniques?

15.2   Explain the following phrases:
(a)   Retention money.
(b)   Work certified.
(c)   Apparent profit.
(d)   Profit reserve.

15.3   The contract account has been described as a sophisticated stock account. Why is this? What else is it?

15.4   The following figures relate to contract No. 44:

Site wages	£5,000
Site salaries	600
Materials to site	4,000
Subcontract costs	900
Other site expenses	300
Hire of special machinery	400
Plant bought for contract	2,000
Work certified by architect	14,000 (all work done to year end is covered)
Cash retention	1,400 (all cash has been paid out but for this)
Plant valuation at year end	1,400
Unused materials at year end	800

Required: prepare the contract account, showing balances brought down and carried down, after calculating profit taken in the normal manner for the construction industry.

15.5   Con-Tractors Ltd has two contracts in progress at the end of its financial year, 31/12/XX, for which the following figures are available:

	Contract 1	Contract 2
Retentions	£52,000	£22,000
Materials delivered to site	194,365	75,180
Site wages	71,390	45,374
Work certified	520,000	220,000
Plant sent to site	10,000	7,400
Site salaries	29,545	31,268

Portable office rental	43,000	25,000
Work not certified	21,000	3,000
Material stocks 31/12/XX	13,400	1,600
Computer costs	3,000	5,282
Plant at valuation 31/12/XX	8,000	5,500
Site management costs	23,000	15,000
Safety equipment	2,516	2,097
Stores plant hire	2,000	1,800
Cranage costs	18,469	3,562
Site employment costs	36,518	27,514

Required: draw up the contract accounts for each contract, recognizing profit in the manner normally adopted in the industry, and showing detailed calculations and balances brought and carried forward. Profit reserves must be clearly shown.

16 Capital expenditure appraisal

Capital expenditure

In earlier chapters it was stated that the word *capital* has at least three meanings in business. It can refer to amounts of money contributed to an enterprise in order to finance its start-up or growth; alternatively the word can be used to describe the total value attributable to the proprietors of a company at a point in time. This is available from the balance sheet and consists of share capital plus reserves and profit retained. It is the third meaning of the term with which this chapter is concerned, capital as distinct from revenue, that is, expenditure on items procured for long term use in a business as opposed to repetitive, cyclical expenditure on such things as raw materials, salaries and expenses.

The impact of capital expenditure on the finances is quite clear. The following balance sheets illustrate the immediate effect of a £1m purchase of plant and machinery:

	'Before'	*'After'*
	£000's	
Land and buildings	5,000	5,000
Plant and machinery	2,000	3,000
Working capital	1,000	1,000
	8,000	9,000
financed by:		
Long-term loan	—	1,000
Capital and reserves	8,000	8,000
	8,000	9,000

The effects on the profit and loss account can be summarized as follows:

(a) The new plant and machinery will generate extra sales revenue.
(b) Extra direct material, labour and overhead costs will be incurred as a result of the additional sales.
(c) Interest on the long-term loan used to finance the capital expenditure will appear as an extra cost.

Obviously, the expectation is that (a) will exceed (b) plus (c) throughout the life of the new machinery, and that the margin will be comfortable enough to justify taking the risks involved in making the new investment.

If the expenditure had been financed by injecting capital or by issuing shares, it is clear that the contributors of capital would be looking for a return on their investment superior to the returns obtainable on safe investments in banks or building societies. (a) would have to exceed (b) by a sufficiently large margin to leave an appropriate profit for contributors of capital.

No mention has yet been made of the cash flow implications. Loans have to be repaid; interest has to be met. If spare cash from the firm's own resources is used, capital expenditure involves the forfeiture of liquidity, always a serious step in a volatile business environment. How, therefore, are these matters to be weighed up prior to capital investment?

Investment appraisal techniques

In view of the fact that capital expenditure is an onerous and risky business, involving heavy cash outlays, four main techniques have been developed in an attempt to help businesses decide whether or not to invest and to compare alternatives. These vary in emphasis and sophistication and are:

- The *payback* calculation.
- The *return on investment* (*ROI*) calculation.
- The *discounted cash flow* (*DCF*) *net present value* calculation (*NPV*).
- The *discounted cash flow internal rate of return* calculation (*IRR*).

Each calculation concerns itself with the flows of *cash* in and out of a business once an investment has been made, recognizing that the cash flow position is more important than the accounting profit. Depreciation is therefore ignored in cash flow projections made in connection with these calculations. The example which follows will be used to demonstrate the four techniques.

A company has £20,000 to invest. Three possible capital expenditure projects are being considered, for which projected cash flows have been produced as follows:

Year	Project	A	B	C
1		£10,000	3,000	2,000
2		8,000	7,000	3,000
3		6,000	10,000	6,000
4		4,000	4,000	9,000
5		2,000	6,000	10,000
		30,000	30,000	30,000

Note: each requires that the £20,000 be spent immediately (year 0). The cash flow projections have been prepared by netting out cash received from sales and cash paid out for costs in each period. Depreciation has been ignored.

The *payback calculation* is designed to answer the question, 'How quickly does each project give us back our cash?' Inspection of the figures provides the following answers:

Project	A	B	C
Years	2⅓	3	4
	(£10,000 +	(£3,000 +	(£2,000 +
	£8,000 +	£7,000 +	£3,000 +
	[⅓ × £6,000] =	£10,000 =	£6,000 +
	£20,000)	£20,000)	£9,000 =
			£20,000)

The payback calculation suggests that A is the best project, since it returns the outlay in the shortest time. This is important from a cash flow standpoint, but there is a false implication that project A will continue to generate cash at a faster rate than the other two. A glance at the inflows for B and C shows that this is not the case. The advantages and disadvantages of payback are as follows:

Advantages	Disadvantages
• Method simple to grasp.	• Ignores the position after payback is reached.
• Quick to calculate.	• Wrong inferences can easily be made
• Emphasizes liquidity.	

The *return on investment* calculation measures the average cash surplus (profit) for the period of the asset's life, as follows:

Cash inflows	£30,000
less Cost	20,000
Profit for 5 years	10,000
Average annual profit	10,000
	5
	= £2,000

$$\therefore \text{ROI} = \frac{£2,000}{£20,000} = 10\% \text{ per annum}$$

Since the total cash inflow for all three projects is £30,000, each has an ROI of 10%. The advantages and disadvantages of ROI are as follows:

Advantages	Disadvantages
• Simple to understand.	• Ignores the timing of cash flows and therefore liquidity
• Quick to calculate.	
• Emphasizes profitability	

Both the payback and ROI calculations suffer from a further defect not yet mentioned – interest, or the 'cost of money', is ignored. To suggest that project A 'pays for itself' in 2⅓ years ignores the fact that the company has, for all or part of that time, either paid extra interest on its overdraft or forfeited the opportunity to earn money as a result of spending £20,000. To suggest that each project earns an average return of 10% not only ignores the fact that the £20,000 invested will cost the company interest or lost earnings, but that each project will cost it a different amount since each repays the original investment at a different time. It was with this in mind that the two *discounted cash flow* techniques were devised. DCF depends on the concept of *present value*.

If I receive £100 one year from now, it is worth less than £100 received today, since I lose interest on it. Assuming interest at 10% per annum, I would only require to invest just over £90 now in order to have £100 in one year's time. The exact figure is £90.91 – £90.91 + 10% = £100. In other words, the *present value* of £100 received one year from now at 10% interest is £90.91. This may be confirmed by applying the actuarial formula:

$$\text{present value (PV)} = \frac{P}{(1 + i)^n} = \frac{100}{(100 + 10)^i} = 90.91$$

where P = future amount, i = interest, and n = number of years.

The DCF techniques of investment appraisal reduce future cash flows to present values in order to reflect the 'cost of money'. The present values are looked up in specially prepared tables rather than calculated each time. Tables are provided in Appendix II. The cost of providing capital is therefore taken into account in the calculation of profits and rates of return.

In order to work out the *DCF net present value calculation* for the three projects, a money cost, or rate of return, will have to be chosen. This is intended to reflect the lost interest or income which the company expects to forfeit over the life of the assets. For illustration purposes, 10% will be used.

Project A

Cash inflows	£	10% discount (NPV) factor	Present value
Yr 1	10,000	0.909	9,090
2	8,000	0.826	6,608
3	6,000	0.751	4,506
4	4,000	0.683	2,732
5	2,000	0.621	1,242
	30,000		24,178
		Cash outflow	20,000
		Net present value	4,178

Project B

Cash inflows	£	10% discount (NPV) factor	Present value
Yr 1	3,000	0.909	2,727
2	7,000	0.826	5,782
3	10,000	0.751	7,510
4	4,000	0.683	2,732
5	6,000	0.621	3,726
	30,000		22,477
		Cash outflow	20,000
		Net Present value	2,477

Project C

Cash inflows	£	10% discount (NPV) factor	Present value
Yr 1	2,000	0.909	1,818
2	3,000	0.826	2,478
3	6,000	0.751	4,506
4	9,000	0.683	6,147
5	10,000	0.621	6,210
	30,000		21,159
		Cash outflow	20,000
		Net present value	1,159

The comparison shows that project A, after taking the cost of money into account, has by far the best return. It should be noted that the apparent surplus, or return, of £10,000 has shrunk to £4,178, the 'cost of money' accounting for the difference. In the case of projects B and C, the returns after applying the 'cost of money' become quite small.

The second of the DCF techniques, the *internal rate of return* calculation, works on similar principles. Its intention is to discount future cash flows to reflect the 'cost of money', and to do so in such a way that a DCF rate is calculated at which inflows and outflows are equal. The rate at which this is achieved is calculated by trial and error, working through each project until it is found, and represents the actual return achieved.

Project A

Cash inflows	£	20% discount (NPV) factor	Present value
Yr 1	10,000	0.833	8,330
2	8,000	0.694	5,552
3	6,000	0.579	3,474
4	4,000	0.482	1,928
5	2,000	0.402	804
			20,088
		Cash inflow	20,000
		Net present value	88

Project B

Cash inflows	£	14% discount (NPV) factor	Present value
Yr 1	3,000	0.877	2,631
2	7,000	0.769	5,383
3	10,000	0.675	6,750
4	4,000	0.592	2,368
5	6,000	0.519	3,114
			20,246
		Cash outflow	20,000
		Net present value	246

Project C

Cash inflows	£	12% discount (NPV) factor	Present value
Yr 1	2,000	0.893	1,786
2	3,000	0.797	2,391
3	6,000	0.712	4,272
4	9,000	0.636	5,724
5	10,000	0.567	5,670
			19,843
		Cash outflow	20,000
		Net present value	(157)

Project A therefore generates a DCF (IRR) return of 20%, project B 14% and project C 12%. The residual NPV values of 88, 246 and (157) disclose that these are not the exact rates. To work them out to decimal places of a percentage is perhaps 'gilding the lily' in view of the number of estimates and assumptions that have been made in getting to this stage. If required, it can nevertheless be done by *interpolation*.

If we work out Project C at 11%, we find that it gives the following values:

Project C

		11% Discount NPV factor	
Yr 1	2,000	0.901	1,802
2	3,000	0.812	2,436
3	6,000	0.731	4,386
4	9,000	0.659	5,931
5	10,000	0.593	5,930
			20,485
		Cash outflow	20,000
		Net present value	485

Since 11% leaves a larger residual NPV than 12%, it is clear the exact rate lies closer to 12% than 11%. The difference between the two rates is (485 + 157) or 642. The exact rate is therefore 12% − (157/642) or 11.76%.

To save the time taken to establish project rates of return by simple trial and error or interpolation, the graphical method may be employed. This involves plotting rates of interest along a central X axis on a piece of graph paper, and monetary values above and below it on the Y axis. By trial and error, two residual DCF values are obtained, one plus, the other minus. The residuals are plotted on the graph beside the DCF rates of return to which they relate. A straight line is drawn between them, the point at which it intersects the X axis giving the DCF rate. While this involves a certain amount of approximation, it has the advantage of speed. Figure 16.1 demonstrates the technique using the data already given for project C above.

What do these DCF (IRR) answers mean? They simply give the annual rates of return which each project is expected to make. Not surprisingly, A

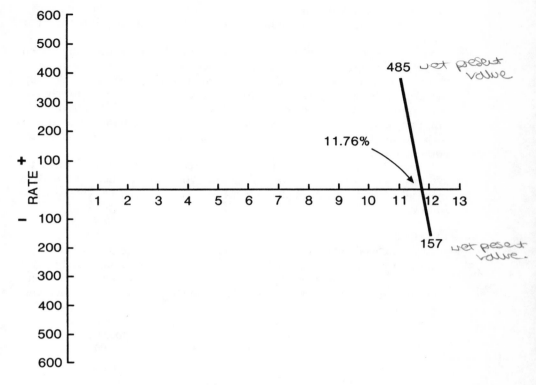

Figure 16.1

again represents the best choice. If the required rate of return chosen for illustration purposes, 10%, was a realistic figure in the light of possible interest rates and returns on capital attainable over the period of the investment, 20% is very handsome indeed. It would, of course, be subject to taxation.

Both the DCF (NPV) and the DCF (IRR) techniques answer the main objections to the payback and ROI methods of investment appraisal; they look at the whole life of the project and also take into account the timing of cash flows and the 'cost of money'. The NPV method establishes at a glance whether or not the target rate of return (sometimes called the *cut-off rate*) will or will not be achieved; the IRR method gives the actual rate of return arising from the project.

Tax and grants

It was noted above that the calculations exclude the effects of tax, nor do they take account of any grants that might be received. While a detailed treatment of both these topics is beyond the scope of this book, the effects of tax and grants can make a significant difference to the figures emerging from project evaluations, and many large organizations take them into account in their calculations. A broad indication of what is involved will therefore be given.

Successive governments in the UK have made the provision of investment grants an important ingredient in regional policy. Under these arrangements, various economically disadvantaged areas have been given 'development' or 'enterprise' status. Firms in such areas making capital investments may apply for initial grants towards their expenditure. The percentage of grant payable will vary with the status of the area in which the expenditure is to be made. Grant is normally received shortly after the assets have been commissioned.

Under the UK tax system, profits are taxed. In common with other tax systems, credit is however given for certain types of investment, particularly plant and machinery, through a scheme of *capital allowances*. This works as follows:

EXAMPLE

A company's taxable profits are £100,000. During the accounting year, new plant and machinery valued £40,000 was acquired. Assuming the firm will pay tax at 30%, and given that plant and machinery attract a 25% capital allowance each year, work out the tax the company will pay for the accounting year in question.

Taxable profits	£100,000
less Capital allowances (25% × £40,000)	10,000
	90,000
Tax at 30%	27,000
Profit after tax	£63,000

Note: under present legislation, capital allowances would continue to be given at 25% on the reducing balance (written down value) of the expenditure. This means that next year, the same assets would attract a capital allowance of (£40,000 − £10,000) × 25%, that is, £7,500, which would be offset against profits, as would *new* allowance on *new* capital investment.

Both investment grant and tax factors will be worked into the example which follows:

EXAMPLE

Bebbington Ltd is considering purchasing a new machine for £50,000 to manufacture and sell potato crisps. It is expected to last five years, and is forecast to generate the following net cash inflows during that period:

Year	1	£15,000
	2	30,000
	3	30,000
	4	30,000
	5	15,000

Bebbington Ltd
Capital expenditure appraisal

Notes	(1) Cash inflow	(2) Capital allowances		(3) Tax payable		(4) Net cash Inflow ((1)–(3))		(5) DCF factor, 35%	(6) NPV at 35%
Yr 1	15,000	(£50,000 × 0.25)	12,500	(£15,000 – 12,500 × 30%)	750	14,250		0.741	10,559
2	30,000	(£37,500 × 0.25)	9,375	(£30,000 – 9,375 × 30%)	6,188	23,812		0.549	13,073
3	30,000	(£28,125 × 0.25)	7,031	(£30,000 – 7,031 × 30%)	6,891	23,109		0.406	9,382
4	30,000	(£21,094 × 0.25)	5,274	(£30,000 – 5,274 × 30%)	7,418	22,582		0.301	6,797
5	15,000	(£15,820 × 0.25)	3,955	(£15,000 – 3,955 × 30%)	3,314	11,686		0.223	2,606
	£120,000				24,561	95,439			42,417
									42,500

Cash outflow (£50,000 – 15% grant)

Net present value   – 83

It will be seen from the above that the DCF (IRR) rate of return is approximately 35%.

Bebbington Ltd is located in an area which attracts 15% government grant. It is assumed that the machine will be eligible for capital allowance of 25% each year, and that profits will be taxed at 30% throughout. A DCF (IRR) calculation is required to show the rate of return the project will earn, taking tax and grant effects into account.

Notes:

(1)   Column 1 contains the net cash inflows originally given.
(2)   Column 2. The capital allowance for year 1 is calculated by taking the cost of the assets, £50,000, times the 25% allowed, giving £12,500. In each succeeding year, the 25% is calculated on the written-down value, that is, after deducting grants given from the previous asset value. For year 2, therefore, the grant is 25% times (£50,000 − £12,500) = £9,375, and so on.
(3)   Column 3 deducts capital allowances, as per column 2, from the net cash inflow, as per column 1, giving taxable profit, then applies the tax rate of 30% to give the tax payable.
(4)   Column 4. The net cash inflow is the figure given originally, as per column 1 less the tax payable calculated in column 3.
(5)   Column 5 contains the DCF factor to be applied to the net cash inflow calculated in column 4.
(6)   Column 6 contains the net present value of the cash flow in column 4.
(7)   It has been assumed that the machine purchased has no residual value at the end of year 5. (If it had, there would be a small tax claw-back.)
(8)   The cash outflow figure, £42,500, has been calculated on the assumption that grant of 15% would be received in year 0.

In practice, alternative projects would be evaluated by the same technique and the results compared.

It should be noted from the above example that DCF techniques can easily accommodate the effects of tax and grants. The other methods of investment appraisal could certainly also incorporate tax effects, but are so unsophisticated that it would not generally be felt worthwhile.

Finally, it must be emphasized that the tax effects and grant position explained above *only apply in certain circumstances* and are subject to change. The figures given are therefore *only illustrative*.

Presenting a case

The financial techniques involved in capital expenditure appraisal have been covered above. In practice, the presentation of a case for capital expenditure involves much more than a few financial calculations. Proper investigations and discusssions with production and/or technical personnel, who may have originated the project, must take place before evaluation. Where possible, at least three tenders for the supply of the capital equipment should be obtained to provide comparable quotations and to ensure probity. The cheapest will not always be recommended. Other factors may play a part, such as:

(a)   Spares compatibility.
(b)   Reliability.

(c)   Delivery.
(d)   Quality of production.
(e)   Ease of maintenance
(f)   Supplier's back-up service.

It should also be borne in mind that, at times, capital expenditure may have to be made on an emergency basis, without stopping to calculate future cash inflows. This might happen when a key item of production plant breaks down. There is then little choice. The investment will have to be quickly weighed up on the basis of the basic cost and other practical criteria.

In the well-run organization, there may be a standard format for capital expenditure requests. It will usually include a summary sheet, comprising:

(a)   Total expenditure requested, with the time scale.
(b)   A précis of the reasons for the expenditure, restricted to a few sentences.
(c)   The return on the chosen project, measured by the methods the organization chooses. (It may choose several, such as DCF (IRR) and also payback, looked at side by side.)
(d)   A note of any working capital involved – to buy a new machine may necessitate holding extra stock.
(e)   The total expenditure requested, broken down by major category, such as plant, machinery, special tooling and installation cost (also part of the capital expenditure).
(f)   How much, if anything has been provided in the budget for the project.

A detailed technical and financial analysis, properly indexed for easy access, will usually be attached.

A final point: capital expenditure appraisals are only as good as the forecasts which underly them. In the well-organized enterprise, a system of *post-investment appraisal* may be operated. This is a system of verification designed to check that the savings and profits forecast are being realized. In this way weaknesses in forecasting can be detected and eliminated from future appraisals.

Other applications of DCF

The examples covered above were based on cases where the capital expenditure generated an inflow of cash, and the various methods compared and quantified outflows and inflows in several ways, as an aid to decision making.

DCF can also be used in situations where there is no cash income from an investment. A local authority paying for a new bridge, a road or even an office block may do so because of benefits which are difficult to quantify, such as increased amenity for the public or staff, or ease of communication.

Even so, the timing and amount of the expenditure will be important to the purchaser. The easier the payments, the less the interest cost will be. A total price that appears dearer than alternatives may cost less when the payment terms are taken into account.

EXAMPLE

A local authority has obtained three quotations for the straightening of a bad stretch of road, as follows:

Tender	A	B	C
Total price	5.2m	4.7m	4.8m
Payment terms	Payable in full after 2 years	Two annual instalments of 50% each	Ist instalment £2m after 1 yr; balance 1 year later

These can be evaluated by applying the present value factors for 12% (the local authority's assumed interest cost over the next two years):

Tender A

	Cash outflow £m	12% discount factor	Net present value
Yr 1	—	—	—
2	5.20	0.797	4.14

Tender B

	Cash outflow £m	12% discount factor	Net present value
Yr 1	2.35	0.893	2.10
2	2.35	0.797	1.87
			3.97

Tender C

	Cash outflow £m	12% discount factor	Net present value
Yr 1	2.00	0.893	1.79
2	2.80	0.797	2.23
			4.02

It can be seen that, taking the terms of payment into account, tender B is the cheapest, but the gap is not so wide as the price, looked at in isolation, would suggest. The use of DCF in this way brings the price and the amounts and timings of payments to a common base.

In the example which follows the evaluation is further complicated by the fact that the payment instalments involve a charge for interest, made by the supplier.

EXAMPLE

An electricity board has received three quotations for the supply, erection and commissioning of a sub-station. Each tender complies with stringent commercial, output and technical criteria. The prices and financial arrangements are as follows:

Tender	Price	Payment Terms
E	£5.55m	£550,000 on signing of contract; balance to be paid over 5 years in equal annual instalments of principal plus interest of 12% on the outstanding balance.
F	£5.8m	£300,000 on placing of contract; balance to be paid in 5 annual instalments of principal plus interest of 8% on the outstanding balance.
G	£6.0m	£2m on placing of order; balance to be paid in 4 annual instalments of principal together with interest at 10% on the outstanding balance.

Bearing all of the above factors in mind, what tender provides the best financial alternative?

A schedule of the cash payments, including interest, has to be made out for each tender, and discounted at the board's cost of money which is put at 12%. (It should be noted that the interest paid to the supplier is quite different to the board's *internal* cost of money. In some ways, the interest charged by the supplier is really just as much part of the price as the basic sum.)

Tender F proves to be the cheapest on a DCF basis, although it is not the cheapest measured by its basic price alone.

Tender E

Yr	Instalment	Bal. o/st'g	Int. @ 12% p.a.	Total pyts	12% disct factor	NPV
	£	£	£	£		£
0	550,000	5,000,000	—	550,000	—	550,000
1	1,000,000	4,000,000	600,000	1,600,000	0.893	1,428,800
2	1,000,000	3,000,000	480,000	1,480,000	0.797	1,795,000
3	1,000,000	2,000,000	360,000	1,360,000	0.712	968,320
4	1,000,000	1,000,000	240,000	1,240,000	0.636	788,640
5	1,000,000	—	120,000	1,120,000	0.567	635,040
	5,550,000		1,800,000	7,350,000		6,166,360

Tender F

Yr	Instalment	Bal. o/st'g	Int. @ 8% p.a.	Total pyts	12% disct factor	NPV
	£	£	£	£		£
0	300,000	5,000,000	—	300,000	—	300,000
1	1,100,000	4,400,000	440,000	1,540,000	0.893	1,375,220
2	1,100,000	3,300,000	352,000	1,452,000	0.797	1,157,244
3	1,100,000	2,200,000	264,000	1,364,000	0.712	971,168
4	1,100,000	1,100,000	176,000	1,276,000	0.636	811,536
5	1,100,000	—	880,000	1,188,000	0.567	673,596
	5,800,000		1,320,000	7,120,000		5,288,764

Tender G

Yr	Instalment	Bal. o/st'g	Int. @ 8% p.a.	Total pyts	12% disct factor	NPV
	£	£	£	£		£
0	2,000,000	4,000,000	—	2,000,000	—	2,000,000
1	1,000,000	3,000,000	320,000	1,320,000	0.893	1,178,760
2	1,000,000	2,000,000	240,000	1,240,000	0.797	988,280
3	1,000,000	1,000,000	160,000	1,160,000	0.712	825,920
4	1,000,000	—	80,000	1,080,000	0.636	686,880
	6,000,000		800,000	6,800,000		5,679,840

Computers and DCF

Most spreadsheet software has an inbuilt DCF capability, operated by simple commands. This means that the tedious arithmetic calculations associated with DCF can be carried out much more quickly than before. In practice this makes it possible for engineers and other non-financial originators of capital expenditure requests to make their own comparisons of financial effects prior to forwarding their proposals to the finance department. Changes in rates can also be fed in at the touch of a key.

Questions

16.1   Why do investment appraisal calculations deal in cash, as opposed to profit figures?

16.2   List the advantages and disadvantages of:
(a) The payback calculation.
(b) The return on investment calculation.
(c) The DCF (NPV) calculation.
(d) The DCF (IRR) calculation.

16.3   'Investment appraisal calculations are only as good as the assumptions which underlie them.' What are these assumptions, and what are the difficulties in making them and working with them?

16.4.   What are the difficulties faced by a firm in selecting an 'acceptable rate of return' on capital expenditure?

16.5   Give examples of circumstances where capital expenditure *has* to be made without there being any tangible benefits.

16.6   (1)   Abacus Engineering Ltd has £20,000 to invest. Advise it as to which of the three undernoted projects represents the best use of its funds, analysing the figures by means of the DCF (NPV) method.

Income

Year	Project A	Project B	Project C
1	£12,000	£6,000	£2,000
2	10,000	14,000	2,000
3	1,000	9,600	8,000
4	1,000	200	8,000
5	6,000	200	10,000

The £20,000 requires to be spent immediately, and the company is currently using 10% as a discount factor.

(2)   In what circumstances is the DCF (IRR) technique more appropriate?

16.7 Strathbungo Ltd would like to replace its inefficient shop-floor lighting system with a more modern one. It has received three quotations from which the following figures have been worked out.

Quotation

	X	Y	Z
Capital cost	£40,000	£35,000	£42,000
Life of Installation	10 yrs	8 yrs	9 yrs
Savings (annual)			
Fuel	£6,500	£7,000	£6,750
Light bulbs	750	850	900
Maintenance wages	520	480	560
Installation cost Add to Capital cost	£2,000	£3,000	£2,000

(1)   Using a discount rate of 15%, compare the three projects on a DCF (NPV) basis.
(2)   Calculate the payback period for each project.
(3)   Calculate the return on investment (ROI) for each project.

16.8   The Wizbit Electronics Company needs a new machine for its manufacturing process, and has obtained quotations from three potential suppliers, A, B and C. The following details are now available:

Machine	A	B	C
Capital cost	£9,000	£8,000	£8,450
Installation cost	350	750	1,200
Annual profits per machine	3,000	3,000	2,800
Life of machine	6 yrs	5 yrs	7 yrs

(1)   Using the NPV discounted cash flow technique, calculate the return for each machine. You may use the company's 'Cut-off rate' as a discounting factor. This is 15%.
(2)   What non-financial factors should be taken into consideration? List five of these factors, discussing each briefly.
(3)   What is the DCF (IRR) for A?
(4)   Calculate the payback and ROI of each option.

16.9.   Patera Ltd is considering investing in one of three projects, each of which has an immediate initial outlay of £10,000. The cash inflows from the projects are as follows.

Year	Project A	B	C
1	£1,500	£4,500	£9,000
2	1,500	10,500	7,500
3	6,000	7,200	750
4	6,000	150	750
5	7,500	150	4,500

(1) Using the DCF (NPV) technique, establish which project gives the best financial return. A discount factor of 12% is to be used.

(2) Using the figures already given, calculate the payback and the return on investment (ROI) for each project.

(3) Discuss the deficiencies of payback and return on investment (ROI) calculations as a guide to project evaluation.

Appendix I
Alternative Companies Act account formats

Balance sheet – format 2 (horizontal presentation)

ASSETS

(A) Called-up shares not paid
(B) Fixed assets
  (1) Intangible assets
    (a) Development costs
    (b) Patents etc.
    (c) Goodwill
    (d) Payments on account
  (2) Tangible assets
    (a) Land and buildings
    (b) Plant and machinery
    (c) Fixtures and fittings
  (3) Investments
(C) Current assets
  (1) Stock
  (2) Debtors
  (3) Investments
  (4) Cash and bank
(D) Prepayments and accruals

LIABILITIES

(A) Capital and reserves
  (1) Called-up share capital
  (2) Share premium account
  (3) Revaluation reserve
  (4) Other reserves
  (5) Revenue reserves
(B) Provisions for liabilities
(C) Creditors
  (1) Debentures
  (2) Bank loans and overdrafts
  (3) Trade creditors
  (4) Accruals
(D) Accruals

Profit and loss account – format 2

(1) Turnover
(2) Changes in stock of finished goods and work in progress
(3) Own work capitalized
(4) Other operating income
(5) Raw materials and consumables
(6) Staff costs
    Wages and salaries
    Social security costs
    Pension costs
(7) Depreciation
(8) Other operating charges
(9) Income from shares in group companies
(10) Income from shares in related companies
(11) Income from other fixed asset investments
(12) Other interest receivable
(13) Amounts written-off investments
(14) Interest payable
(15) Tax on profit from ordinary activities

(16)   Profit or loss on ordinary activities after tax
(17)   Extraordinary income
(18)   Extraordinary charges
(19)   Extraordinary profit or loss
(20)   Tax on extraordinary profit
(21)   Other taxes
(22)   Profit or loss for the year.

Appendix II
Discounted cash flow
(present value) tables

Years hence	1%	2%	3%	4%	5%	6%	7%	8%	9%	10%	11%	12%	13%	14%	15%
1	.990	.980	.971	.962	.952	.943	.935	.926	.917	.909	.901	.893	.885	.877	.870
2	.980	.961	.943	.925	.907	.890	.873	.857	.842	.826	.812	.797	.783	.769	.756
3	.971	.942	.915	.889	.864	.840	.816	.794	.772	.751	.731	.712	.693	.675	.658
4	.961	.924	.888	.855	.823	.792	.763	.735	.708	.683	.659	.636	.613	.592	.572
5	.951	.906	.863	.822	.784	.747	.713	.681	.650	.621	.593	.567	.543	.519	.497
6	.942	.888	.837	.790	.746	.705	.666	.630	.596	.564	.535	.507	.480	.456	.432
7	.933	.871	.813	.760	.711	.665	.623	.583	.547	.513	.482	.452	.425	.400	.376
8	.923	.853	.789	.731	.677	.627	.582	.540	.502	.467	.434	.404	.376	.351	.327
9	.914	.837	.766	.703	.645	.592	.544	.500	.460	.424	.391	.361	.333	.308	.284
10	.905	.820	.744	.676	.614	.558	.508	.463	.422	.386	.352	.322	.295	.270	.247
11	.896	.804	.722	.650	.585	.527	.475	.429	.388	.350	.317	.287	.261	.237	.215
12	.887	.788	.701	.625	.557	.497	.444	.397	.356	.319	.286	.257	.231	.208	.187
13	.879	.773	.681	.601	.530	.469	.415	.368	.326	.290	.258	.229	.204	.182	.163
14	.870	.758	.661	.577	.505	.442	.388	.340	.299	.263	.232	.205	.181	.160	.141
15	.861	.743	.642	.555	.481	.417	.362	.315	.275	.239	.209	.183	.160	.140	.123
16	.853	.728	.623	.534	.458	.394	.339	.292	.252	.218	.188	.163	.141	.123	.107
17	.844	.714	.605	.513	.436	.371	.317	.270	.231	.198	.170	.146	.125	.108	.093
18	.836	.700	.587	.494	.416	.350	.296	.250	.212	.180	.153	.130	.111	.095	.081
19	.828	.686	.570	.475	.396	.331	.277	.232	.194	.164	.138	.116	.098	.083	.070
20	.820	.673	.554	.456	.377	.312	.258	.215	.178	.149	.124	.104	.087	.073	.061
21	.811	.660	.538	.439	.359	.294	.242	.199	.164	.135	.112	.093	.077	.064	.053
22	.803	.647	.522	.422	.342	.278	.226	.184	.150	.123	.101	.083	.068	.056	.046
23	.795	.634	.507	.406	.326	.262	.211	.170	.138	.112	.091	.074	.060	.049	.040
24	.788	.622	.492	.390	.310	.247	.197	.158	.126	.102	.082	.066	.053	.043	.035
25	.780	.610	.478	.375	.295	.233	.184	.146	.116	.092	.074	.059	.047	.038	.030
30	.742	.552	.412	.308	.231	.174	.131	.099	.075	.057	.044	.033	.026	.020	.015
40	.672	.453	.307	.208	.142	.097	.067	.046	.032	.022	.015	.011	.008	.005	.004
50	.608	.372	.228	.141	.087	.054	.034	.021	.013	.009	.005	.003	.002	.001	.001

Years hence	16%	18%	20%	22%	24%	25%	26%	28%	30%	35%	40%	45%	50%	55%	60%
1	.862	.847	.833	.820	.806	.800	.794	.781	.769	.741	.741	.690	.667	.645	.625
2	.743	.718	.694	.672	.650	.640	.630	.610	.592	.549	.510	.476	.444	.416	.391
3	.641	.609	.579	.551	.524	.512	.500	.477	.455	.406	.364	.328	.296	.269	.244
4	.552	.516	.482	.451	.423	.410	.397	.373	.350	.301	.260	.226	.198	.173	.153
5	.476	.437	.402	.370	.341	.328	.315	.291	.269	.223	.186	.156	.132	.112	.095
6	.410	.370	.335	.303	.275	.262	.250	.227	.207	.165	.133	.108	.088	.072	.060
7	.354	.314	.279	.249	.222	.210	.198	.178	.159	.122	.095	.074	.059	.047	.037
8	.305	.266	.233	.204	.179	.168	.157	.139	.123	.091	.068	.051	.039	.030	.023
9	.263	.225	.194	.167	.144	.134	.125	.108	.094	.067	.048	.035	.026	.019	.015
10	.227	.191	.162	.137	.116	.107	.099	.085	.073	.050	.035	.024	.017	.012	.009
11	.195	.162	.135	.112	.094	.086	.079	.066	.056	.037	.025	.017	.012	.008	.006
12	.168	.137	.112	.092	.076	.069	.062	.052	.043	.027	.018	.012	.008	.005	.004
13	.145	.116	.093	.075	.061	.055	.050	.040	.033	.020	.013	.008	.005	.003	.002
14	.125	.099	.078	.062	.049	.044	.039	.032	.025	.015	.009	.006	.003	.002	.001
15	.108	.084	.065	.051	.040	.035	.031	.025	.020	.011	.006	.004	.002	.001	.001
16	.093	.071	.054	.042	.032	.028	.025	.019	.015	.008	.005	.003	.002	.001	.001
17	.080	.060	.045	.034	.026	.023	.020	.015	.012	.006	.003	.002	.001	.001	
18	.069	.051	.038	.028	.021	.018	.016	.012	.009	.005	.002	.001	.001		
19	.060	.043	.031	.023	.017	.014	.012	.009	.007	.003	.002	.001	.001		
20	.051	.037	.026	.019	.014	.012	.010	.007	.005	.002	.001				
21	.044	.031	.022	.015	.011	.009	.008	.006	.004	.002	.001				
22	.038	.026	.018	.013	.009	.007	.006	.004	.003	.001	.001				
23	.033	.022	.015	.010	.007	.006	.005	.003	.002	.001					
24	.028	.019	.013	.008	.006	.005	.004	.003	.002	.001					
25	.024	.016	.010	.007	.005	.004	.003	.002	.001	.001					
30	.012	.007	.004	.003	.002	.001	.001	.001							
40	.003	.001													
50	.001														

Appendix III
Two software applications: cash flow forecasting and budgeting

The solution to question 10.8, Chapter 10, and the example contained on pages 175–6 of Chapter 11 now follow, reworked on the SuperCalc 4 software package. In addition to the revised answers, a sample printout of the information in each cell is given. This is to enable readers to inspect the formulas used and the precise contents of the cells. Only part of this information has been given for the budgeting example since a large number of pages would be need to show it in full. It should be noted that the quote marks on these lists denote text and are not part of the commands.

	A		B		C		D		E		F		G		H	
1																
2							I.B.GOOD - FINANCIAL PLAN									
3																
4	VARIABLES															
5	Own Cash		5000				Sale price				4					
6	Loan		3600				Int. rate				.12					
7	Labour		.8				Raw material price				1.3					
8	Personal		500				Depreciation				.2					
9	Loan term						Sales for:									
10	(months)		36				cash				.45					
11							1 mth cr				.4					
12							2 mths cr				.15					
13																
14	Sales volume															
15	JAN	FEB			MARCH		APRIL		MAY		JUNE		TOTAL			
16		600		750		1150		1500		1050		900		5950		
17																
18							I.B. GOOD									
19							CASH FLOW FORECAST									
20			JAN		FEB		MARCH		APRIL		MAY		JUNE		TOTAL	
21	Capital		5000												5000	
22	Loan		3600												3600	
23	Sales:														0	
24	cash		1080		1350		2070		2700		1890		1620		10710	
25	1 mth		0		960		1200		1840		2400		1680		8080	
26	2 mths		0		0		360		450		690		900		2400	
27			----		----		----		----		----		----		----	
28			9680		2310		3630		4990		4980		4200		29790	
29			----		----		----		----		----		----		----	
30	Loan Int		0		36		36		36		36		36		180	
31	Repays		0		100		100		100		100		100		500	
32	Assets		4500												4500	
33	Van		3000												3000	
34	Material		0		780		975		1495		1950		1365		6565	
35	Labour		480		600		920		1200		840		720		4760	
36	Power		0		0		435		0		435		0		870	
37	Personal		500		500		500		500		500		500		3000	
38	Stock		350												350	
39			----		----		----		----		----		----		----	
40			8830		2016		2966		3331		3861		2721		23725	
41			----		----		----		----		----		----		----	
42	Diffce		850		294		664		1659		1119		1479			
43	b/f		0		850		1144		1808		3467		4586			
44			----		----		----		----		----		----		----	
45	BALANCE		850		1144		1808		3467		4586		6065		6065	
46			----		----		----		----		----		----		----	
47																

```
     |  A    ||   B   ||   C   ||   D   ||   E    ||   F   ||   G   ||   H
52
53                  PROJECTED PROFIT AND LOSS ACCOUNT
54
55   SALES                                        23800
56   lESS/COST OF SALES                            7735
57                                             ---------
58   GROSS PROFIT                                          16065
59   LESS/ COSTS
60          Loan Interest          216
61          Labour                4760
62          Power                 1305
63          Depreciation           750
64          Rates                 1500
65                             ---------           8531
66                                             ---------
67   NET PROFIT                                            7534
68                                             ---------
69
70                  PROJECTED BALANCE SHEET
71   FIXED ASSETS
72   Equipment                                     4050
73   Van                                           2700
74                                             ---------
75                                                 6750
76   CURRENT ASSETS
77   Stock                                          350
78   Debtors                                       2610
79   Bank                                          6065
80                                             ---------
81                                                 9025
82   less/CURRENT LIABILITIES
83   Creditors for:
84          Material              1170
85          Interest                36
86          Rates                 1500
87          Power                  435
88                             ---------          3141
89                                             ---------   5884
90                                                      ---------
91                                                        12634
92                                                      ---------
93             as financed by
94
95   Owners capital                                5000
96   add/ Profit                                   7534
97                                             ---------
98                                                12534
99   less/ Personal Drawings                       3000
100                                            ---------
101                                                9534
102  add/ Loans outstanding                        3100
103                                            ---------
104                                               12634
105                                            ---------
106
```

```
C2      =  "I.B.GOOD - FINANCIAL PLAN
A4      =  "VARIABLES
A5      =  "Own Cash
B5      =  5000
D5      =  "Sale price
F5      =  4
A6      =  "Loan
B6      =  3600
D6      =  "Int. rate
F6      =  .12
A7      =  "Labour
B7      =  0.8
D7      =  "Raw material price
F7      =  1.3
A8      =  "Personal
B8      =  500
D8      =  "Depreciation
F8      =  .2
A9      =  "Loan term
D9      =  "Sales for:
A10     =  "(months)
B10     =  36
E10     =  "cash
F10     =  .45
E11     =  "1 mth cr
F11     =  .4
E12     =  "2 mths cr
F12     =  .15
A14     =  "Sales volume
A15     =  "JAN
B15     =  "FEB
C15     =  "MARCH
D15     =  "APRIL
E15     =  "MAY
F15     =  "JUNE
G15     =  "TOTAL
A16     =  600
B16     =  750
C16     =  1150
D16     =  1500
E16     =  1050
F16     =  900
G16     =  SUM(A16:F16)
C18     =  "I.B. GOOD
C19     =  "CASH FLOW FORECAST
B20     =  "JAN
C20     =  "FEB
D20     =  "MARCH
E20     =  "APRIL
F20     =  "MAY
G20     =  "JUNE
H20     =  "TOTAL
A21     =  "Capital
B21     =  B5*1
H21     =  SUM(A21:G21)
A22     =  "Loan
B22     =  B6*1
H22     =  SUM(A22:G22)
A23     =  "Sales:
H23     =  SUM(A23:G23)
A24     =  "cash
B24     =  A16*F5*F10
C24     =  B16*F5*F10
D24     =  C16*F5*F10
```

```
E24          = D16*F5*F10
F24          = E16*F5*F10
G24          = F16*F5*F10
H24          = SUM(A24:G24)
A25          = "1 mth
B25          = 0
C25          = A16*F5*F11
D25          = B16*F5*F11
E25          = C16*F5*F11
F25          = D16*F5*F11
G25          = E16*F5*F11
H25          = SUM(A25:G25)
A26          = "2 mths
B26          = 0
C26          = 0
D26          = A16*F5*F12
E26          = B16*F5*F12
F26          = C16*F5*F12
G26          = D16*F5*F12
H26          = SUM(A26:G26)
B27          = "------------
C27          = "------------
D27          = "------------
E27          = "------------
F27          = "------------
G27          = "------------
H27          = "------------
B28          = SUM(B21:B26)
C28          = SUM(C21:C26)
D28          = SUM(D21:D26)
E28          = SUM(E21:E26)
F28          = SUM(F21:F26)
G28          = SUM(G21:G26)
H28          = SUM(H21:H26)
A29          = "------------
B29          = "------------
C29          = "------------
D29          = "------------
E29          = "------------
F29          = "------------
G29          = "------------
H29          = "------------
A30          = "Loan Int
B30          = 0
C30          = (B6*F6)/12
D30          = (B6*F6)/12
E30          = (B6*F6)/12
F30          = (B6*F6)/12
G30          = (B6*F6)/12
H30          = SUM(B30:G30)
A31          = "Repays
B31          = 0
C31          = B6/B10
D31          = B6/B10
E31          = B6/B10
F31          = B6/B10
G31          = B6/B10
H31          = SUM(B31:G31)
A32          = "Assets
B32          = 4500
H32          = SUM(B32:G32)
A33          = "Van
B33          = 3000
H33          = SUM(B33:G33)
```

```
A34    = "Material
B34    = 0
C34    = A16*F7
D34    = B16*F7
E34    = C16*F7
F34    = D16*F7
G34    = E16*F7
H34    = SUM(B34:G34)
A35    = "Labour
B35    = A16*B7
C35    = B16*B7
D35    = C16*B7
E35    = D16*B7
F35    = E16*B7
G35    = F16*B7
H35    = SUM(B35:G35)
A36    = "Power
B36    = 0
C36    = 0
D36    = 435
E36    = 0
F36    = 435
G36    = 0
H36    = SUM(B36:G36)
A37    = "Personal
B37    = B8*1
C37    = B8*1
D37    = B8*1
E37    = B8*1
F37    = B8*1
G37    = B8*1
H37    = SUM(B37:G37)
A38    = "Stock
B38    = 350
H38    = SUM(B38:G38)
B39    = "------------
C39    = "------------
D39    = "------------
E39    = "------------
F39    = "------------
G39    = "------------
H39    = "------------
B40    = SUM(B30:B38)
C40    = SUM(C30:C38)
D40    = SUM(D30:D38)
E40    = SUM(E30:E38)
F40    = SUM(F30:F38)
G40    = SUM(G30:G38)
H40    = SUM(H30:H38)
B41    = "------------
C41    = "------------
D41    = "------------
E41    = "------------
F41    = "------------
G41    = "------------
H41    = "------------
A42    = "Diffce
B42    = B28-B40
C42    = C28-C40
D42    = D28-D40
E42    = E28-E40
F42    = F28-F40
G42    = G28-G40
A43    = "b/f
```

```
B43          =  0
C43          =  B42+B43
D43          =  C42+C43
E43          =  D42+D43
F43          =  E42+E43
G43          =  F42+F43
B44          =  "-------------
C44          =  "-------------
D44          =  "-------------
E44          =  "-------------
F44          =  "-------------
G44          =  "-------------
H44          =  "-----------
A45          =  "BALANCE
B45          =  B42+B43
C45          =  C42+C43
D45          =  D42+D43
E45          =  E42+E43
F45          =  F42+F43
G45          =  G42+G43
H45          =  H28-H40
B46          =  "-------------
C46          =  "-------------
D46          =  "-------------
E46          =  "-------------
F46          =  "-------------
G46          =  "-------------
H46          =  "-------------
C53          =  "PROJECTED PROFIT AND LOSS ACCOUNT
A55          =  "SALES
E55          =  G16*F5
A56          =  "lESS/COST OF SALES
E56          =  ((G16*F7)+H38)-H38
E57          =  "---------
A58          =  "GROSS PROFIT
E58          =  E55-E56
A59          =  "LESS/ COSTS
B60          =  "Loan Interest
D60          =  H30+((B6*F6)/12)
B61          =  "Labour
D61          =  H35*1
B62          =  "Power
D62          =  H36+435
B63          =  "Depreciation
D63          =  ((H32+H33)*F8)/2
B64          =  "Rates
D64          =  1500
D65          =  "---------
E65          =  SUM(D60:D64)
E66          =  "---------
A67          =  "NET PROFIT
E67          =  E58-E65
E68          =  "---------
C70          =  "PROJECTED BALANCE SHEET
A71          =  "FIXED ASSETS
A72          =  "Equipment
E72          =  H32-((H32*F8)/2)
A73          =  "Van
E73          =  H33-((H33*F8)/2)
E74          =  "---------
E75          =  E72+E73
A76          =  "CURRENT ASSETS
A77          =  "Stock
D77          =  H38*1
```

```
A78      = "Debtors
D78      = (G16*F5)-(H24+H25+H26)
A79      = "Bank
D79      = H45*1
D80      = "---------
D81      = SUM(D77:D79)
A82      = "less/CURRENT LIABILITIES
A83      = "Creditors for:
B84      = "Material
C84      = (G16*F7)-H34
B85      = "Interest
C85      = B6*F6/12
B86      = "Rates
C86      = D64*1
B87      = "Power
C87      = 435
C88      = "---------
D88      = SUM(C84:C87)
D89      = "---------
E89      = D81-D88
E90      = "---------
E91      = E75+E89
E92      = "---------
B93      = "as financed by
A95      = "Owners capital
E95      = H21*1
A96      = "add/ Profit
E96      = E67*1
E97      = "---------
E98      = E95+E96
A99      = "less/ Personal Drawings
E99      = H37*1
E100     = "---------
E101     = E98-E99
A102     = "add/ Loans outstanding
E102     = H22-H31
E103     = "---------
E104     = E101+E102
E105     = "---------
```

```
  |   A    ||    B    ||    C    ||    D    ||    E    ||    F    ||    G    ||    H    |
1 BUDGETARY CONTROL
2
3 VARIABLES
4                              Product 1Product 2
5 Sales Volume                    100       200
6 sale price                      100        60
7 Costs                                 ,
8          Material                 50        30
9          Labour                   10         5
10
11 No. of clerks          2        Employ costs          .3
12 Clerk's wage         400        Price inc            .05
13 No. of inspectors      2        wages inc            .03
14 Inspector's wage     500
15 Misc overheads      1000
16
17
18                      SALES BUDGET
19 product                      months
20              JAN      FEB      MAR      APR      MAY      JUNE     JULY
21       1     10000    10000    10000    10000    10000    10500    10500
22       2     12000    12000    12000    12000    12000    12600    12600
23           ------------------------------------------------------------
24 Total       22000    22000    22000    22000    22000    23100    23100
25           ------------------------------------------------------------
26              AUG      SEP      OCT      NOV      DEC     Total
27             10500    10500    10500    10500    10500   123500
28             12600    12600    12600    12600    12600   148200
29           --------------------------------------------------
30             23100    23100    23100    23100    23100   271700
31           --------------------------------------------------
32
33
34                   DIRECT MATERIALS BUDGET
35
36 Product      JAN      FEB      MAR      APR      MAY      JUNE     JULY
37       1      5000     5000     5000     5000     5000     5000     5000
38       2      6000     6000     6000     6000     6000     6000     6000
39           ------------------------------------------------------------
40            11000    11000    11000    11000    11000    11000    11000
41           ------------------------------------------------------------
42              AUG     SEPT      OCT      NOV      DEC     TOTAL
43             5000     5000     5000     5000     5000    60000
44             6000     6000     6000     6000     6000    72000
45           --------------------------------------------------
46            11000    11000    11000    11000    11000   132000
47           --------------------------------------------------
48
49
50                   DIRECT LABOUR BUDGET
51
52 Product      JAN      FEB      MAR      APR      MAY      JUNE     JULY
53       1      1000     1000     1000     1000     1000     1000     1000
54       2      1000     1000     1000     1000     1000     1000     1000
55           ------------------------------------------------------------
56             2000     2000     2000     2000     2000     2000     2000
57           ------------------------------------------------------------
58              AUG      SEP      OCT      NOV      DEC     TOTAL
59             1000     1030     1030     1030     1030    12120
60             1000     1030     1030     1030     1030    12120
61           --------------------------------------------------
62             2000     2060     2060     2060     2060    24240
```

```
 |  A   ||   B   ||   C   ||   D   ||   E   ||   F   ||   G   ||   H   |
63        --------------------------------------------------------------
64
65
66              LABOUR OVERHEAD BUDGET
67
68               JAN     FEB     MAR     APR     MAY     JUNE    JULY
69  Clerks       800     800     800     800     800     800     800
70  Inspector    1000    1000    1000    1000    1000    1000    1000
71           ----------------------------------------------------------
72               1800    1800    1800    1800    1800    1800    1800
73           ----------------------------------------------------------
74               AUG     SEPT    OCT     NOV     DEC     TOTAL
75               800     824     824     824     824     9696
76               1000    1030    1030    1030    1030    12120
77           ----------------------------------------------------------
78               1800    1854    1854    1854    1854    21816
79           ----------------------------------------------------------
80
81
82              OTHER OVERHEAD BUDGET
83
84               JAN     FEB     MAR     APR     MAY     JUNE    JULY
85  Emp costs    1140    1140    1140    1140    1140    1140    1140
86  Misc         1000    1000    1000    1000    1000    1000    1000
87           ----------------------------------------------------------
88               2140    2140    2140    2140    2140    2140    2140
89           ----------------------------------------------------------
90
91               AUG     SEP     OCT     NOV     DEC     TOTAL
92               1140    1174.2  1174.2  1174.2  1174.2  13816.8
93               1000    1000    1000    1000    1000    12000
94           ----------------------------------------------------------
95               2140    2174.2  2174.2  2174.2  2174.2  25816.8
96           ----------------------------------------------------------
97
98
99              BUDGETED PROFIT AND LOSS ACCOUNT
100
101  SALES                          271700
102  DIRECT MATERIALS      132000
103  DIRECT LABOUR          24240
104  OVERHEADS:
105  labour                 21816
106  other                 25816.8
107                        --------  203872.8
108                                  ---------
109  NET PROFIT                      67827.2
110                                  ---------
```

```
A1              =  "BUDGETARY CONTROL
A3              =  "VARIABLES
D4              =  "Product 1
E4              =  "Product 2
A5              =  "Sales Volume
D5              =  100
E5              =  200
A6              =  "sale price
D6              =  100
E6              =  60
A7              =  "Costs
B8              =  "Material
D8              =  50
E8              =  30
B9              =  "Labour
D9              =  10
E9              =  5
A11             =  "No. of clerks
C11             =  2
E11             =  "Employ costs
G11             =  .3
A12             =  "Clerk's wage
C12             =  400
E12             =  "Price inc
G12             =  .05
A13             =  "No. of inspectors
C13             =  2
E13             =  "wages inc
G13             =  .03
A14             =  "Inspector's wage
C14             =  500
A15             =  "Misc overheads
C15             =  1000
C18             =  "SALES BUDGET
A19             =  "product
D19             =  "months
B20             =  "JAN
C20             =  "FEB
D20             =  "MAR
E20             =  "APR
F20             =  "MAY
G20             =  "JUNE
H20             =  "JULY
A21             =  1
B21             =  D5*D6
C21             =  D5*D6
D21             =  D5*D6
E21             =  D5*D6
F21             =  D5*D6
G21             =  D5*D6*(1+G12)
H21             =  D5*D6*(1+G12)
A22             =  2
B22             =  E5*E6
C22             =  E5*E6
D22             =  E5*E6
E22             =  E5*E6
F22             =  E5*E6
G22             =  E5*E6*(1+G12)
H22             =  E5*E6*(1+G12)
B23             =  "---------
C23             =  "---------
D23             =  "---------
E23             =  "---------
F23             =  "---------
G23             =  "---------
H23             =  "---------
A24             =  "Total
B24             =  B21+B22
C24             =  C21+C22
D24             =  D21+D22
```

```
E24              = E21+E22
F24              = F21+F22
G24              = G21+G22
H24              = H21+H22
B25              = "---------
C25              = "---------
D25              = "---------
E25              = "---------
F25              = "---------
G25              = "---------
H25              = "---------
B26         TR = "AUG
C26         TR = "SEP
D26         TR = "OCT
E26         TR = "NOV
F26         TR = "DEC
G26         TR = "Total
B27              = D5*D6*(1+G12)
C27              = D5*D6*(1+G12)
D27              = D5*D6*(1+G12)
E27              = D5*D6*(1+G12)
F27              = D5*D6*(1+G12)
G27              = SUM(B21:H21)+SUM(B27:F27)
B28              = E5*E6*(1+G12)
C28              = E5*E6*(1+G12)
D28              = E5*E6*(1+G12)
E28              = E5*E6*(1+G12)
F28              = E5*E6*(1+G12)
G28              = SUM(B22:H22)+SUM(B28:F28)
B29              = "---------
C29              = "---------
D29              = "---------
E29              = "---------
F29              = "---------
G29              = "---------
B30              = B27+B28
C30              = C27+C28
D30              = D27+D28
E30              = E27+E28
F30              = F27+F28
G30              = G27+G28
B31              = "---------
```

Appendix IV
Solutions to numerical questions

Chapter 2

Q2.7   (Note: all figures are in £s)

			Debit	Credit
(a)		Bank	7,000	
		Capital		7,000
(b)		Machinery	3,600	
		Bank		3,600
(c)		Purchases	1,200	
		Bank		1,200
(d)		Sales		600
		Bank	250	
		Cash	350	
(e)		Rent	250	
		Cash		250
(f)		Wages	190	
		Bank		190
(g)		Fixed assets	60	
		Cash		60

Q2.8

			Debit	Credit
	Opening entries			
		Bank	1,750	
		Capital		1,000
		Bank loan		750
(a)		Cash	700	
		Sales		700
(b)		Purchases	235	
		Bank		235
(c)		Sales		525
		Cash	525	
(d)		Bank	1,100	
		Cash		1,100
(e)		Creditors		315
		Purchases	315	
(f)		Wages	60	
		Cash		60
(g)		Sales		100
		Debtors	100	

Bank	
1,000	235
750	
1,100	
2,850	235
2,615	

Capital	
	1000

Bank loan	
	750

Cash	
700	1,100
525	60
1,225	1,160
65	

Sales	
	700
	525
	100
	1,325

Creditors	
	315

Purchases	
235	
315	
550	

Wages	
60	

Debtors	
100	

Trial balance

	Debit	Credit
Bank	2,615	
Capital		1,000
Bank loan		750
Cash	65	
Sales		1,325
Creditors		315
Purchases	550	
Wages	60	
Debtors	100	
	3,390	3,390

Q2.9

Trial balance

	Debit	Credit
Cash	500	
Purchases	12,000	
Capital		7,500
Loans		2,500
Rent paid	2,500	
Debtors	2,000	
Sales		22,500
Machinery	3,000	
Personal drawings	3,000	
Interest received		500
Wages	4,000	
Interest paid	200	
Car	5,800	
	33,000	33,000

Q2.11

	Debit	Credit
Purchases	1,100	
Bank	500	
Debtors	1,250	
Stall	1,000	
Opening capital		3,850
Sales		3,000
Cash	3,000	
Sales		1,250
Debtors	1,250	
Cash	350	
Debtors		350
Purchases	2,150	
Cash		2,150
Bank	500	
Cash		500
Purchases		1,150
Closing stock	1,150	

Bank		Debtors		Stall	
500		1,250	350	1,000	
500		1,250			
1,000		2,500	350		
		2,150			

Capital		Sales		Cash	
	3,850		3,000	3,000	2,150
			1,250	350	500
			4,250	3,350	2,650
				700	

Purchases		Closing stock	
1,100	1,150	1,150	
2,150			
3,250	1,150		
2,100			

Trial balance

	Debit	Credit
Bank	1,000	
Debtors	2,150	
Stall	1,000	
Capital		3,850
Sales		4,250
Cash	700	
Purchases	2,100	
Closing stock	1,150	
	8,100	8,100

Q2.12

Bank		Capital		Bank loan	
6,000	2,000		6,000		14,000
	800		2,000		
	300				
	300		8,000		
6,000	3,400				
2,600					

Shop		Fittings		Creditors	
14,000		2,500		2,000	2,500
					1,900
				2,000	4400
					2,400

Purchases		Car		Personal	
2,700		2,000		300	
				300	
				600	

Q2.13

Capital		Equipment		Vehicles	
	9,600	6,500		2,700	
	5,000	6,300			
	14,600	12,800			

Loans	
	3,000

Opening stock	
2,900	2,900

Bank	
	1,500
44,584	32,200
44,584	33,700
10,884	

Debtors	
2,000	400
1,600	

Sales	
2,000	39,584
	1,600
	4,420
2,000	45,604
	43,604

Purchases	
10,950	3,600
1,500	570
2,900	
15,350	4,170
11,180	

Wages	
4,700	
570	
5,270	

Heat and light	
1,900	
370	
2,270	

Rent and rates	
3,500	

Personal	
4,420	

Administration	
400	

Miscellaneous	
4,450	

Creditors	
	2,295

Accounts fee	
425	

Closing stock	
3,600	

Trial balance

	Debit	Credit
Capital		14,600
Equipment	12,800	
Vehicles	2,700	
Loans		3,000
Debtors	1,600	
Bank	10884	
Sales		43,604
Purchases	11,180	
Wages	5,270	
Heat and light	2,270	
Rent and rates	3,500	
Administration	400	
Miscellaneous	4,450	
Creditors		2,295
Accounts fee	425	
Closing stock	3,600	
Personal	4,420	
	63,499	63,499

Chapter 3

Q3.10   Equipment

– Value at 31/12/19x8	£76,800
Depreciation (20% of opening value)	15,360
Value at 31/12/19x9	£61,440

Vehicles

Value at 31/12/19x8	£48,000
Depreciation (20% of cost)	16,000
Value at 31/12/19x9	£32,000

(a)   Total depreciation charge for year –   £31,360

(b)   *Fixed assets*

	Premises	Equipment	Vehicles
Cost	£75,000	120,000	80,000
less Depreciation to date	—	58,560	48,000
Value as at 31/12/19x9	£75,000	61,440	32,000

Q3.11   As at 31/12/19x8:

Machinery

Cost	£200,000	Depreciation	£87,500
less Disposals	60,000	*less* Depreciation on disposals	22,500
	£140,000		£65,000

Opening cost	£140,000
less Depreciation to date	65,000
	£ 75,000
add Acquisition	60,000
	£135,000
less Depreciation	33,750
	£101,250

Vehicles

Cost	£120,000	Depreciation	£60,000
less Disposals	28,000	*less* Depreciation on disposals	14,000
	£92,000		£46,000

Opening cost	£92,000
less Accumulated depreciation	46,000
	£46,000
less Depreciation	23,000
Value as at 31/12/19x9	£23,000

(a)   Total depreciation charge for 19x9 –   £56,750

(b)   *Fixed assets*

	Machinery	Vehicles
Cost	£200,000	92,000
less Accumulated depreciation	98,750	69,000
Value as at 31/12/19x9	£101,250	23,000

Q3.12

Date	In	Out	Balance	Value
1/1/x9	1,200 @ £2		1,200 @ £2	£2,400
1/2/x9	16,400 @ £2.5		1,200 @ £2 16,400 @ £2.5	£43,400
1/4/x9		1,200 @ £2 12,800 @ £2.5	3,600 @ £2.5	£9,000
1/5/x9		400 @ £2.5	3,200 @ £2.5	£8,000
1/6/x9	11,000 @ £3		3,200 @ £2.5 11,000 @ £3	£41,000
1/7/x9	4,000 @ £3.5		3,200 @ £2.5 11,000 @ £3 4,000 @ £3.5	£55,000
1/9/x9		3,000 @ £2.5	200 @ £2.5 11,000 @ £3 4,000 @ £3.5	£47,500
1/10/x9		200 @ £2.5 3,800 @ £3	7,200 @ £3 4,000 @ £3.5	£35,600
1/11/x9		3,000 @ £3	4,200 @ £3 4,000 @ £3.5	£26,600

Q3.13

Date	In	Out	Average cost	Balance Number	Value £
Jan. 1	100 @ £2		£2	100	200
10	300 @ £2		£2	400	800
15		90	£2	310	620
31		150	£2	160	320
Feb. 10	240 @ £2.5		$\frac{£320 + (240 \times 2.5)}{160 + 240}$ = £2.3	400	920
15		200	£2.3	200	460
28		170	£2.3	30	69

Mar. 10	270 @ £3	£69 + (270 × 3)		
		30 + 270		
		= £2.93	300	879
11	50	£2.93	250	732.5
15	110	£2.93	140	410.2
31	50	£2.93	90	263.7

If FIFO: 90 @ £3 = £270

Q.3.14

Jane Smith
Profit and loss account
for the year ended 31/3/19x9

Sales			£164,000
less Cost of sales			72,500
Gross profit			£91,500
less Manufacturing cost		£24,000	
Overheads		31,000	
Depreciation		11,000	
			66,000
Net profit			£25,500

Jane Smith
Balance sheet
as at 31/12/19x9

Fixed assets			
Premises			£96,000
Machinery			44,000
			£140,000
Current assets			
Stock		£14,000	
Debtors		24,000	
		£38,000	
less Current liabilities			
Creditors	£25,000		
Overdraft	2,000	27,000	11,000
			£151,000
as financed by:			
Opening capital			£73,500
add Profit			25,500
			£99,000
less Personal drawings			10,000
			£89,000
add Long-term loans			62,000
			£151,000

Q3.15

Eagle Co. Ltd
Profit and loss account
for the year ended 31/7/19x9

Sales		£390,000
less Cost of sales		142,000
Gross profit		£248,000
less Expenses		
Wages	£75,000	
Heat and light	2,000	
Phone	3,000	
Insurance	1,000	
Loan interest	1,000	
Other costs	36,000	
Depreciation	14,000	
		132,000
Net profit		£116,000

Balance sheet
as at 31/7/19x9

Fixed assets			
Premises			£160,000
Plant and machinery			81,000
Vehicles			20,000
			£261,000
Current assets			
Stock		£25,000	
Debtors		12,000	
Bank		5,000	
		£42,000	
less Current liabilities			
Creditors	£15,000		
Accruals	2,000		
		17,000	25,000
			£286,000
as financed by:			
Opening capital			£160,000
add Profit			116,000
			£276,000
add Long-term loans			10,000
			£286,000

Q3.16

Vanilla Cone
Profit and loss account
for the year ended 31/12/19x9

Sales		£176,400
less Cost of sales		122,800
Gross profit		£53,600
less Expenses		
Wages	£14,100	
General	4,100	
Motor costs	6,245	
Insurance	800	
Depreciation	10,000	
Bad debt provision	900	36,145
Net profit		£17,455

Vanilla Cone
Balance sheet
as at 31/12/19x9

Fixed assets			
Vans			£5,000
Current assets			
Stock		£18,000	
Debtors		16,500	
Bank		18,400	
Prepayment		200	
		£53,100	
less Current liabilities			
Creditors	£18,200		
Employer's NIC	100		
Bad debt provision	900	19,200	33,900
			£38,900
as financed by:			
Opening capital			£30,000
add Profit			17,455
			£47,455
less Personal drawings			8,555
			£38,900

Chapter 4

Q.4.5

Draft manufacturing and profit and loss account

Sales			£275,000
Direct costs			
Opening stock of raw material		£20,000	
Purchases		100,000	
		£120,000	
less Closing stock of raw materials		35,000	
		£85,000	
Direct labour		80,000	
Prime cost		£165,000	
Indirect costs			
Factory insurance	£9,000		
Glue and nails	2,300		
Paint	4,500		
Factory rent	1,500	17,300	
Work in progress adjustment			
Opening value	£15,000		
less Closing value	10,000	5,000	
Finished goods adjustment			
Opening value	£50,000		
less Closing value	55,000	(5,000)	
Production cost			182,300
Gross profit			£92,700
less Administration insurance	£2,000		
Other administration costs	3,000		
Sales reps' salaries	5,000		10,000
Net profit			£82,700

Q4.6

Wares, Fino and Morrison
Profit and loss account
for the year ended 31/12/19x9

Sales			£250,000
less Cost of sales			122,500
Gross profit			£127,500
less Expenses			
Wages		£50,000	
Rent and rates		5,000	
Other costs		35,000	
Depreciation		4,600	94,600
			£32,900

Net profit
less Partners' salaries:

Wares	£6,000	
Fino	3,000	
Morrison	2,000	11,000
		£21,900

divisible thus:

Wares	£10,950
Fino	7,300
Morrison	3,650
	£21,900

Wares, Fino and Morrison
Balance sheet
as at 31/12/19x9

Fixed assets

Plant and equipment		£12,000
Vehicles		6,400
		£18,400

Current assets

Stock	£18,000	
Debtors	29,000	
Bank	3,000	
	£50,000	
less Current liabilities		
Creditors	12,000	38,000
		£56,400

as financed by:
Partners' capital accounts
Current accounts

	Wares	Fino	Morrison	Total
Opening balance	£4,000	(500)	2,000	£5,500
add Profit share	10,950	7,300	3,650	21,900
	£14,950	6,800	5,650	£27,400
less Transfers	1,000	800	600	2,400
	£13,950	6,000	5,050	£25,000
Fixed accounts	11,000	8,800	6,600	26,400
	£24,950	14,800	11,650	£51,400
Long term loans				5,000
				£56,400

Q4.7

Appropriation account

Net profit			£40,000
adjusted as follows:			
Partner's salary – Frances		4,000	
Interest on capital:			
– Andrew	£3,000		
– Pat	2,000		
– Frances	1,000		
		6,000	
			10,000
Distributable profit			£30,000
Divisible thus:			
Andrew			£12,000
Pat			9,000
Frances			9,000
			£30,000

Current accounts

	Andrew	Pat	Frances	Total
Opening balance	£25,000	15,000	5,000	£45,000
add Interest on capital	3,000	2,000	1,000	6,000
	£28,000	17,000	6,000	£51,000
add Profit share	12,000	9,000	9,000	30,000
	£40,000	26,000	15,000	£81,000
Fixed accounts				
	£5,000	5,000	5,000	15,000
	£45,000	31,000	20,000	£96,000

Chapter 5

Q5.7

The Nairn Company Ltd
Profit and loss account
for the year ended 31/3/19x9

Turnover		£3,475,000
Cost of sales		2,498,000
Gross profit		£977,000
Distribution costs	£40,000	
Administrative costs	176,500	
		216,500
Operating profit		£760,500
Interest received		37,500
		£798,000
Interest paid		28,500
Profit on ordinary activities before tax		£769,500
Tax on profits on ordinary activities		58,000

Profit for year on ordinary activities after taxation	£711,500
Dividends paid and proposed	63,000
Undistributed profits carried to reserves	£648,500

Q5.8

S. O. Poor Ltd
Balance sheet
as at 31/12/xx

notes

Fixed assets			
Intangible assets			£2,500
Tangible assets	(1)		11,000
			£13,500
Current assets			
Stock		£4,000	
Debtors		7,000	
		£11,000	
less Creditors: amounts falling Due within one year			
	(2)	10,500	
Net current assets			500
Total assets less current liabilities			£14,000
less Creditors: Amounts falling due in more than one year			
			2,000
			£12,000
Capital and reserves			
Called-up Share capital			£5,000
Revenue reserves			7,000
			£12,000

Notes
(1) *Tangible assets*

	Cost	Depn	Net
Plant and Equipment	£11,000	3,000	£ 8,000
Vehicles	4,000	1,000	3,000
			£11,000

(2) *Creditors: amounts falling due within one year*

Trade creditors	£8,000
Overdraft	2,500
	£10,500

Q5.9

Alpha Company Ltd
Profit and loss account
for the year ended 31/12/19x1

		£
Turnover		540,000
Cost of sales		248,400
Gross profit		291,600
Distribution costs	15,500	
Administrative expenses	172,000	
		187,500
Operating profit		104,100
Interest payable		2,500
Profit on ordinary activities before tax and profit for year		101,600
Dividends paid and proposed:		
Preference shares	900	
Ordinary shares	35,320	
		36,220
Profit for year carried to reserves		65,380

Alpha Company Ltd
Balance sheet
as at 31/12/19x1

		£
Fixed assets		
Tangible assets		241,600
Current assets		
Stock	50,000	
Debtors	65,000	
Bank	5,000	
	120,000	
Creditors: amounts falling due within one year	81,220	
Net current assets		38,780
Total assets less current liabilities		280,380
Creditors: amounts falling due in more than one year		25,000
		255,380
Capital and reserves		
Called-up share capital		115,000
Revenue reserves		140,380
		255,380

Q5.10

Iona Plc
Profit and loss account
for the year ended 31/12/19x2

		£
Turnover		1,000,000
Cost of sales		498,000
Gross profit		502,000
Distribution costs	110,000	
Administration expenses	154,000	
		264,000
Operating profit		238,000
Interest payable		2,000
Profit on ordinary activities before tax: profit for year		236,000
Dividends paid and proposed		
Ordinary shares	20,000	
Preference shares	3,500	
		23,500
Profit transferred to reserves		212,500

Iona Plc
Balance sheet
as at 31/12/19x2

Fixed assets		
Tangible assets		100,000
Current assets		
Stock	150,000	
Debtors	300,000	
Cash	200,000	
	650,000	
Creditors: amounts falling due within one year	107,500	
Net current assets		542,500
Total assets less *Current liabilities*		642,500
Creditors: amounts falling due in more than one year		20,000
		622,500
Capital and reserves		
Called-up share capital		270,000
Share premium reserve		90,000
Revenue reserves		262,500
		622,500

Q5.11

I.B.K. Ltd
Statement of sources and uses of funds
for the year ended 31/3/19x9

Sources of Funds		
Profit before tax		£3,500,000
add back Non-cash movements		
(depreciation)		1,000,000
Total generated from operations		£4,500,000
Funds from other sources		
Issue of shares at a premium	£1,050,000	
Bank loan	300,000	
		1,350,000
		£5,850,000
Uses of funds		
Acquisition of fixed assets	£3,500,000	
Repayment of debentures	1,500,000	
Tax paid	210,000	
Dividends paid	300,000	
		5,510,000
		£340,000
Movement in working capital		
Stock	£400,000	
Debtors	350,000	
Creditors	(450,000)	
		300,000
		£40,000
Movement in liquid assets		
Increase in bank balance		£40,000

Chapter 6

Q6.4

Clydecare Ltd
Value added statement
for the year ended 31/12/19x9

Turnover		£22,000,000	
less bought-in materials and services		13,250,000	
Value added		£8,750,000	
Distribution of value added			%
To pay employees		£4,100,000	46.9
To pay providers of capital			
– Dividends	£1,200,000		
– Loans	100,000	1,300,000	14.9

To pay the government	1,100,000	12.6
To maintain and expand capital		
– Depreciation	£750,000	
– Retained	1,500,000	
	2,250,000	25.6
	£8,750,000	100.0

Chapter 7

Q7.7

	Scribble	Scrawl
Profitability		
Profit: sales	2.00%	8.00%
Gross profit	22.3%	66.7%
Wages etc.: sales	19.2%	51.3%
Profit: total assets	10.00%	8.22%
Liquidity		
Current ratio	0.93:1	1.89:1
Acid test	0.33:1	0.68:1
Debtors turnover	0.69 wks	13.17 wks
Stock turnover	4.02 wks	70.72 wks
Stability		
Sales: fixed assets	9.38x	3.75x
Gearing	—	0.33%

Q7.8

	Eddie	Adie
Profit: sales	6.00%	5.50%
Gross profit	16.66%	14.28%
Expenses: sales	10.67%	8.79%
Profit: total assets	7.00%	12.59%
Current ratio	4.5:1	0.9:1
Acid test	2.4:1	0.7:1
Sales: fixed assets	2.68x	4.14x
Net worth: total assets	87.4%	50.3%

Chapter 8

Q8.6

$$\text{Raw materials} = \frac{200,000}{14,000,000} \times 365 = 5.2 \text{ days}$$

$$\text{Work-in-progress} = \frac{1,500,000}{14,000,000} \times 365 = 39.1 \text{ days}$$

$$\text{Finished goods} = \frac{400,000}{14,000,000} \times 365 = 10.4 \text{ days}$$

Debtors $= \dfrac{2,500,000}{20,000,000} \times 365 = 45.6$ days

$\overline{}$

100.3 days

less Creditors $= \dfrac{3,000,000}{14,000,000} \times 365 = 78.2$ days

$\overline{}$

22.1 days

Chapter 9

Q9.9

Costs incurred by selling on credit:	
1,000 posts @ 17p	£170
Bad debts lost	650
Overdraft interest	400
	£1,220
'Cash Only' profit	£7,360
add Cost of giving credit	1,220
Revised profit	£8,580
Actual profit	£8,000

Mary should change her sales policy to one of cash only and increase her net profit by £580. The net cost to her of giving credit is £580.

Chapter 10

Q10.6

	Sales schedule					
	Jan.	Feb.	March	April	May	June
Value	£2,000	4,000	5,000	9,000	8,000	7,000
20% cash	£400	800	1,000	1,800	1,600	1,400
48% 1 month	—	960	1,920	2,400	4,320	3,840
24% 2 months	—	—	480	960	1,200	2,160
8% 3 months	—	—	—	160	320	400
Cash in	£400	1,760	3,400	5,320	7,440	7,800

Q10.7

Megan Roberts

	Jan.	Feb.	March	April	May	June
Sales value	£25,000	30,000	30,000	40,000	50,000	4,0000

Cash flow forecast

	Jan.	Feb.	March	April	May	June
Cash in						
Opening balance	£1,500					
Debtors	7,500	8,200				
Cash	5,000	6,000	6,000	8,000	1,0000	8,000
1 month	—	12,500	15,000	15,000	2,0000	25,000
2 months	—	—	7,500	9,000	9,000	12,000
Total in	£14,000	26,700	28,500	32,000	39,000	45,000
Cash out						
Creditors	£15,000					
Purchases		15,000	18,000	18,000	24,000	3,0000
Rent	2,000		2,000		2,000	
Other	5,000	5,000	5,000	5,000	5,000	5,000
Total out	£22,000	20,000	25,000	23,000	31,000	35,000
Difference	£(8,000)	6,700	3,500	9,000	8,000	10,000
Balance b/f	—	(8,000)	(1,300)	2,200	11,200	19200
Balance	£(8,000)	(1,300)	2,200	11,200	19,200	29,200

Q10.8

I. B. Good
Cash flow forecast

	Jan.	Feb.	March	April	May	June	Total
Cash in							
Own cash	£5,000						5,000
Loan	3,600						3,600
Sales	1,080	2,310	3,630	4,990	4,980	4,200	21,190
Total in	£9,680	2,310	3,630	4,990	4,980	4,200	29,790
Cash out							
Loan Int. £	—	36	36	36	36	36	180
Loan repaid	—	100	100	100	100	100	500
Equipment	4,500						4,500
Van	3,000						3,000
Material	—	780	975	1,495	1,950	1,365	6,565
Wages	480	600	920	1,200	840	720	4,760
Power			435		435		870
Personal	500	500	500	500	500	500	3,000
Stock	350						350
Total out	8,830	2,016	2,966	3,331	3,861	2,721	23,735
Difference	£850	294	664	1,659	1,119	1,479	
Balance b/f	—	850	1,144	1,808	3,467	4,586	
Balance	£850	1,144	1,808	3,467	4,586	6,065	6,065

I. B. Good
Projected profit and loss account

Sales		£23,800
less Cost of sales		7,735
Gross profit		£16,065
less Expenses		
Loan interest	£216	
Wages	4,760	
Power	1,305	
Rates	1,500	
Depreciation	750	8,531
Net profit		£7,534

Projected balance sheet

Fixed assets			
Equipment			£4,050
Van			2,700
			£6,750
Current assets			
Stock		£350	
Debtors		2,610	
Bank		6,065	
		£9,025	
less Current liabilities			
Creditors			
– Material	£1,170		
– Rates	1,500		
– Power	435		
– Loan Interest	36	3,141	
			5,884
			£12,634
as financed by:			
Capital introduced			£5,000
add profit			7,534
			£12,534
less Personal drawings			3,000
			£9,534
add Loan outstanding			3,100
			£12,634

Q10.9

Cash flow forecasts

Year 1	Spring	Summer	Autumn	Winter	Total
Sales	£100,000	250,000	100,000	50,000	£500,000
Capital	200,000				200,000
	£300,000	250,000	100,000	50,000	£700,000
Purchases	£80,000	200,000	80,000	40,000	400,000
Wages, etc.	15,000	15,000	15,000	15,000	60,000
Equipment	220,000				220,000
	£315,000	215,000	95,000	55,000	£680,000
Difference	£(15,000)	35,000	5,000	(5,000)	
Balance b/f	—	(15,000)	20,000	25,000	
Balance	£(15,000)	20,000	25,000	20,000	£20,000

Year 2

	Spring	Summer	Autumn	Winter	Total
Balance from previous year	£20,000				£20,000
Sales	100,000	250,000	100,000	50,000	500,000
	£120,000	250,000	100,000	50,000	£520,000
Purchases	£80,000	200,000	80,000	40,000	£400,000
Wages, etc	15,000	15,000	15,000	15,000	60,000
	£95,000	215,000	95,000	55,000	£460,000
Difference	£25,000	35,000	5,000	(5,000)	
Balance b/f	—	25,000	60,000	65,000	
Balance	£25,000	60,000	65,000	60,000	£60,000

Profit and loss accounts

	Year 1		Year 2	
Sales		£500,000		£500,000
less Cost of sales				
Purchases	£480,000		£480,000	
– Closing stock	80,000	400,000	80,000	400,000
Gross profit		£100,000		£100,000
less Wages, etc.	£60,000		£60,000	
Depreciation	22,000	82,000	22,000	82,000
Net Profit		£18,000		£18,000

Balance sheets

	Year 1		Year 2	
Fixed assets		£198,000		£176,000
Current assets				
Stock	£80,000		£80,000	
Bank	20,000		60,000	
	£100,000		£140,000	
less				
Current liabilities				
(Stock – Spring)	80,000	20,000	80,000	60,000
		£218,000		£236,000
Owner's capital		£200,000		£200,000
Profits retained		18,000		36,000
		£218,000		£236,000

Q. 10.10

Ivor Payne
Sales schedule

Cash flow forecast

	1	2	3	4	5	6	7	8	9	
Value	£16,000	16,000	16,000	16,000	17,600	17,600	17,600	20,600	20,600	£158,000
Cash in										
Own cash	£25,000									25,000
Loan	10,000									10,000
Sales – cash	1,600	1,600	1,600	1,600	1,760	1,760	1,760	2,060	2,060	15,800
– credit	—	14,400	14,400	14,400	14,400	15,840	15,840	15,840	18,540	123,660
	£36,600	16,000	16,000	16,000	16,160	17,600	17,600	17,900	20,600	174,460
Cash out										
Loan interest	£100	100	100	100	100	100	100	100	100	900
Loan repays							116	167	167	500
Materials		12,800	12,800	12,800	12,800	14,080	14,080	14,080	16,480	109,920
Equipment	12,000									12,000
Vehicles	8,000									8,000
Wages	3,000	3,000	3,000	3,000	3,000	3,000	3,000	3,000	3,000	27,000
Rent	600	300	300	300	300	300	300	300	300	3,000
Phone				250			250			500
Motoring	150	150	150	150	150	150	150	150	150	1,350
Personal	600	600	600	600	600	600	600	600	600	5,400
	£24,450	16,950	16,950	17,200	16,950	18,230	18,646	18,397	20,797	168,570
Difference	£12,150	(950)	(950)	(1,200)	(790)	(630)	(1,046)	(497)	(197)	
Balance b/f	—	12,150	11,200	10,250	9,050	8,260	7,630	6,584	6,087	
Balance	£12,150	11,200	10,250	9,050	8,260	7,630	6,584	6,087	5,890	

Ivor Payne
Projected profit and loss account

Sales		£158,000
less Purchases		126,400
Gross profit		£31,600
less Expenses		
Loan interest	£900	
Wages	27,000	
Rent	2,700	
Rates	3,750	
Phone	750	
Motoring	1,350	
Depreciation	2,850	
		39,300
Net loss		£(7,700)

Projected balance sheet

Fixed assets		
Equipment		£10,650
Vehicles		6,500
		£17,150
Current assets		
Debtors	£18,540	
Bank	5,890	
Prepayments (rent)	300	
	£24,730	
less Current liabilities		
Creditors:		
– Materials	£16,480	
– Phone	250	
– Rates	3,750	
	20,480	4,250
		£21,400
Opening capital		£25,000
less Loss	£7,700	
Personal drawings	5,400	
		13,100
		£11,900
add Loans outstanding		9,500
		£21,400

Mel Bourne
Sales schedule

	1	2	3	4	5	6	7	8	9	10	11	12	Total
Value	£2,500	3,000	5,000	5,500	15,000	1,000	2,250	3,250	4,500	6,000	9,000	22,500	

Cash flow forecast

	1	2	3	4	5	6	7	8	9	10	11	12	Total
Cash in													
Own cash	£5,000												5,000
Loan	6,000												6,000
Sales – cash	625	750	1,250	1,375	3,750	250	562	813	1,125	1,500	2,250	5,625	19,875
– 1 month	—	1,000	1,200	2,000	2,200	6,000	400	900	1,300	1,800	2,400	3,600	22,800
– 2 month	—	—	875	1,050	1,750	1,925	5,250	350	787	1,138	1,575	2,100	16,800
	£11,625	1,750	3,325	4,425	7,700	8,175	6,212	2,063	3,212	4,438	6,225	11,325	70,475
Cash out													
Purchases	£1,750	2,100	—	3,500	3,850	10,500	700	1,575	2,275	3,150	4,200	6,300	39,900
Equipment	5,000												5,000
Rent				500			500			500			1,500
Power and phone				340			340			340			1,020
Delivery	50	60	100	110	300	20	45	65	90	120	180	450	1,590
Wages	350	350	350	350	350	350	350	350	350	350	350	350	4,200
Personal	450	450	450	450	450	450	450	450	450	450	450	450	5,400
Other costs	160	160	160	160	160	160	160	160	160	160	160	160	1,920
Loan interest	200	100	100	100	100	100	100	100	100	100	100	100	1,300
Loan repays	100	100	100	100	100	100	100	100	100	100	100	100	1,200
	£8,060	3,320	1,260	5,610	5,310	11,680	2,745	2,800	3,525	5,270	5,540	7,910	63,030
Difference	£3,565	(1,570)	2,065	(1,185)	2,390	(3,505)	3,467	(737)	(313)	(832)	685	3,415	
Balance b/f	—	3,565	1,995	4,060	2,875	5,265	1,760	5,227	4,490	4,177	3,345	4,030	
Balance	£3,565	1,995	4,060	2,875	5,265	1,760	5,227	4,490	4,177	3,345	4,030	7,445	7,445

Mel Bourne
Projected profit and loss account

Sales		£79,500
less Cost of sales		55,600
Gross Profit		£23,900
less Expenses		
Rent	£2,000	
Power and phone	1,360	
Delivery	1,590	
Wages	4,200	
Other costs	1,920	
Loan interest	1,200	
Depreciation	1,500	
		13,770
Net Profit		£10,130

Balance sheet

Fixed assets			
Equipment			£4,500
Car			3,000
			£7,500
Current assets			
Stock		£50	
Debtors		20,025	
Bank		7,445	
Prepayments (interest)		100	
		£27,620	
less Current liabilities			
Creditors:			
– Rent	£500		
– Power and phone	340		
– Purchases	15,750		
		16,590	11,030
			£18,530
Opening capital			£9,000
add Profit			10,130
			£19,130
less Personal drawings			5,400
			£13,730
add Loans outstanding			4,800
			£18,530

Chapter 11

Q11.5

(1)

	Production	Sales	Budget stock balance
Opening			5,750
Jan.	2,850	3,050	5,550
Feb.	2,850	3,050	5,350
March	2,850	3,050	5,150
April	3,135	3,050	5,235
May	3,135	3,050	5,320
June	3,135	2,565	5,890
July	3,135	2,565	6,460
Aug.	2,508	2,565	6,403
Sept.	2,508	2,565	6,346
Oct.	2,508	4,000	4,854
Nov.	4,000	4,000	4,854
Dec.	4,000	4,000	4,854
Totals	36,614	37,510	

(2)   £55 × 4,854 = £266,970.

(3)   The budgeted balance sheet will reflect the need for increased working capital in the middle of the year and a reduced requirement at the year end. Creditors and debtors will be affected, as will cash/bank.

Q11.6

		£000s	
Land		1,200	
Buildings		575	
		1,775	
Stock	825		(£3.3/4 = £825,000)
Debtors	763		(1.5 × 1/12 × £6.1m = £762,500)
Cash (note 1)	694		
	2,282		
Creditors	550		(1/6 × £3.3m = £550,000)
Working capital		1,732	
		3,507	
Share capital		1,500	
Reserves		2,007	(£1,262,000 + £754,000 = £2,007,000)
		3,507	

*   The cash figure has been derived as follows:

Share capital + reserves = £3,507 net assets.

∴ Working capital is (£3,507 − £1,775) = £1,732.

∴ Current assets = £550 + 1,732 = £2,282. Cash = £2,282 − 1,588 = £694.

Q11.7

Sales 40 × 0.8 × 52 (£190 × 1.05)		£331,968
less: Food costs 40 × 0.8 × 52 × £20		£33,280
Matron	£14,500 + (0.07 × ¾ × £14,500)	15,261
Care assistants	£7,450 + (0.07 × ¾ × £7,450)	
	= (£7,450 + £391) × 18	141,138
Kitchen staff	£6,745 + (0.07 × ¾ × £6,745)	
	= £7,099 × 3	21,297
Employment costs	0.2 × (£15,261 + £141,138	35,539
	+ £21,297)	
Interest		21,500
Rates		25,000
Miscellaneous		15,750
Budget Profit		£23,203

Q11.8

Sales

Product 1 3,300 × £23	£75,900	
2 5,195 × £17	88,315	
3 1,850 × £13	24,050	
	£188,265	
add Increase 3/12 × 0.08 = 0.02	3,765	
	£192,030	

Material cost   *Retained in stock*

Product 1 3,400 × £3	£10,200	100 × 3 = 300
2 5,195 × £6	31,170	
3 1,900 × £4	7,600	50 × 4 = 200
	£48,970	500
add Increase	—	
	£48,970	

Labour cost   *Retained in stock*

Product 1 3,400 × £5	£17,000	100 × 5.40 = 540
2 5,195 × £4	20,780	
3 1,900 × £3	5,700	50 × 3.24 = 162
	£43,480	702
add Increase 8/12 × 0.08 = 0.053	2,304	
	£45,784	

Maintenance and administrative expense
£3,980 + £7,465 = £11,445 × 1.06 (av. inflation)
         = £12,132

Non-production workers   *Salaried staff*

	3 × £7,090 = £21,270	2 × £6,750	£13,500
add Increase 8/12 × 0.08 = 0.053 =	1,127	*add* Increase 0.053	716
	£22,397		£14,216

Employment costs
£45,784 + £22,397 + £14,216 = £82,397
    × 0.20   =   £16,479

Budgeted profit and loss account

Sales		£192,030
less Material costs (£48,970 − £500)	£48,470	
Labour costs (£45,784 − £702)	45,082	93,552
Gross margin		£98,478
less Expenses:		
Maintenance and administration	£12,132	
Non-production labour	22,397	
Salaried costs	14,216	
Employment costs	16,479	
Depreciation	5,750	70,974
Net profit		£27,504

Note: It has been assumed that stock is valued at direct (prime) cost.

Chapter 12

Q12.6

$$\text{Flexing factor} = \frac{32,656}{35,406} = 0.9223$$

Schinkel Ltd

£'000's	Flexed Budget	Actual	Variance
Sales	32,656	32,656	—
Cost of sales			
Material (note 1)	10,694	12,314	(1,620)
Labour (note 2)	8,267	7,968	299
Gross margin	13,695	12,374	(1,321)
Expenses			
Indirect labour	998	1,014	(16)
Salaries	1,451	1,427	24
Indirect materials (note 3)	2,469	2,400	69
Services (note 4)	1,351	1,395	(44)
Depreciation	550	564	(14)
Profit	6,876	5,574	(1,302)

Notes
(1)   0.9223 × 11,595 = 10,694.
(2)   0.9223 × 8,963 = 8,267.
(3)   2,569 × 0.5 = 1,285 fixed.
      2,569 × 0.5 = 1,284 variable.
      Variable 1,284 × 0.9223 = 1,184.
      Flexed budget = 1,285 + 1,184 = 2,469.

(4)   1,372 × 0.8 = 1,098 fixed.
      1,372 × 0.2 = 274 variable.
      Variable 274 × 0.9223 = 253.
      Flexed budget = 1,098 + 253 = 1,351.

Q12.7

Flexing Factor – 120 per cent
Production Control Department
Budget Statement
period 3

	Flexed Budget	Actual	Variance
Progress salaries (note 1)	£5,200	4,650	550
Material control – salaries (note 2)	3,640	3,908	(268)
Production control – salaries (note 3)	2,860	2,804	56
Overtime premiums (note 4)	690	907	(217)
Employee benefits	3,950	3,681	269
Computer costs	1,750	1,800	(50)
Misc. costs (note 5)	900	700	200
	18,990	18,450	321 540

Notes:
(1)   5,000 × 0.8 = 4,000 fixed.
      ∴ 5,000 × 0.2 = 1,000 variable.
      Variable 1,000 × 1.2 = 1,200.
      ∴ Flexed budget = 4,000 + 1,200 = 5,200.
(2)   3,500 × 0.8 – 2,800 fixed.
      3,500 × 0.2 = 700 variable.
      Variable 700 × 1.2 = 840.
      ∴ Flexed budget = 2,800 + 840 = 3,640.
(3)   2,750 × 0.8 = 2,200 fixed.
      2,750 × 0.2 = 550 variable.
      Variable 550 × 1.2 = 660
      ∴ Flexed budget = 2,200 + 660 = 2,860.
(4)   575 × 1.2 = 690.
(5)   750 × 1.2 = 900.

Labour variances

Labour efficiency variance
Units difference × budgeted
  labour cost
= (36,355–35,000) × £1.25
= 1,355 × £1.25
= £1,694 unfav.

Labour rate variance
Actual units × cost difference
= 36,355 × (1.30–1.25)
= 36,355 × 0.05
£1,818 unfav.

(Total variance £3,512)

Variable overhead variances

Volume element
Units difference × budgeted variable overhead
= (36,355–35,000) × £1.15
= 1,355 × 1.15
= £1,588 unfav.

Cost element
Actual units × cost difference
= 36,355 × (1.15–1.10)
= 36,355 × 0.05
= £1,817 fav.

(Total variance £259)

Sales variances

Sales quantity variance
Units difference × budgeted selling price
= (36,355–35,000) × £9.50
= 1,355 × £9.50
= £12,873 fav.

Sales price variance
Actual units sold × price difference
= 36,355 × (9.75–9.50)
= 36,355 × 0.25
£9,088 fav.

(Total variance £21,961)

Material variances

Material usage variance
Units difference × budgeted cost
= (36,355–35,000) × £4.20
= 1,355 × 4.20
= £5,691 unfav.

Material price variance
Actual units × cost difference
= 36,355 × (4.30–4.20)
= 36,355 × 0.10
= £3,636 unfav.

(Total variance £9,327)

Chapter 13

Q13.6

	Machine shop	Assembly shop
Salaries	£4,500	£3,000
Indirect wages	9,900	5,500
Maintenance	3,120	780
Depreciation	2,500	1,000 (Allocation)
Heat, light, power	2,400	3,600
Computer costs	—	2,750
Miscellaneous	1,633	327
	£24,053	£16,957

Q13.7 *Absorption (recovery) rates:*

	Machine shop	Assembly shop
=	$\dfrac{£24,053}{10,000}$	$\dfrac{£16,957}{15,000}$
=	£2.41 per machine hour	£1.13 per man hour

Cost, product C

M			£15.00
L			7.00
O M/c	£2.41 × 12		
	=	28.92	
Assy	£1.13 × 0.333		
	=	£0.38	29.30
Selling and admin.			
(150% × £22.00)			33.00
			84.30

Selling price
£84.30 + 25% = £105.38

Q13.8

Overhead Rates

Assembly	Fly press	Guillotine	Finishing
£15,800/£10,000	£4,000/£2,000	£1,150/£500	£6,750/£3,000
£1.58 per £1 of	= £2 per	= £2.30 per	£2.25 per £1 of
direct labour	machine-hour	machine-hour	direct labour

Cost of 1 kw fire:

Material	
Flex (2 × 35p)	0.70
Sundries	0.75
MS sheet (1.5 × £1.6)	2.40
Formers (2 × £2.05)	4.10
Switch	2.16
Metal finishing	1.00
Wooden trim (3 × 40p)	1.20
Bar	1.90
Total material cost	£14.21

Labour

Fly press $2 \times \dfrac{£2.50}{60}$ £0.08

Guillotine $\dfrac{£2.50}{60}$ 0.04

Assembly $10 \times \dfrac{£2.25}{60}$ 0.38

Finishing $6 \times \dfrac{£2.25}{60}$ 0.23

Total labour cost £1.73

Overheads

$$\text{Fly press } \frac{£2.00}{60} \qquad\qquad £0.03$$

$$\text{Guillotine } \frac{£2.30}{120} \qquad\qquad 0.02$$

Assembly (0.38p × 158%)	0.60
Finishing (23p × 225%)	0.52
Total overhead cost	£1.17
Total cost	£16.11

Q13.9

Overhead absorption rates

$$\text{Machining} = £\frac{500,000}{625,000} = \text{80p per machine-hour}$$

$$\text{Assembly} = £\frac{250,000}{100,000} = £2.50 \text{ per direct labour hour}$$

$$\text{Finishing} = £\frac{125,000}{62,500} = 200\%$$

Product cost

Direct material	£75

Direct labour

$$\text{Machining } £\frac{93,750}{18,750} \times 2 = 10$$

$$\text{Assembly } £\frac{450,000}{100,000} \times 2 = 9$$

$$\text{Finishing } £\frac{62,500}{15,625} \times 2 = 8 \qquad \frac{27}{£102}$$

Administration overheads
10% × £102   £10.20

Production overheads
Machining 15 × 0.80 = 12
Assembly 2 × 2.50 = 5
Finishing 8 × 200% = 16
                  —   33

Total cost	£145.20
∴ Selling price = £145.20 × 1.2 =	£174.24

Q13.10

(1)   *Overhead absorption rates*

	Sub-assembly	Final assembly	Total
	£77,760	19,440	97,200
– by	£60,000	10,080	
∴ Rate	129.6%	192.9%	

Product cost
Material

2 mouldings at 30p	£0.60	
1 motor at	3.71	
3 metres flex at 75p	2.25	
1 rotor	0.73	
Sundries	0.65	
	7.94	
5% scrap	£0.40	£8.34

Labour

Sub-assembly	$\dfrac{£60,000}{20,000} \times \dfrac{7}{60}$	£0.35	
Final assembly	$\dfrac{£10,080}{2,800} \times \dfrac{5}{60}$	0.30	0.65

Overheads

Sub-assembly	£129.6 × 0.35 = £0.45	
Final assembly	£192.9 × 0.30 = 0.58	1.03
Total		£10.02

(2)   Total overhead rate = £97,200/70,080 = 138.7%
∴ Revised cost = £8.34 + 0.65 + (0.65 × 138.7)
= £8.99 + 0.90 = £9.89

(3)   Selling price = 100/70 × £9.89 = £14.13

Chapter 14

Q14.4   Return required = 0.3 × £175,000 = £52,500

∴ Profit per golf club = $\dfrac{£52,500}{10,000}$ = £5.25

∴ Selling price of golf club = £5.25 + £16 = £21.25

Q14.5   (1)   Returned required = 0.2 × £1.1 million = £220,000

∴ Profit to sales % required = $\dfrac{220,000}{1,500,000}$ = 14.66%

(2) Old percentage uplift on cost = $\dfrac{102}{1{,}457 - 102} \times \dfrac{100}{1} = 7.53\%$

New percentage uplift and cost = $\dfrac{220}{1{,}500 - 220} \times \dfrac{100}{1} = 17.19\%$

∴ Increase = 17.19% − 7.53% = 9.66%

Q14.7 (1) *Projected profit*

	A	B	C	D	Total
Contribution × volume	(8 × 3,500)	(11 × 2,750)	(11 × 2,000)	(10 × 1,500)	
=	£28,000	30,250	22,000	15,000	95,250
Fixed costs × volume	(3 × 3,500)	(5 × 2,750)	(12 × 2,000)	(14 × 1500)	
=	£10,500	13,750	24,000	21,000	69,000
Profit	£17,500	16,500	(2,000)	(6,000)	26,000

(2) If D was discontinued, then profits would be:
(A + B + C) − fixed costs D
= £(17,500 + 16,500 + [2,000]) − 21,000
= £32,000 − £21,000 = £11,000 profit

∴ D's closure is *not* advised because it makes a contribution to fixed costs of £15,000.

(3) If 2,000 units of C were sold at £40 each, instead of D, the position would be:
Contribution lost from D = £15,000
Contribution gained from C
= 2,000 × (£40 − £30 v.c.)
= 2,000 × £10 = £20,000
∴ Changeover to C would be a better option than carrying on with D. Profits would increase from £26,000 to £30,000 since C would generate an extra £5,000 contribution.

Q14.8 (1) 'In-house' contribution = £121 − (41 + 19 + 17) = £44

'Outsourced' contribution = £121 − (£72)   = £49

∴ Outsource, and, if possible, utilize the facility for something else, or dispose of it.

(2) If the exchange rate worsens by 10%, 'outsourced' contribution becomes £121 − (£72 + 10%)

= £121 − £79.20 = £41.80

In these circumstances, outsourcing would not be advisable.

Q14.9 (2) As long as the price is greater than marginal cost, i.e. £43, it makes a contribution.

(3) Fixed overheads = 50,000 × 12 = £600,000.

Price at	60,000	75,000	100,000 units
= V	£48	£48	48
F	10	8	6
	£58	56	54

(4) Unit profit:

$80 - 58$	$80 - 56$	$80 - 54$
$- 22$	$= 24$	$= 26$
$\times 60,000$	$\times 75,000$	$\times 100,000$
$= £1.32m$	$£1.8m$	$£2.6m$

Q14.10

(1) Profit (normal) $= 10,000 \times (75 - 32) =$ 430,000 contribution

$-$ 95,000 fixed

£335,000

Profit (reduced) $= 5,000 \times (75 - 32) =$ 215,000

$-$ 95,000 fixed

120,000

Alternatively, £335,000 $-$ £215,00 $= £120,000$

(2) If SE Asian option accepted,
Profit $= £120,000 + 5,000 \times (40 - 32)$ contribution
$= £120,000 + 40,000 = £160,000$

(3) Extra profit required $= £335,000 - £120,000 = £215,000$

$\therefore$ Increase per unit needed $= \dfrac{215,000}{5,000} = £43$

Making new price $= £75 + 43$
$= £118$

(4)
$$BEP = \frac{95,000}{£43} \text{ FC/cont.} = 2,209 \text{ units}$$

(5)

M	£14	
L	8	
VO	10	
FC	19	$\left(\dfrac{95,000}{5,000}\right)$
Total cost	£51	
SP	90	
Profit	£39	

Q14.11 *Variable expenses (overheads)*

Maintenance materials		*Other materials*		*Heat, light, power*		*Total variable*
F	V	F	V	F	V	
	9		2		19(½)	30
19		4		18	(½)	

Contribution = gross margin $-$ variable overheads
$= £2,741 - £30 = £2,711$

Fixed costs (unadjusted) $= £2,741 - £589 = £2,152$

Fixed costs (adjusted) = £2,152-£30 = £2,122

Contribution as a % of sales = $\dfrac{£2,711}{4,865} \times \dfrac{100}{1}$ = 55.72 %

∴ Breakeven sales = $\dfrac{£2,122}{0.5572}$ = £3,808

Q.14.13 (1)

	Sousaphone	Bass saxophone	Alto saxophone
Contribution	750 – 532	1,100 – 662	550 – 347
	= 218 unit	= 438 unit	= 203 unit
	× 5,000	× 2,750	× 6,050
	= 1,090,000	1,204,500	1,228,150
	− FC 438,125	438,125	438,125
Profit	£651,875	£766,375	£790,025

Alto saxophone
Profit and loss account

Sales	£3,327,500
Materials	£477,950
Labour	901,450
VO	719,950
FO	438,125
	£790,025

(2) BEP = $\dfrac{FC}{Contribution}$ = 2,158 units

(3) Profit at 2,379 units (BEP + 10%)
= 2,379 × 203 = 482,937 − 438,125
= £44,812

(4) VC = 347 + 10% = £382
SP = 550 + 6% = £583
∴ Contribution = £201

Chapter 15

Q11.4

Contract 44
Contract account for the y/e 19xx

Site wages	£5,000	Architect's certificates	£14,000
Site salaries	600	Stock of unused materials	
Materials	4,000	c/d	800
Subcontract costs	900	Value of plant c/d	1,400
Other site expenses	300		
Hire of special machinery	400		
Plant bought	2,000		
Profit taken to			
profit and loss account	1,800		
Reserve c/d	1,200		
	£16,200		£16,200
Stock b/d	800	Reserve b/d	£1,200
Plant b/d	£1,400		

Profit calculation

$$\tfrac{2}{3} \text{ apparent profit} \times \frac{\text{cash received}}{\text{work certified}}$$

$$= \tfrac{2}{3} \times (16,200 - 13,200) \times £\frac{12,600}{14,000}$$

$$= \tfrac{2}{3} \times £3,000 \times 90\%$$
$$= \quad £1,800$$

Q11.5

Contract 1

Materials	£194,365	Work certified	£520,000
Wages	71,390	Work in progress c/d	21,000
Plant	10,000	Material stocks c/d	13,400
Salaries	29,545	Plant valuation c/d	8,000
Office rental	43,000		
Computer costs	3,000		
Management costs	23,000		
Safety costs	2,516		
Plant hire	2,000		
Cranage	18,469		
Equip. costs	36,518		
Profit reserve	51,435		
Profit taken	77,162		
	£562,400		£562,400
Profit reserve b/d			£51,435
Stocks b/d	13,400		
Plant b/d	8,000		
WIP b/d	21,000		

Contract 2

Materials	£75,180	Work certified	£220,000
Wages	45,374	Work in progress c/d	3,000
Plant	7,400	Material stocks c/d	1,600
Salaries	31,268	Plant valuation c/d	5,500
Office rental	25,000		
Computer costs	5,282		
Management costs	15,000		
Safety costs	2,097		
Plant hire	1,800		
Cranage	3,562		
Equip. costs	27,514		
Loss	(9,377)		
	£230,100		£230,100
Stocks b/d	£1,600		
Plant b/d	5,500		
W/P b/d	3,000		

Contract 1

Profit taken:

Formula: apparent profit $\times \dfrac{\text{cash received}}{\text{work certified}}$

$= \frac{2}{3} \times 128{,}597 \times \dfrac{468{,}000}{520{,}000}$

$= \quad 85{,}736 \times 0.9 = £77{,}162$

Contract 2

Loss, $\therefore$ shown in full.

Chapter 16

Q16.6   Abacus:

A

Yr.	Income	10% factor	NPV
1	12,000	0.909	10,908
2	10,000	0.826	8,260
3	1,000	0.751	751
4	1,000	0.683	683
5	6,000	0.621	3,726
			24,328
		Cost	20,000
		NPV	4,328

B
Yr.

1	6,000	0.909	5,454
2	14,000	0.826	11,564
3	9,600	0.751	7,210
4	200	0.683	137
5	200	0.621	124
			24,489
		Cost	20,000
		NPV	4,489

C
Yr.

1	2,000	0.909	1,818
2	2,000	0.826	1,652
3	8,000	0.751	6,008
4	8,000	0.683	5,464
5	10,000	0.621	6,210
			21,152
		Cost	20,000
		NPV	1,152

Q16.7   (1)   Strathbungo:
X

Yrs.	Savings	15% factor	NPV
1	7,770	0.870	6,760
2	7,770	0.756	5,874
3	7,770	0.658	5,113
4	7,770	0.572	4,444
5	7,770	0.497	3,862
6	7,770	0.432	3,567
7	7,770	0.376	2,922
8	7,770	0.327	2,541
9	7,770	0.284	2,207
10	7,770	0.247	1,919
	77,700		39,209
		Cost	42,000
		NPV	(2,791)

Y
Yrs.

1	8,330	0.870	7,247
2	8,330	0.756	6,297
3	8,330	0.658	5,481
4	8,330	0.572	4,765
5	8,330	0.497	4,140
6	8,330	0.432	3,959
7	8,330	0.376	3,132
8	8,330	0.327	2,724
	66,640		37,745
		Cost	35,000
		NPV	2,745

Z
Yrs.

1	8,210	0.870	7,143
2	8,210	0.756	6,207
3	8,210	0.658	5,402
4	8,210	0.572	4,696
5	8,210	0.497	4,080
6	8,210	0.432	3,547
7	8,210	0.376	3,087
8	8,210	0.327	2,685
9	8,210	0.284	2,332
	73,890		39,179
			42,000
		NPV	(2,821)

(2) Payback
Yrs.

	X	Y	Z
	5.41	4.20	5.12

(3) ROI

Annual profit

$$\frac{77,700 - 42,000}{10} \qquad \frac{66,640 - 35,000}{8} \qquad \frac{73,890 - 42,000}{9}$$

Return %

$$\frac{3,570}{42,000} \qquad \frac{3,955}{35,000} \qquad \frac{3,543}{42,000}$$

=   8.5%   11.3%   8.4%

Q16.8   Wizbit:

(1)
15% factor

0.8686	Yr. 1	3,000	2,609	3,000	2,609	2,800	2,435
0.7651	2	3,000	2,268	3,000	2,268	2,800	2,117
0.6575	3	3,000	1,973	3,000	1,973	2,800	1,841
0.5718	4	3,000	1,715	3,000	1,715	2,800	1,601
0.4972	5	3,000	1,992	3,000	1,492	2,800	1,392
0.4323	6	3,000	1,297			2,800	1,210
0.3759	7					2,800	1,053
			11,354		10,057		11,649
			−9,350		−8,750		−9,650
			2,004		1,307		1,999

(2)   Quality, reliability, backup, services, spares, etc.

(3)

A		22% gives:		24% gives:	
1	3,000	0.820	2,460		2,420
2	3,000	0.672	2,016		1,951
3	3,000	0.551	1,653		1,574
4	3,000	0.451	1,353		1,269
5	3,000	0.370	1,110		1,023
6	3,000	0.303	909		825
			9,501		9,062
			−9,350		9,350
			151		(288)

Total difference 151 + 288 = 439
Rate lies between 22 and 24%

$\therefore$ Rate is $\dfrac{151}{439} \times 2\%$ difference = 22.69%

(4)   Payback

	A	B	C
	3.12	2.92	3.45
	yrs	yrs	yrs

ROI

$$\text{Annual profit} = \dfrac{18,000 - 9,350}{6} \qquad \dfrac{15,000 - 8,750}{5} \qquad \dfrac{19,600 - 9,650}{7}$$

$$\text{Return \%} \quad \dfrac{1,442}{9,350} \qquad \dfrac{1,250}{8,750} \qquad \dfrac{1,421}{9,650}$$

$$= \quad 15.4\% \qquad 14.3\% \qquad 14.7\%$$

Q16.9   Patera:

A

Yr.	Income	12% factor	NPV
1	1,500	0.893	1,340
2	1,500	0.797	1,196
3	6,000	0.712	4,272
4	6,000	0.636	3,816
5	7,500	0.567	4,253
			14,877
		Cost	10,000
		NPV	4,877

B

Yr.			
1	4,500	0.893	4,019
2	10,500	0.797	8,369
3	7,200	0.712	5,126
4	150	0.636	95
5	150	0.567	85
			17,694
		Cost	10,000
		NPV	7,694

C

Yr.			
1	9,000	0.893	8,037
2	7,500	0.797	5,978
3	750	0.712	534
4	750	0.636	477
5	4,500	0.567	2,552
			17,578
		Cost	10,000
		NPV	7,578

(2)   Payback A

$1,500 + 1,500 + 6,000 + (0.167 \times 6,000) = 10,000$

∴ 3.167 years

B

$4,500 + (0.523 \times 10,500) = 10,000$

∴ 1.523 years

C

$9,000 + (0.133 \times 7,500) = 10,000$

∴ 1.133 years

Index

Page numbers in italic refer to figures